JOURNAL FOR THE STUDY OF THE OLD TESTAMENT
SUPPLEMENT SERIES

405

Theory and Practice in
Old Testament Ethics

John Rogerson

edited and with an Introduction by

M. Daniel Carroll R.

T&T CLARK INTERNATIONAL
A Continuum imprint
LONDON • NEW YORK

Copyright © 2004 T&T Clark International
A Continuum imprint

Published by T&T Clark International
The Tower Building, 11 York Road, London SE1 7NX
15 East 26th Street, Suite 1703, New York, NY 10010

www.tandtclark.com

British Library Cataloguing-in-Publication Data
A catalogue record for this book is available from the British Library

Typeset and edited for Continuum by Forthcoming Publications Ltd
www.forthcomingpublications.com

Printed on acid-free paper in Great Britain by MPG Books Ltd

ISBN 0-8264-7165-X (HB)
ISBN 0-5670-8259-8 (PB)

CONTENTS

Part III
THE RELEVANCE OF THE OLD TESTAMENT
FOR MODERN SOCIAL ISSUES

Part IV
OLD TESTAMENT ETHICS AND CHRISTIAN FAITH

PREFACE

Professor John Rogerson is one of those rare individuals who passionately tries to live out what he writes. For him, biblical ethics is not just an academic exercise; it is a call to a certain kind of lifestyle and to concrete social and political commitments. This is not true of all who write in the field of Old Testament ethics.[1]

Professor Rogerson lives without a car because of a concern for the environment and as a protest against the fact that the daily loss of life and serious injuries in road accidents on British (and other!) roads is accepted as a normal fact of modern life. From 1964 until five years after his arrival in Sheffield in 1979 he was an active leader in the (Boy) Scout Association in order to work with young people; for him, these organizations are upholders of the moral values 'of my station' within British society. He himself was a member of the scouts as a boy and young adult. Professor Rogerson and his wife Rosalind are vegetarians and use 'green' electricity, since it is generated by renewable natural resources. Some years ago they purchased a larger home in order to care for aging parents and another ailing family member; they now house university students and make them part of the family. They also are members of the Green Party and volunteer for activities as time permits.

These and other commitments have grown out of his life experience and Christian faith. In this volume's final chapter Rogerson recounts a bit of that pilgrimage. This Preface supplements what is told there with more details in order to gain greater insight into his interdisciplinary interests and his desire to integrate biblical study with theological and ethical concerns. What follows is not intended to lift Professor Rogerson up as a moral exemplar—something with which he would be very uncomfortable—but rather to reveal the origin of several features of his thinking that are foundational to the essays reproduced in this book.[2]

1. Rogerson's Ethics in Personal Context

Having discovered Christian faith as a young man and being interested in dedicating his life to church ministry, Rogerson started the ordination process at the

---

1. One of the most extreme examples of this incongruence was the German scholar J. Hempel, author of *Das Ethos des Alten Testament* (BZAW, 67; Berlin: W. de Gruyter, 2nd edn, 1964), who supported the Nazi regime. Note C. Weber, *Altes Testament und völkische Frage: Der biblische Volksbegriff in der alttestamentlichen Wissenschaft der nationalsozialisteschen Zeit, dargestellt am Beispiel von Johannes Hempel* (FAT, 28; Tübingen: Mohr Siebeck, 2000).

2. This information comes from an extensive interview with Professor Rogerson in his home in Sheffield in late August, 2003.

University of Manchester. In those days (the 1950s–60s) the usual process was to go to university and then move on to two years at theological college. Rogerson first became interested in ethics during his studies for the B. D. at Manchester, and in his second year he took a course in moral philosophy. From Manchester he went to Ripon Hall at Oxford. There he did two years of theological studies, but he also was fascinated with languages and took classical and medieval Hebrew, classical Arabic, as well as Ugaritic as a special subject.

At that time he should have been ordained, but his tutor, G.R. Driver, was able to secure him a scholarship to spend a year at the Hebrew University in Jerusalem (1963–64). While there Rogerson did a lot of exploring of the land, an interest that is evident in the publication of an atlas.[3] It was a much less violent place then, so he was able to travel freely all over the countryside (putting to use his background as a scout in all kinds of unforeseen ways!). While in Jerusalem he studied linguistics with Chaim Rabin, and this led to an interest in social linguistics and eventually to social anthropology. He quickly recognized that these disciplines could help him and others understand the context of the Old Testament world. In particular, his reading of the social anthropologist E.E. Evans-Pritchard showed him how it is possible to go to a totally different culture and mediate it into one's own. In other words, background studies of the Bible, which would need to be informed by these and other disciplines, were clearly important.

While in Jerusalem he was appointed to a post at the University of Durham. Rogerson returned to England and was ordained in September 1964, just before he began his first term of teaching there. Various strands of his experience during the years at Durham helped him to begin to formulate an approach that would wed a pastoral and theological focus with a critical methodology. To begin with, for the first three years he was a lecturer in theology and a curate of a local congregation of the Church of England. In time, Rogerson became a full-time lecturer, but he maintained (and continues to maintain) his commitment to preaching and church involvement. Second, during his tenure at Durham Rogerson was able to put into practice what he had learned from a writer who had earlier deeply influenced his passage into Christian faith, the Methodist Leslie D. Weatherhead. Weatherhead saw the importance of clarity in method and recognized the value of interdisciplinary work (he appealed to psychology and English literature). Weatherhead also held to some of the critical views of his day, but was at the same time a great preacher and evangelist. Here, in other words, was an example of the possibility of combining Christian piety and ministry with intellectual integrity. Third, while he was researching his book on myth (1968–69),[4] Rogerson came upon the nineteenth century German Old Testament scholar W.M.L. de Wette. At this time he was also travelling regularly to Germany to do research and attended some Lutheran services. Within that tradition Rogerson discovered a theological perspective not well known in England: the special emphasis on the Fall and the grace of God and the Law-Gospel distinction. The latter allows for holding together in healthy tension a

---

3.   *The New Atlas of the Bible* (London: Macdonald, 1985).
4.   *Myth in Old Testament Interpretation* (BZAW, 134; Berlin: W. de Gruyter, 1974).

critical perspective of the Bible and Christian faith, a tension embodied in de Wette and others. This contact also spurred him on in his study of German. He realized that to be a first-rate Old Testament scholar he would need to be as fluent in German as he was in English. This conviction would soon bear fruit for his ethics in another unexpected turn of events.

With the move to the University of Sheffield to be Professor and Head of the Department of Biblical Studies in 1979, the concern for ethics sprang up again. At that time, Rogerson belonged to a German academic book club and acquired coincidentally a volume by E. Meinberg titled *Das Menschenbild der modernen Erziehungswissenschaft.*[5] This book, along with the work of Jürgen Habermas, triggered for him the key question for Old Testament ethics: What does it mean to be human? The thinking of Habermas and others of the Frankfurt School have continued to inform his thinking in ethics.

These various brief vignettes, along with the opening list of moral stances, help explain the multi-dimensional and interdisciplinary nature of Professor Rogerson's Old Testament ethics. It strives to be grounded in the exegesis of the biblical text (the interest in languages), informed by the realities of the ancient and modern worlds (background studies, the social sciences), articulated in a way that can engage broader ethical discourse (philosophical ethics), and deeply theological, pastoral, and practical.

2. *Concluding Remarks*

The work in Old Testament ethics by John Rogerson has been extensive, but scattered. This volume was conceived as a means to gather these materials in order to enrich the discourse that is now going on in the field. The selection represents a timeframe spanning from 1982 to 2001, and the essays in each major part are arranged chronologically. The dates of previously published pieces are available in the Acknowledgments; the dates and places of presentation for each unpublished piece is noted in an initial footnote to the title.

I would like to thank the secretary to the Biblical Studies Division at Denver Seminary, Jeanette Freitag, for her tireless work in transcribing several essays to disk. One of my students, Jonathan Jameson, has been a wonderful help in carefully proofreading the chapters. A word of thanks also is extended to Philip Davies, a former member of the faculty at the University of Sheffield and head of Sheffield Academic Press, who was a great encouragement in the conception and development of this project.

Finally, I am, of course, especially grateful to Professor John Rogerson. He was an exceptional advisor during my days as a doctoral student at Sheffield, where he introduced me to the necessity (and the fascinating adventure) of interdisciplinary study for Old Testament ethics. Professor Rogerson has been supportive of my own work over the years, but, more importantly, he has always been open to share his

---

5. E. Meinberg, *Das Menschenbild der modernen Erziehungswissenschaft* (Darmstadt: Wissenschaftliche Buchgesellschaft, 1988).

thoughts on Christian faith and mission with a characteristic graciousness and self-effacing sense of humour. Even though Professor Rogerson and I do come from different theological persuasions, he continues to be for me a model of serious scholarship committed to God, the Bible, the church, and the world. The publication of this volume is a small attempt to express my respect for him as a scholar and mentor, with the hope that others might profit as I have from his reflections on Old Testament ethics and the Christian life.

Advent, 2003
M. Daniel Carroll R.

ACKNOWLEDGMENTS

The editor would like to thank the respective publishers for allowing the repro-
duction in this volume of the following articles by Professor Rogerson:

'The Old Testament and Social and Moral Questions', *ModChm* NS 25 (1982), pp. 28-35.

'Christian Morality and the Old Testament', *HeyJ* 36.4 (1995), pp. 422-30. (Copyright for this article belongs to the Trustees for R. R. Purposes and Blackwell Publishing.)

'The Old Testament and Christian Ethics', in R. Gill (ed.), *The Cambridge Companion to Christian Ethics* (Cambridge: Cambridge University Press, 2001), pp. 29-41.

'What Does It Mean to Be Human? The Central Question of Old Testament Theology?', in D.J.A. Clines, S.E. Fowl and S.E. Porter (eds.), *The Bible in Three Dimensions: Essays in Celebration of Forty Years of Biblical Studies in the University of Sheffield* (JSOTSup, 87; Sheffield: JSOT Press, 1990), pp. 285-98.

'Discourse and Biblical Ethics', in J.W. Rogerson, Margaret Davies and M.D. Carroll R. (eds.), *The Bible and Ethics: The Second Sheffield Colloquium* (JSOTSup, 207; Sheffield: Sheffield Academic Press, 1995), pp. 17-26.

'Using the Bible in the Debate about Abortion', in J.H. Channer (ed.), *Abortion and the Sanctity of Human Life* (Exeter: Paternoster Press, 1985), pp. 77-92.

'The Enemy in the Old Testament', in A.G. Auld (ed.), *Understanding Poets and Prophets: Essays in Honour of George Wishart Anderson* (JSOTSup, 152; Sheffield: JSOT Press, 1993), pp. 284-93.

'The Family and Structures of Grace in the Old Testament', in S.C. Barton (ed.), *The Family in Theological Perspective* (Edinburgh: T. & T. Clark, 1996), pp. 25-42.

'Exegesis and World Order', *EpRev* 14.2 (1987), pp. 54-62.

ABBREVIATIONS

AnBib	Analecta biblica
AV	Authorized Version
BJRL	*Bulletin of the John Rylands University Library of Manchester*
BKAT	Biblischer Kommentar: Altes Testament
BTB	*Biblical Theology Bulletin*
BZAW	Beihefte zur *ZAW*
CBC	Cambridge Bible Commentary
EpRev	*Epworth Review*
ExpTim	*Expository Times*
FAT	Forschungen zum Alten Testament
FOTL	The Forms of the Old Testament Literature
GGJ	Grundriss der Gesamtwissenschaft des Judentums
GNB	Good News Bible
HeyJ	*Heythrop Journal*
JSOT	*Journal for the Study of the Old Testament*
JSOTSup	*Journal for the Study of the Old Testament*, Supplement Series
JTS	*Journal of Theological Studies*
ModChm	*Modern Churchman*
NEB	*New English Bible*
NIV	New International Version
NRSV	New Revised Standard Version
NTD	Das Neue Testament Deutsch
OTG	Old Testament Guides
RAC	*Reallexikon für Antike und Christentum*
RSV	Revised Standard Version
SAM	Sheffield Archaeological Monographs
SBM	Stuttgarter biblische Monographien
SBT	Studies in Biblical Theology
TRE	*Theologische Realenzyklopädie*
VTSup	*Vetus Testamentum*, Supplements
WBC	Word Biblical Commentary
ZAW	*Zeitschrift für die alttestamentliche Wissenschaft*

AN INTRODUCTION TO THE ETHICS OF JOHN ROGERSON

M. Daniel Carroll R.

When the first essay in this volume, 'The Old Testament and Social and Moral Questions', was published in 1982, no new significant monographs on the subject of Old Testament ethics had appeared for a decade and a half.[1] This situation, however, was beginning to be remedied. Barton had recently written several articles on the concept of natural law and how it could illuminate prophetic thinking on moral issues, and McKeating had produced an important piece that probed how the legal penalties of the Old Testament might actually have been applied in ancient Israel.[2] Since that time, of course, there has been a veritable explosion of publications in the field of Old Testament ethics. Today one can benefit from a growing number of studies that use different textual methodologies and represent a wide range of views regarding the possible bearing of the text on modern life. The list is now quite a long one. Of the many works published since 1990 mention can be made, for example, of book-length studies by Bruce Birch, Christopher Wright, Waldemar Janzen, William Brown, Eckart Otto, Gordon Wenham, Cyril Rodd, David Pleins, Mary Mills, and John Barton.[3] In addition, the fruit of several

1.   E.g. J. Hempel, *Das Ethos des Alten Testament* (BZAW, 67; Berlin: W. de Gruyter, 2nd edn, 1964); H. Van Oyen, *Die Ethik des Alten Testaments* (Gütersloh: Gütersloher Verlagshaus Gerd Mohn, 1967). Also note W. Eichrodt, *Theology of the Old Testament* (trans. J.A. Baker; Philadelphia: Westminster Press, 1967), II, pp. 316-79.

2.   J. Barton, 'Understanding Old Testament Ethics', *JSOT* 9 (1978), pp. 44-64; 'Natural Law and Poetic Justice in the Old Testament', *JTS* 30 (1979), pp. 1-14; *idem*, 'Ethics in Isaiah of Jerusalem', *JTS* 32 (1981), pp. 1-18; H. McKeating, 'Sanctions against Adultery in Ancient Israelite Society, with Some Reflections on Methodology in the Study of Old Testament Ethics', *JSOT* 11 (1979), pp. 57-72.

3.   B.C. Birch, *Let Justice Roll Down: The Old Testament, Ethics, and the Christian Life* (Louisville, KY: Westminster/John Knox Press, 1991); C.J.H. Wright, *God's People in God's Land: Family, Land, and Property in the Old Testament* (Grand Rapids: Eerdmans, 1990); *idem, Walking in the Ways of the Lord: The Ethical Authority of the Old Testament* (Downers Grove, IL: Inter-Varsity, 1995); E. Otto, *Theologische Ethik des Alten Testaments* (Stuttgart: W. Kohlhammer, 1994); W. Janzen, *Old Testament Ethics: A Paradigmatic Approach* (Louisville, KY: Westminster/John Knox Press, 1994); W.P. Brown, *Character in Crisis: A Fresh Approach to the Wisdom Literature of the Old Testament* (Grand Rapids: Eerdmans, 1996); G.J. Wenham, *Torah as Story: Reading the Old Testament Ethically* (Edinburgh: T. & T. Clark, 2000); C.S. Rodd, *Glimpses of a Strange Land: Studies in Old Testament Ethics* (Edinburgh: T. & T. Clark, 2001); J.D. Pleins, *The Social Visions of the Hebrew Bible: A Theological Introduction* (Louisville, KY: Westminster/John Knox Press, 2001); M.E. Mills, *Biblical Morality: Moral Perspectives in Old Testament Narratives* (Heythrop

symposia,[4] as well as a whole host of monographs on a variety of topics, are now available.

A vital voice in this renaissance in Old Testament ethics has been John Rogerson. For the last two decades he has been publishing articles in various journals and books of collected essays and giving presentations in all kinds of venues on different matters related to Old Testament ethics. This volume gathers together for the first time many of these publications and papers under one cover.[5] Several expound the theoretical and biblical foundations of his thinking on ethics; others apply these to specific moral challenges in contemporary life.

The purpose of this introductory essay is to offer the reader a brief, systematic outline of the essential features of Rogerson's approach. The discussion is divided into three major sections. The first puts forward his methodological concerns in the study of the biblical text. Rogerson is unswerving in his desire to show that the Old Testament is significant for Christian ethics today, but he refuses to try to approach the Bible in any sort of simplistic or uninformed way. The second section surveys the interdisciplinary nature of his work. One of the goals of Rogerson's forays into other fields has been to probe the Old Testament for ethical insights in new and creative ways and to ground his biblical study on broader foundations. The third and final section presents the basic framework of Rogerson's own proposal for an Old Testament ethics.

1. *Discerning How Best to Study the Text for Old Testament Ethics*

Fundamental to John Rogerson's ethics is a firm commitment to the Bible as the scripture of the Christian Church. He believes that the Old Testament discloses the true condition of humanity as fallen and in need of divine redemption. It also recounts the involvement of God within history and with a particular people, Israel, in order to effect this redemption. This nation was to model a different set of values in its lifestyle and institutions and so be a light to others in order that they, too, might know and follow Yahweh. Ultimately, this hope for a transformed world finds its fulfillment in the life, death, and resurrection of Jesus Christ. Consequently, Rogerson has concentrated on working out a method by which Christians can understand the Old Testament and then appropriate its truths for the modern world. The concerns of this project, in other words, are at once biblical, theological, and hermeneutical.

Studies in Contemporary Philosophy, Religion & Theology; Aldershot: Ashgate, 2001); J. Barton, *Understanding Old Testament Ethics: Approaches and Explorations* (Louisville, KY: Westminster/ John Knox Press, 2003).

    4.   E.g. D.A. Knight (ed.), *Ethics and Politics in the Hebrew Bible* (= *Semeia* 66 [1995]); J.W. Rogerson, M. Davies and M.D. Carroll R. (eds.), *The Bible and Ethics: The Second Sheffield Colloquium* (JSOTSup, 207; Sheffield: Sheffield Academic Press, 1995); W.P. Brown (ed.), *Character and Scripture: Moral Formation, Community, and Biblical Interpretation* (Grand Rapids: Eerdmans, 2003).

    5.   One important essay not able to be included is 'Old Testament Ethics', in A.D.H. Mayes (ed.), *Text in Context: Essays by Members of the Society for Old Testament Study* (Oxford: Oxford University Press, 2000), pp. 116-37.

There are two areas in which it is crucial to establish methodological clarity. First, it is impossible to speak about what the Old Testament might offer for ethics unless one has determined how *to analyze the text itself*. An important initial purpose of biblical study is to try to reconstruct how believers in ancient times comprehended and lived out the moral obligations of their faith. On the one hand, this need to grasp as fully as possible the setting within which Israel lived has fueled Rogerson's continuing efforts in the areas of geography, history, sociology, and anthropology.[6] All of these contribute to the task of reconstructing the contours of that ancient society.

On the other hand, Rogerson has explored how Christians across the centuries have interpreted the Old Testament, because to study the past is to glean clues about pitfalls to avoid and more constructive avenues to pursue.[7] He judges that a critical approach is the best way to be intellectually honest with the data.[8] His is not purely an intellectual stance for the academic guild, however; it is also a deeply felt ecclesiastical and pastoral principle. He is convinced that critical studies provide the surest avenue for the Christian Church to get at what the Old Testament truly is saying. Only then will it be able to see what is of value for the present.[9] Therefore, of special interest to him are those critical scholars of previous generations, who maintained their sincere Christian convictions even as they engaged in types of study that sometimes made the Church of their day uncomfortable. These individuals, among whom for him the nineteenth-century German scholar de Wette is the most stellar figure, exemplify the possibility of wedding academic integrity with Christian faith and mission.[10]

---

6. E.g. Geography: *The New Atlas of the Bible* (London: Macdonald, 1985); history: *Chronicle of the Old Testament Kings: The Reign-by-Reign Record of Ancient Israel* (London: Thames & Hudson, 1999); sociology: 'The Use of Sociology in Old Testament Studies', in J.A. Emerton (ed.), *Congress Volume, Salamanca 1983* (VTSup, 36; Leiden: E.J. Brill, 1985), pp. 245-56; anthropology: *Myth in Old Testament Interpretation* (BZAW, 134; Berlin: W. de Gruyter, 1974); *Anthropology and the Old Testament* (The Biblical Seminar; Sheffield: JSOT Press, 1984); 'Was Early Israel a Segmentary Society?', *JSOT* 36 (1986), pp. 17-26; 'Anthropology and the Old Testament', in R.E. Clements (ed.), *The World of Ancient Israel: Sociological, Anthropological and Political Perspectives* (Cambridge: Cambridge University Press, 1989), pp. 17-37.

7. J.W. Rogerson, 'The Old Testament', in J.W. Rogerson, C. Rowland and B. Lindars (eds.), *The Study and Use of the Bible: The History of Christian Theology* (Basingstoke: Marshall Pickering; Grand Rapids: Eerdmans, 1988), I, pp. 1-150. This interest in the use of the Bible is also reflected in volumes that he has edited. Note *The Oxford Illustrated History of the Bible* (Oxford: Oxford University Press, 2001).

8. J.W. Rogerson, *An Introduction to the Bible* (London: Penguin Books, 1999); J.W. Rogerson with P.R. Davies, *The Old Testament World* (Cambridge: Cambridge University Press, 1989). Rogerson is also sensitive to the fact that critical approaches might be disconcerting to students coming from more conservative backgrounds. This concern, in part, led to his editing *Beginning Old Testament Study* (London: SPCK, 1983), which was designed as a primer on method.

9. J.W. Rogerson, 'Biblical Criticism and the Churches: A Plus or a Minus?', *ExpTim* 113.8 (2002), pp. 255-58.

10. J.W. Rogerson, *Old Testament Criticism in the Nineteenth Century: England and Germany* (London: SPCK, 1984); *W.M.L. de Wette, Founder of Modern Biblical Criticism: An Intellectual Biography* (JSOTSup, 126; Sheffield: Sheffield Academic Press, 1992); 'Synchrony and Diachrony

In Rogerson's estimation, Eckart Otto's *Theologische Ethik des Alten Testaments* is a helpful model of how to pursue the dynamics of moral thinking in Israel.[11] Otto compares how laws were conceived and drafted in the ancient Near East with what, according to his reconstruction, occurred in Israel and, in turn, in the production of the Old Testament. He focuses his attention primarily on the Book of the Covenant (Exod. 21–23) and Deuteronomy 12–26 and points out the differences between the two. Although some similarities to the law codes of surrounding peoples do exist, Otto contends that Israel fused its secular laws in a unique way with a theology of the compassion of Yahweh—especially the divine solidarity with the poor and oppressed. Laws now were founded on the character and acts of God, resulting in the exceptional content and motivations of Israel's laws. These norms originally had arisen within the extended family but, as they were molded anew, they were transferred to the responsibility of the state. This was an important development, as traditional social structures began to break down over time because of economic and political pressures.

Otto's formulation is attractive to Rogerson for at least two reasons. To begin with, it works from the premise that ancient Israel's moral thinking was not stagnant. The people engaged the changing realities of their circumstances in connection with their view of God. In addition, and correlatively, it recognizes that the Old Testament is a record of this engagement. What we discover through a study of the redaction of the legal material, Otto claims (and Rogerson would agree), are distinct attempts over time to legislate ethical demands in a way that would be faithful to Israel's sense of divine calling as well as appropriate to the context. Israel apparently was aware of other law codes and the mores of the larger world, yet strove for a distinct lifestyle because of its special relationship with Yahweh.

This biblical study cannot be limited to a descriptive exercise. At this juncture, therefore, Rogerson moves to the second methodological area, the necessity of working out how *to move from the text to today*. The move from the Old Testament to our context, though, is not an easy one. To begin with, ancient Israel's society (primarily composed of small villages made up of extended families) and economy (essentially agrarian, within a feudal and simple market system) were very unlike the modern (especially Western) world, and that is precisely the kind of society to which the text's ethical material was directed. It deals with issues foreign to us and ignores (or is ignorant of) other things that are now considered important. What is more, the Old Testament contains narratives (like the Conquest) and legal material (such as passages dealing with the treatment of women and capital punishment) that

in the Work of de Wette and its Importance for Today', in J.C. de Moor (ed.), *Synchronic or Diachronic? A Debate on Method in Old Testament Exegesis* (Leiden: E.J. Brill, 1995), pp. 145-58; *The Bible and Criticism in Victorian Britain: Profiles of F.D. Maurice and William Robertson Smith* (JSOTSup, 201; Sheffield: Sheffield Academic Press, 1995); 'What Is Religion? The Challenge of Willhelm Vatke's *Biblische Theologie*', in C. Bultmann, W. Dietrich and C. Levin (eds.), *Vergegenwärtigung des Alten Testaments: Beiträge zur biblische Hermeneutik* (Festschrift R. Smend; Göttingen: Vandenhoeck & Ruprecht, 2002), pp. 272-84.

11.   J. Barton also interacts extensively with Otto; see Barton's reviews in *TRE* 64.4 (1999), pp. 425-31, and *Understanding Old Testament Ethics*, pp. 162-75.

can offend moral sensibilities if they are brought over without remainder into today's societies. Nevertheless, the divide between these two worlds is not so wide so that the Old Testament can have little or nothing to say to ethical thought and practice today.[12]

In the articulation of his own view, Rogerson surveys attempts from across the theological spectrum to cross this bridge between the ancient and contemporary worlds.[13] For instance, among those on the evangelical wing, Rogerson has interacted with the views of Walter Kaiser and Christopher Wright.[14] Kaiser, he believes, has an inadequate understanding of the nature of the Old Testament in general and of the Law in particular. Kaiser's portrayal of the Old Testament as the revelation of the eternal will of God is incapable of doing justice to the complexities and moral problems found in the text. A by-product of this shortcoming is that a sizeable portion of Kaiser's work naturally must be dedicated to the task of apologetics, trying to defend the Old Testament from an assortment of critiques of perceived moral deficiencies. In addition, Rogerson feels that Kaiser's suggestions for drawing universal and enduring principles from the text based on the notion of an infallible prepositional revelation are not very helpful either. In contrast, his evaluation of Wright is more positive. He appreciates Wright's awareness of the history of Old Testament interpretation and ethics. The paradigm strategy that Wright employs in order to avoid mere imitation of Israelite practices also is closer to the approach that Rogerson himself champions, but he does disagree with the confidence that Wright shows in the historicity of the text and in the sociological method of Norman Gottwald's *Tribes of Yahweh*.[15]

In sum, Rogerson holds that critical approaches are the best means to comprehend both the text and the ancient world. The results of this study are foundational for elaborating an Old Testament social ethics. Nevertheless, the biblical text and classic critical methods alone are not sufficient in and of themselves for that task. The input of other disciplines is required to craft a more comprehensive system.

2. *The Contributions of Interdisciplinary Study to Old Testament Ethics*

Rogerson's work in Old Testament ethics is no exception to his characteristic willingness to draw upon other fields of study in significant ways. For example, he has utilized material from anthropology (e.g. C. Lévi-Strauss and kinship studies)[16] and

---

12. This negative assessment characterizes Rodd's *Glimpses*.

13. See the essay 'The Old Testament and Christian Ethics', in R. Gill (ed.), *The Cambridge Companion to Christian Ethics* (Cambridge: Cambridge University Press, 2001), pp. 29-41 [Editor's note: this article appears as Chapter 3 of the present volume]. Cf. 'Old Testament Ethics'.

14. W.C. Kaiser, *Toward Old Testament Ethics* (Grand Rapids: Zondervan, 1983). For Wright, see *supra*, n. 3.

15. N.K. Gottwald, *The Tribes of Yahweh: A Sociology of the Religion of Liberated Israel, 1250–1050 B.C.E.* (Maryknoll, NY: Orbis Books, 1979).

16. See 'The Family and Structures of Grace in the Old Testament', in S.C. Barton (ed.), *The Family in Theological Perspective* (Edinburgh: T. & T. Clark, 1996), pp. 25-42 [Editor's note: this article appears as Chapter 13 of the present volume].

social theory (e.g. T.W. Adorno and Z. Bauman).[17] An area of special importance for his Old Testament ethics has been moral philosophy. Three authors particularly stand out: A.D. Lindsay, N.H.G. Robinson, and Jürgen Habermas. Insights from all three help conceptualize the issues of moral life within ancient Israel and today.

It will be remembered from the preceding section that a key concern is how believers, whether they be the people of God in biblical times or in the present, are to interact with and differentiate themselves from the moral standards of the surrounding world. How should one try to discern the demands of faith in God in different situations and eras? Two publications have guided Rogerson's thinking in this regard. The first comes from A.D. Lindsay. In *The Two Moralities: Our Duty to God and to Society*, Lindsay distinguishes between the 'morality of my station and its duties' and the 'morality of grace'.[18] The former is the basic moral framework of any culture or society at any given time and place; it is those standards that most citizens would agree to be correct and reasonable. These are the minimum values and corresponding rules that any society must have in order to function and maintain a sense of order. In other words, they are context-specific (although there will be overlap between cultures due to common human needs and aspirations). Everyone in a society is encouraged to observe these mores and regulations—even Christians (within the bounds of their conscience, of course)—and this is why they constitute what Lindsay labels the 'morality of my station and its duties'. At the same time, and just as importantly, these social duties are incomplete and flawed, precisely because they are a social creation and are enforced by human institutions.

The 'morality of grace', on the other hand, is that morality of perfection grounded in Christian love (the greatest expression of which, in Lindsay's view, is the Sermon on the Mount). Because of the very nature of things and human limitations and constraints, these two moralities have been and will always be in tension. Therefore, the challenge for Christians is to discern how to maneuver this conflict responsibly and creatively in their own life settings, in humble recognition that our moral life is a pilgrimage of growth in character. The 'morality of grace' ideally should influence and, when necessary, even confront that of 'my station' and work to contribute in constructive ways to everyday existence.

The second significant source is N.H.G. Robinson's *The Groundwork of Christian Ethics*.[19] This book moves in much the same direction as Lindsay's book, but

17. For Adorno, see 'The Potential of the Negative: Approaching the Old Testament through the Work of Adorno', in M.D. Carroll R. (ed.), *Rethinking Contexts, Rereading Texts: Contributions from the Social Sciences to Biblical Interpretation* (JSOTSup, 299; Sheffield: Sheffield Academic Press, 2000), pp. 24-47; for Bauman, 'Old Testament Ethics', pp. 129-31; 'Measurable and Immeasurable: Themes in Old Testament Theology', in J.C. Exum and H.G.M. Williamson (eds.), *Reading from Right to Left: Essays on the Hebrew Bible in Honour of David J.A. Clines* (JSOTSup, 373; London: Sheffield Academic Press, 2003), pp. 377-89.

18. A.D. Lindsay, *The Two Moralities: Our Duty to God and Society* (London: Eyre & Spottiswoode, 1940). For Rogerson's use of Lindsay, see 'Christian Morality and the Old Testament' [Editor's note: this article appears as Chapter 2 of the present volume].

19. N.H.G. Robinson, *The Groundwork of Christian Ethics* (London: Collins, 1971). For Rogerson's use of Robinson, see 'The Old Testament and Social and Moral Questions' and 'The

employs a different terminology. Instead of a 'morality of my station and its duties', Robinson speaks of 'natural morality'. This is not the same as what is commonly understood in philosophical ethics as natural law. Whereas natural law, classically conceived, is the moral insights embedded in creation and accessible in some measure to all human beings, natural morality is the moral consensus among sensitive people within a society and even across societies. This, then, is a phenomenological, not an ontological category. This natural morality obviously is imperfect and sometimes contradictory, but it is still the moral framework within which all Christians must live. This consensus also changes over time and can even be said to have evolved in some positive ways (witness, for example, changes in views concerning slavery, the rights of minorities, and ecological matters). Rogerson is not naïve in claiming this moral development; there is no denying, for example, the unspeakable horrors of human behavior in the last century. Still, it must be admitted that there have been advances in some dimensions of human life that should not be ignored. It is also true that Christians can share the moral opinions of others on a variety of topics. Robinson, then, as does Lindsay, provides Rogerson with a conceptual framework to pursue an ethics within the biblical and modern worlds that is engaged yet distinct, adaptable yet faithful.

More recently Rogerson has explored the possible contributions that the discourse ethics of the German philosopher Jürgen Habermas can make to Old Testament ethics. It is not that the Old Testament actually is written from a discourse ethics perspective. Rather, discourse ethics can stimulate a fresh appreciation for what the text says.

Discourse ethics defines humans as interdependent beings, whose interdependence depends upon their ability to communicate with others. This communicative attribute assigns a unique worth to all persons; on the basis of this crucial starting point, it also establishes a universal moral responsibility to allow for all of humanity to be able to achieve and enjoy meaningful communication through familial, social, and institutional means. Humans, then, should not be reduced to the rational creatures of modernity or be manipulated in the style of the *homo economicus* of market-driven culture. They are not to be neglected, exploited, and eliminated for political and economic gain. In other words, discourse ethics offers a particular answer to the fundamental ethical question, 'What does it mean to be human?'[20] The answer to this question determines how humans evaluate and treat each other, at whatever level.

In accordance with this view of the nature of humans, discourse ethics proposes a procedure for doing ethics.[21] It is important to notice that this approach self-

Old Testament and Christian Ethics' [Editor's note: these are articles appear as Chapters 1 and 3 of the present volume, respectively].

20. See 'Life and Death Between Creation and Fall: Some Theological Reflections on Life Issues' and 'What Does It Mean to Be Human? The Central Question of Old Testament Theology?' [Editor's note: these articles appear as Chapters 4 and 5 of the present volume, respectively].

21. See 'Discourse and Biblical Ethics' and 'Ethical Experience in the Old Testament, Legislative or Communicative Rationality?' [Editor's note: these appear as Chapters 6 and 7 of the present volume, respectively].

consciously does not propose or defend a specific content for morality; instead, it describes the optimum conditions under which ethical discussion can take place in a productive and non-coercive manner in any context. Put very simply (and here I do not do justice to the complexities and subtleties of Habermas's position),[22] ethical norms should be argued and agreed upon, with the free and active participation of all parties, before they can be enforced. Obviously, discourse ethics makes it clear that ethics can never be a solely private affair.

Discourse ethics can open a window into the canonical story. From the very beginning of the biblical narrative, humans are pictured as communicating with God and among themselves. One way of describing human sin and its consequences, then, is the rupture of both of these kinds of communication. There are several other ways in which ethics as discourse is reflected within the Old Testament. For example, not every law is apodictic, nor is every legal action predetermined. There are passages that assume that some cases would require more careful consideration and deliberation (compare Exod. 20.13 with 21.13). The Old Testament also presents scenes where God and certain individuals have an exchange about the fairness of moral decisions and actions as part of the process of moral formation. Abraham's dialogue with his visitors in Gen. 18.23-33, Job's complaints, and the give-and-take of the book of Malachi are good illustrations of this. It is interesting to note, too, that Israel's laws and narratives envision institutions that would give a voice to the underprivileged so that the impact of legal decisions, economic structures, and public policy on them might be taken into consideration. The monarchy and the prophets were to safeguard the rights of the less fortunate—the former as a final court of appeal and as the guarantor of justice, the latter as spokespersons before oppressors.

Habermas's discourse ethics is realistic enough to recognize that these ideal conditions cannot be entirely satisfied. Consequently, there will always be levels of conflict in the adjudication of ethical quandaries, their legislation, and social embodiment. In Rogerson's mind, for Christians this pragmatism should reinforce the importance of engagement with the culture within which they live; what is more, it opens the horizon to an eschatological expectation of a future, ethically different from the present. This hope finds expression in the Old Testament. Utopian-like arrangements, like the Jubilee (Lev. 25), and visions of a time of universal peace and prosperity that transcend national boundaries (e.g. Ps. 96.10-13; Isa. 65.17-25; Mic. 4.1-4), can be interpreted as ideal communicative situations. Then, everyone will be able to participate in the good life together and will submit to moral rules that will benefit all of humanity and creation. In this time between the present and the end, though, the doing of ethics will not be easy, and it very well might prove costly. Thus, the eschatological dimension could require a prophetic witness and courage (cf. Mic. 2.6; the experience of Jeremiah).

---

22.   Habermas's discussion deals with other dimensions that Rogerson does not utilize. For example, Habermas relates his system to L. Kohlberg and R. Selman's theories of human moral development. Note, e.g., J. Habermas, *Moral Consciousness and Communicative Action* (trans. C. Lenhardt and S. Weber Nicholsen; Cambridge: Polity Press, 1990).

These three authors, Lindsay, Robinson, and Habermas—each in their own way —underscore the difficulties in living out a moral life in an imperfect and fallen world. They wrestle with the necessity of negotiating between the ideal and the mundane, which for Christians means between what the Gospel might demand and what is achievable on the ground. This is as true for us today as it was for those who lived in ancient Israel.

3. *A Methodological Proposal*

This final section now turns to Rogerson's own proposal for Old Testament ethics. It will be evident that his approach builds off of the material presented in the two preceding sections.

There are three fundamental points to his approach. The first is that ethics is embedded within definite contexts. That is, moral absolutes do exist, but these always are historically situated. They are incarnated in individual lives and communities and expressed in customs and legislation in diverse ways over time. Accordingly, the morality of those who follow God should strive to be representative of the enduring principles of the tradition while simultaneously being in contact with the context. This conviction harkens back to the discussion of the work of Lindsay and Robinson regarding the challenges of pursuing moral ideals (Lindsay's 'morality of grace') in a fallen world. Rogerson has chosen to use Robinson's phrase *natural morality* to label that ethical consensus of the people and place within which believers are embedded and within which they must live out their faith.

A proper appreciation of this natural morality can help those wanting to utilize the Old Testament to recognize the multidimensional distance between their world and that of ancient Israel. The natural morality of a society thousands of years ago along the eastern Mediterranean cannot match that of the present, and so how believers relate to today's natural morality should vary from what was done in that distant past. To recognize the existence of natural morality also requires a healthy realism about the complexity of modern moral debates. It is to be expected that society will not agree with Christian values and positions. Nonetheless, Christians are called to impact their world. This commitment to moral relevance explains Rogerson's interest in Habermas's discourse ethics: it is important to think through what might be the best socio-cultural arrangement for constructive ethical dialogue, both among Christians and between the Christian Church and the broader society.

If the first crucial point of Rogerson's ethics is an awareness of the moral realities of society, the next two concern the motivation and strategy of Christian ethics in any given context. To begin with, and this is the second essential point, Rogerson points out that moral living for the community of faith is to be grounded in *imperatives of redemption*. The imperatives of redemption are those reasons for commending a particular action that are based on the gracious acts of God. In the Old Testament laws, for instance, there is a repeated reminder to recall the Exodus: because Yahweh had mercifully redeemed Israel from slavery in Egypt, the Israelites should be merciful to the less fortunate among them (e.g. Exod. 22.21 [Heb. 22]; 23.9; Lev. 19.34, 36; 25.42, 55; 26.45). For the Christian, of course, the supreme motivation should be based on God's redemptive undertaking for sinful humanity through the cross of Jesus Christ (note Rom. 5.8; Gal. 2.20).

Ethical attitudes and behavior, in other words, are not generated in a vacuum. They should be motivated by gratitude to God and the desire to reflect his character in the world. The next step then is to try to bring those values to bear in the world. This brings us to Rogerson's third point. The imperatives of redemption should inform and orient what he calls 'structures of grace'. These are those social arrangements that are designed to work out this divine graciousness in practical and concrete ways. The hope, too, is that they be a means by which the beneficiaries might be able to stand on their own; these are not to be just isolated acts of charity (although those too are important), but rather constructive measures to help people establish and experience more fully their humanity before God and others. These structures of grace, therefore, are inseparable from and are geared to their context; or, to use the phrase used earlier, they are historically situated. Different eras and social, political, and economic settings require ethical insights and solutions specifically intended for their particular problems. That is why Christians today cannot duplicate the details of the legal system or the practices of the Old Testament. Today's needs are not the same as ancient Israel's, and the ethical challenges of modern societies cannot be met by reproducing what was done among and for that people so long ago. What can be emulated in our time, however, is that creative dynamic of the application of the ethical principles, which now are recorded for us in the Old Testament text—that is, the elaboration and championing of structures of grace for our own time based on those imperatives of redemption. What counts is the moral process visible in the Bible, Rogerson holds, not its contextually conditioned prescriptions. In sum, the Old Testament can best contribute to Christian ethics by its examples of moral reasoning and efforts, rather than by direct, literal imitation.

The best means to understand this proposal is by citing an example of its application. One prominent illustration that Rogerson uses in his publications concerns the practice of slavery.[23] In the ancient Near East and in Israel slavery was an accepted social institution. Yet, as was mentioned above, the attitudes of the people of God towards slaves and servants were to be shaped by an *imperative of redemption*— the release from bondage in Egypt (e.g. Deut. 5.13-15; cf. Deut. 7.7-9; 24.17-22). The Old Testament laws appropriately, therefore, contain *structures of grace* that humanized to a degree that common but cruel institution, which was part of the fabric of the *natural morality* of the time. Exodus 21.1-11, for example, sets a time-limit for servitude and expects some level of benevolence on the part of the master. It is interesting to compare this passage with Deut. 15.12-18. Generosity is expected of the master and is plainly commanded in v. 14. Nevertheless, notice that this passage does not quantify the master's duty; his is a moral obligation based on an appeal to hark back to the mercy of God. Note, too, that the injunction of Exod. 21.2 is expanded in Deut. 15.12 to include explicitly women slaves, thereby giving

---

23. See 'Christian Morality and the Old Testament' and 'The Old Testament and Christian Ethics', which appear as Chapters 2 and 3, respectively, of the present volume.

it a broader reach. For Rogerson, who considers the material in Deuteronomy to be later than what is found in the Book of the Covenant of Exodus 21–23, these differences point to a movement toward greater moral sensitivity within the Old Testament tradition and the people of God. What we have is an ethics interacting with its world and that is attempting to relate continually the character of God to its social life.

The essays in section three of this volume offer a number of examples of this approach. Topics include war, abortion, work, and the family. In every case, Rogerson eschews simple prooftexting. Each is a complicated and sensitive matter. They require that Christians give much careful thought to the issues and demonstrate a judicious use of the Old Testament scripture. Christians must appreciate the importance of suitably arguing for and embodying in the world today the values of the kingdom of God found in the biblical text.

4. *Conclusion*

John Rogerson has developed his Old Testament ethics from the perspective of the convictions of his Christian faith (note especially the last two essays of this volume). He has tried to demonstrate faithfulness to the God of the Bible and to the spirit of its ethical teaching, even as he has explored ways to be intellectually honest with both the historical and textual data and the challenges of modern life. In addition, for him, ethical reflection and practice cannot be exercised apart from the world, so it is necessary to interact with society—both by working through other ancillary disciplines to enrich Old Testament ethics itself and in order to speak to and act on today's social problems more effectively. His coordination of natural morality, the imperatives of redemption, and the structures of grace are his attempt to make the biblical text relevant today and is foundational to his significant contribution to Old Testament ethics.

Part I

THE OLD TESTAMENT AS A SOURCE
FOR CHRISTIAN ETHICS

Chapter 1

The Old Testament and Social and Moral Questions

In 1907, the Deceased Wife's Sister's Marriage Act received the Royal Assent, and a situation was created in which the Canon Law of the Church of England was in conflict with Statute Law. Canon 99 of 1603 and the Table of Kindred and Affinity which it adopted made marriage with a man's deceased wife's sister contrary to 'the laws of God'. The Canon was based upon the principles 'that as husband and wife are one flesh he who is related to the one by consanguinity is related to the other by affinity in the same degree' and 'consanguinity and affinity alike bar marriage to the third degree collaterally'.[1]

The Old Testament basis for this view of 'the laws of God' is clear. Not only is there a direct reference to Gen. 2.24 'they shall become one flesh', but the Table of Kindred and Affinity rests largely upon Lev. 18.6-18. The revision of Canon 99 in 1946 removed the conflicts between Canon Law and Statute Law that the Act of 1907 and subsequent legislation had created, by bringing Canon Law into line with Statue Law. The new Canon made no reference to 'the laws of God'.[2] That not all anomalies were removed seems to be indicated by the fact that a man and his deceased wife's daughter from another marriage were obliged to obtain special legislation recently in order to marry, a bill introduced by Baroness Wootton to allow this type of marriage in general having failed.[3]

Deceased wife's sister marriage highlights what appears to be the relationship between the Old Testament and social and moral issues. Some legislation and some moral attitudes among Christians have an Old Testament origin, going back into pre-Reformation Canon Law, and reinforced after the Reformation in England by the use of the Old Testament as a law book.[4] However, as society has changed, and as moral attitudes have changed, there has been a steady erosion of these laws or

---

1.   G.K.A. Bell, *Randall Davidson, Archbishop of Canterbury* (Oxford: Oxford University Press, 1952–53), pp. 550-57.

2.   *The Constitutions and Canons Ecclesiastical* (made in the year 1603 and amended in the years 1865, 1887, 1936, 1946, and 1948) (London: SPCK, 1961), pp. 43-44.

3.   At the time of writing, March 1982, Baroness Wootton has introduced a new bill dealing with this matter.

4.   For an account of the use of the Old Testament in the Church of England from the Reformation to the eighteenth century, see H. Graf Reventlow, *Bibelautorität und Geist der Moderne* (Göttingen: Vandenhoeck & Ruprecht, 1980); English translation, *The Authority of the Bible and the Rise of the Modern World* (trans. J. Bowden; London: SPCK, 1984).

attitudes based upon the Old Testament. This is most obvious in regard to Sunday observance. It can also be seen in connection with discussions about capital punishment and about attitudes to homosexual relationships.

The belief that the Old Testament contained authoritative information about the origin and constitution of the universe, and about the origin and dispersion of the 'races' of mankind began to retreat in earnest in the face of secular knowledge from the seventeenth century onwards.[5] Ultimately, in the nineteenth century in Britain at any rate, the boundaries between science and theology were re-drawn, to the great benefit of biblical studies. For the Old Testament, it was accepted that it could not be regarded as a scientific or geographical handbook, and that even in the realm of history it was not always accurate in the light of modern canons of historical accuracy.

No such radical re-drawing of the boundaries appears to have taken place regarding the relation between the Old Testament and social and moral questions. True, there has been the gradual erosion of legislation and attitudes based upon the Old Testament as described above; but instead of this bringing about the conclusion that a completely new approach is called for, one can be forgiven for thinking that the Church can still conceive of only one way to use the Old Testament in social and moral issues, and that is to use it as a law book in cases where its content is not too obviously at variance with modern attitudes.

In the 1979 report of the Working Party on homosexual relationships, a complete section is devoted to the biblical evidence, including the biblical evidence from the Old Testament.[6] The main aim of this section appears to be to suggest reasons why this evidence cannot be determinative for the current discussion. But the reasons given appear to be *ad hoc*, and nowhere is the question raised as to exactly how the Bible should be used in the discussion. The method of the report, namely, the discussion of the biblical evidence before the attempt is made to minimize its relevance, seems to suggest a relic of the view that biblical statements on moral matters are fairly directly applicable to the modern situation. In the comments made upon the report of the Working Party by the Board for Social Responsibility it is stated that 'some members of the Board would regard the biblical testimony on homosexual behaviour as by itself settling the matter once and for all'.[7]

It is not the purpose of this article to suggest that there is no way in which the Old Testament can be used in the discussion about homosexual relationships, neither should the above remarks be taken to imply that for Christians, all things are lawful so long as they are done in love. What is being objected to is the apparently unexamined assumption that the starting point for using the Old Testament in social and

5.   K. Scholder, *Ursprünge und Probleme der Bibelkritik im 17 Jahrhundert* (Munich: Chr. Kaiser Verlag, 1966); English translation, *The Birth of Modern Critical Theology: Origins and Problems of Biblical Criticism in the Seventeenth Century* (trans. J. Bowden; London: SCM Press; Philadelphia: Trinity Press International, 1990).

6.   *Homosexual Relationships: A Contribution to Discussion* (London: Church Information Society, 1979).

7.   *Homosexual Relationships*, p. 88.

moral questions is that it is there to provide laws that should be enforced on modern society or Church discipline, provided that the difference between the Old Testament and modern attitudes on the issue concerned is not insuperable.

What might be called the 'legalistic' use of the Old Testament has become prominent in recent discussions of moral issues in theologically conservative circles. The approach known as 'creation ethics' states in a modern form the Calvinistic view that in the Old Testament (as well as in the New), God's ideal will for his creation is disclosed. This revelation serves both as a standard which indicates what is sinful when behaviour falls short of the standard, and it provides guidance for what Christian life and indeed society in general should be like. Creation ethics rejects the traditional use of 'natural law' in Christian ethics, and it claims to provide an approach which is both biblical, and relevant to the modern world.[8]

A specific conservative example is the discussion on homosexual relationships by Michael Green and others, produced in response to the report of the Working Party mentioned above.[9] The book firmly states that 'homosexual activity is wrong, as fornication, adultery, bestiality are wrong' and goes on to give as the reason for this the fact that 'it is written into creation'. By this is meant that Gen. 2.24 is the Creator's instructions for mankind, and that its 'one-man-one-woman—for keeps' teaching rules out homosexual activity just as it rules out fornication, adultery and bestiality.[10]

Although one must respect the sincerity and integrity of those who believe in and practise creation ethics, at the level of method it seems to me that such an approach can only succeed if the biblical material, especially that in the Old Testament, is used selectively. People who cite Gen. 9.6 in support of capital punishment do not normally add that the Old Testament requires the death penalty not only for homicide, but for cursing one's parents, for blasphemy and for adultery.[11] Unless I have overlooked it, I am not aware that the book by Green and others on homosexual activity mentions the fact that the Old Testament demands the death penalty also for homosexual actions.[12] The material from the Old Testament quoted by Green appears to stop short of including the references to the death penalty, yet the book wishes to stress that the Church and clergy should be guided by 'this unambiguous teaching of the Bible'.[13]

It is not being claimed here that it is impossible to devise a hermeneutic that will allow creation ethics to be worked out in modern discussions. One of the contributors to Green's book, David Holloway, implies such a hermeneutic, the centre of

8. For a presentation of creation ethics see the essay by O. Barclay, 'The Nature of Christian Morality', in B.N. Kaye and G.J. Wenham (eds.), *Law, Morality and the Bible* (Leicester: Inter-Varsity Press, 1978), pp. 125-50.

9. Michael Green *et al.*, *The Church and the Homosexual: A Positive Answer to the Current Debate* (London: Hodder & Stoughton, 1980).

10. Green *et al.*, *The Church and the Homosexual*, p. 27.

11. Exod. 21.17; Lev. 24.16; Deut. 22.22.

12. Lev. 20.13. This verse is partly quoted in Green *et al.*, *The Church and the Homosexual*, pp. 76-77, the reference to the death penalty being omitted.

13. Green *et al.*, *The Church and the Homosexual*, p. 28.

which is that the Old Testament can be modified if this is already done in the New Testament, for example, in relation to slavery, where Holloway perceives in Philemon the germs of a rejection of slavery.[14] However, for various reasons, I find it impossible to accept this hermeneutic, and for the remainder of the article an attempt is made to suggest a different way of looking at the Old Testament in relation to social and moral issues. This is based upon two key ideas: natural morality and the imperative of redemption.

Natural morality is a notion found in N.H.G. Robinson's *The Groundwork of Christian Ethics*.[15] He uses it in criticisms of the theological ethics of continental neo-protestantism, where the latter has tried to work out theological ethics purely on the basis of what is revealed (however revelation is understood). Natural morality is not the same as 'natural law'. It is not an attempt to work out from the nature of a person or of an institution what is proper to them, so that a norm is obtained by which to order behaviour. Natural morality is more like a moral consensus common to sensitive and thoughtful people, religious and non-religious alike. In today's world, the consensus would uphold the rights of coloured peoples and of oppressed minorities. It would oppose modern forms of slavery and exploitation, and it would seek to establish justice wherever this was denied in whatever form.

It must be admitted at the outset that the idea of natural morality can be criticized in many ways. Because it implies an intuitionist or deontologist view of ethics, it can be attacked by those who champion the emotive view of ethics, and for whom ethical statements are simply statements about personal preferences. It can be pointed out that on some issues, for example, capital punishment, a majority of citizens, if polled, would favour the opposite of what sensitive and thoughtful people wanted. There are some areas of moral concern, for example, abortion, where sensitive and thoughtful people would be divided between championing the right to life of the unborn, and championing the right of women to do what they please with their own bodies.

Yet when due allowance has been made for these and other objections, it still seems reasonable to suggest that in the course of the history of mankind, there has been an increasing sensitivity to justice, and to the needs and rights of minorities. No doubt this increasing sensitivity has had, and continues to have numerous sources, including religious convictions, philosophical reflection and cultural conditioning backed by legislation. However, the end product at any given point in time has been some sort of consensus among sensitive and intelligent people about things that seemed to be self-evidently right, even if the consensus went against the prejudices of vested interests and the uninformed morality of the majority.

The idea of natural morality has possibilities of application to the Old Testament. At least since the discovery and decipherment of Assyrian and Babylonian cuneiform texts in the nineteenth century, it has been apparent that many of the laws in the Old Testament are not unique, but are ancient Israel's share in a much wider

14.   Green *et al.*, *The Church and the Homosexual*, p. 92.
15.   N.H.G. Robinson, *The Groundwork of Christian Ethics* (London: Collins, 1971), pp. 31-54, 193-205. In what follows, Robinson is not responsible for the presentation of natural morality.

heritage of law in the ancient Near East. It is also clear that Israel was not alone in believing that its laws had been handed down from God or the gods.[16] If we ask what was the basis of these laws, it can be reasonably replied that it was natural morality: a moral consensus of what was self-evidently just and right.

It is difficult to see what is responsible for the law about the goring ox in Exod. 21.28-29 other than a recognition of what was self-evidently just and right. According to this law, an ox that gores a man or a woman to death must be stoned to death. Its owner is not responsible. If, however, an ox is known to be dangerous, its owner has been warned of this fact, he has taken no steps to protect innocent people, and then someone is gored to death by the ox, then not only the ox but also its owner is liable to death. Of course, modern attitudes would regard the death of the owner as an unacceptably high penalty for his negligence, and they might even protest about killing the ox; but otherwise, it would be difficult to fault the intention of the law.

A quite different example of natural morality can be found in the opening chapters of the book of Amos, where the prophet denounces what we would call crimes against humanity. Gaza is accused of taking into exile a whole people (Amos 1.6), the Ammonites of ripping up pregnant women in an attempt to enlarge territory (Amos 1.13) and Moab of desecrating the human remains of slain enemies (Amos 2.1). It is unlikely that Amos was referring to international conventions ratified by members of an ancient precursor of the United Nations, and more likely that he was referring to generally accepted standards of what did, and what did not constitute fair standards in time of war—standards which Israel itself violated if it treated the Canaanites in the way described in the book of Joshua.[17]

If it can be accepted that many of the laws and moral attitudes in the Old Testament constituted the natural morality that obtained in Old Testament times, the following further suggestions can be made. First, by regarding the laws as expressions of human moral sensitivity rather than as expressions of an unalterable divine will, we are better placed to distinguish between what is culturally no longer acceptable (e.g. the death penalty for the negligent owner of a known dangerous ox that gores someone to death) and what is morally important (e.g. that lives should not be put at risk by dangerous animals). Second, we can say that those who believe in God should observe natural morality because it is natural morality; that is to say, God commands it because it is good. This, in turn, leads to a third point, which is that as natural morality changes in accordance with deepening sensitivity in moral matters, so the obligation upon believers changes. In short, the Old Testament does not lay down timeless laws or principles that express God's blueprint for creation. It teaches us that God approves what moral sensitivity at its best holds to be right. A dynamic

16. See G.R. Driver and J.C. Miles, *The Babylonian Laws* (2 vols.; Oxford: Clarendon Press, 1952–55), I, p. 516 gives references to Old Testament passages cited in the discussion.

17. See Robinson, *The Groundwork of Christian Ethics*, p. 32: 'It is not too much to say that Scripture as a whole treats men throughout as moral beings… Whatever changes the Christian religion may work in the moral outlook of men, and however radical these changes may be, morality, it would plainly seem, is not the product but the indispensable presupposition of the Christian revelation and the Christian gospel'. See also J. Barton, 'Understanding Old Testament Ethics', *JSOT* 9 (1978), pp. 44-64.

model is introduced by the idea of natural morality altering in accordance with deepening moral sensitivity.

That the Old Testament goes on to provide more than this will be argued shortly. It is necessary at this point, however, to enter an important qualification with regard to the idea of development that has been associated above with natural morality.

There is no doubt that as mankind has grown older, there has been a development of moral attitudes. To take the well-known example of slavery, here is a case of something that is accepted in the Bible, was presupposed in graeco-roman society, and which endured in Christendom until the nineteenth century. Its abolition is a good example of how deepening sensitivity to rights can result in a change in natural morality. On the other hand, if there has been moral progress in mankind at one level, it does not follow from this that mankind has become 'better'. No one can suppose that mankind is getting 'better' who lives in a century in which the techniques of mass murder, human degradation, ill-treatment of animals and destruction of the environment have been brought to levels of 'effectiveness' of which our great-grandparents could have had no inkling. There is a paradox here. Man's inhumanity to man assumes more subtle and sophisticated forms at the same time that there are real advances in outlawing certain manifestations of that inhumanity. From the Christian point of view, it is a way of recognising both that mankind remains ever in need of redemption by God, and that there is undeniable moral progress in mankind.

The second important key to thinking about the Old Testament and moral issues is what is described above as the imperative of redemption. It is based initially upon those parts of the Old Testament where the motive clause of commandments or instructions mentions God's deliverance of Israel from slavery. The thrust of these commandments or pieces of instruction is that because God showed mercy in redeeming Israel, Israelites must show mercy in dealings with each other; that because Israel is the redeemed people of God, the fact of their being redeemed must affect their lives.

Many of the commands about generous behaviour concern behaviour towards the weak and the poor. Thus, in the Deuteronomy version of the Ten Commandments, where it is enjoined that the manservant and maidservant must rest on the Sabbath, the motive clause is 'you shall remember that you were a servant in the land of Egypt' (Deut. 5.13). Where it is commanded that legal justice must be upheld for the sojourners or the fatherless, and that a widow's garment must not be taken in pledge, the motive clause reads 'you shall remember that you were a slave in Egypt' (24.17-18). Where it is enjoined that the sojourner, the fatherless and the widow are to benefit from a sheaf that is accidentally left in a field, and from what remains of olive trees and grape vines after they have been beaten once only, the motive clause is 'you shall remember that you were a slave in the land of Egypt' (24.19-22).

We have a sort of *imitatio dei* here, in which the imitation centres upon the fact that God in his grace and mercy redeemed Israel, a weak and insignificant people who were oppressed in slavery (cf. Deut. 7.7). Thus the strong have a responsibility to the weak and to the oppressed, to provide for them and to see that they receive justice. The leaders of the community especially have a responsibility here. The prayer for the well-being of the king contains the petitions:

> May he judge thy people with righteousness,
>   and thy poor with justice!
> May he defend the cause of the poor of the people,
>   give deliverance to the needy,
>   and crush the oppressor! (Ps. 72.3-4)

The bitter condemnations of the leaders in Ezekiel 34 are because

> the weak you have not strengthened, the sick you have not healed, the crippled you have not bound up, the strayed you have not brought back, the lost you have not sought, and with harshness you have ruled them. (v. 4)

In Psalm 82, the 'gods' appointed to watch over the nations are judged because they failed to

> Give justice to the weak and the fatherless;
>   maintain the right of the afflicted and the destitute.
> Rescue the weak and the needy;
>   deliver them from the hand of the wicked. (vv. 3-4)

The Psalm ends with the prayer 'Arise, O God, judge the earth; for to thee belong all the nations!'[18]

But not only do we have this imperative which derives from God's salvation of a weak and oppressed people that were enslaved, we can actually see within the Old Testament tradition this imperative being exerted upon what I have called the natural morality, forcing it into deeper sensitivity. If the section on the freeing of slaves in Exod. 21.1-11 is compared with that in Deut. 15.12-18, it will be noticed that the woman slave is dealt with far more generously in the Deuteronomy passage. The exact meaning of Exod. 21.7-11 is disputed, but a reasonable interpretation is that a female slave has no right of freedom (a male slave must be freed after six years) unless her master has married her himself, or has married her to his son, and she has then been denied the rights of a wife. In the Deuteronomy passage, the female slave is given the same right to freedom after six years as male slave; and it can be discerned even by a non-hebraist reading a formal equivalence translation such as the RSV that the reference to the female slave is a gloss. But it is a very important gloss, for it indicates the extending of rights so as to include female slaves, in a passage which has the motive clause 'you shall remember that you were a slave in the land of Egypt, and the LORD your God redeemed you' (Deut. 15.15).

If we put together the two ideas of natural morality and the imperative of redemption, we obtain the following synthesis. Natural morality is something to which we must be responsive. God commands it because it is good. But it is not static; it must change in accordance with deepening insights, and part of this change is to be brought about from the pressure provided by the imperative of redemption.

---

18.   See J.W. Rogerson and J.W. McKay, *Psalms 51–100* (CBC; Cambridge: Cambridge University Press, 1977), pp. 163-65.

In the situation of the fellowship of the redeemed, the strong must protect and support the weak, but also, the quest to identify the weak must be never-ending. In the Old Testament, the female slave was thus identified, and was given the same rights as the male slave. In eighteenth-century Britain the slave was given the rights of any citizen. In the twentieth century the equal rights of women and of coloured minorities have been identified and championed. There is now growing discussion about the rights of unborn children, of handicapped children, even of animals.

The purpose of this article is to urge that the Old Testament cannot be used like a law book. The approach suggested here is that much of the Old Testament material about command and instruction is the natural morality of Old Testament times. This is often illuminating in its principles but often superseded in its details, because natural morality alters in response to new moral insights. If we are to take seriously the Old Testament demands for righteousness, and its stress upon God's demand for righteousness, we do this by participating to the full in the natural morality of our own day. But we do this, if we are Christians, in the light of the Old Testament imperatives of redemption. These remind us of the duty of the strong to support the weak; but also, they remind us of our total dependence upon God, of our constant need for his grace, and on the need for the vision of his kingdom which the Bible alone supplies.

Much more needs to be said on this subject than a short article can contain, and no doubt what has been said will alarm those who wish to use the Bible in order to obtain some sort of fixed morality. What is envisaged here is an attempt to be truly and fully biblical, an attempt to use the Bible honestly. It is also designed to deliver us from the security of precisely defined rules, into the insecurity, and the freedom of the children of God.

Chapter 2

CHRISTIAN MORALITY AND THE OLD TESTAMENT

Robert Murray's work has been distinguished not only by the highest scholarship, but by a concern that the Bible should shed light on today's world. The present article seeks to set down some thinking that I have been doing in recent years about the use of the Old Testament in Christian morality in today's world, as a contribution to one side of Robert Murray's interests.[1]

A necessary prelude to thinking about how to use the Old Testament in today's world is a very brief consideration of how previous generations of Christian writers have tackled the problem; for however sketchy and inadequate such a consideration might be, it will at least pre-empt the misleading view that, until recently, Christian moralists fully accepted the Old Testament as part of Christian ethics, and that any hesitations that may now be found result from the biblical criticism of the eighteenth century onwards, or even the liberal trends of the 1960s.

The use of the Old Testament in the moral teaching of the New Testament is a matter for New Testament experts; and I am not such an expert. Yet one simple example will indicate the complexity of the matter. In Exod. 21.1-6 and Deut. 15.12-18 there are laws specifying that a male (in Deut. 15.12 also a female) slave must not serve a master for more than six years. At the end of this period, the slave is either released or, in a publicly witnessed ceremony, pledges his (or her) service to the master for life. In Deut. 23.15-16 there is a law which prescribes that if a slave escapes from his [*sic*] master, the Israelite to whom he flees must not return him to his master, but must let him dwell in a town 'where it pleases him best'.

In the New Testament, Paul refers to the duties of slaves at Eph. 6.5-9 and Col. 3.22–4.1. It has to be recognized, of course, that probably a majority of scholars disputes the Pauline authorship of Ephesians while opinions on the Pauline authorship of Colossians are more equally divided.[2] This issue is not important here. What is important is that a writer (or writers) whose work was accepted into the New Testament canon wrote about slavery without any reference to the Old Testament laws on the matter. Slaves are told to serve their masters, 'fearing the Lord' (Col. 3.22), while masters are told to treat their slaves justly and fairly, knowing that they have 'a Master in heaven' (Col. 4.1). There is no hint that the Old Testament limits

1.   See also my article, 'The Old Testament and Social and Moral Questions', *ModChm* 25 (1982), pp. 28-35.

2.   The matter is discussed, for example, in A.T. Lincoln, *Ephesians* (WBC, 42; Dallas: Word Books, 1990), pp. xlvii-lxxiii.

the period of the service of slaves to six years; there is no warning to slave-owners that they should ensure that they release their slaves at the proper time.

Now there are several ways in which this apparent discrepancy could be explained. It could be argued that it was common ground between slave-owners and the writer(s) of Ephesians and Colossians that the slaves would be released after six years, and that it did not need to be spelled out. Or, Paul or a disciple believed that the parousia was imminent, and would end the world before slaves needed to be released. Against this, it can be said that if Christian slave-owners needed to be reminded that they should treat their slaves 'justly and fairly', it was over-optimistic to expect them to be assiduous about the laws of release. There remains the possibility that the Old Testament laws on slavery were being ignored, a possibility that is strengthened when Philemon is considered.

Again, the matter of the Pauline authorship of Philemon is irrelevant. What is important is that a writing was accepted into the New Testament canon that appears to fly directly in the face of the Deut. 23.15-16 law about not returning a runaway slave. Philemon is a letter written on the occasion of the *return* of a slave, One-simus, to his master, Philemon. Again, some of the details are not clear and the apparent difficulty may be capable of satisfactory explanation. Thus the writer speaks of the returned Onesimus as 'no longer...a slave but more than a slave'. But Paul (or his disciple) did not have the power of manumission; only the master had that. And if Paul hints in v. 21 that it would be good if Onesimus were freed, this is done without any reference to the Old Testament laws on the subject. Indeed, by sending Onesimus back to his master Paul is denying him the independence that the law in Deut. 23.15-16 appears to guarantee to escaped slaves.

If, on this one example, the use or non-use of the Old Testament in New Testament moral practice is shown to be problematic, it will come as no surprise that the early Church adopted various strategies to cope with the application of the Old Testament to moral problems. Three such strategies will be considered briefly: allegorization, dispensationalism and classification.[3]

Allegorization is found in the Epistle of Barnabas, where the laws about avoiding unclean animals are taken to mean that Christians should not associate with certain types of persons, whose characters resemble those of the forbidden creatures.[4] There are at least two types of dispensationalism. The Apostolical Constitutions distinguish between the laws that were given prior to the making of the Golden Calf in Exodus 32, and those that were given afterwards.[5] It is argued that the post-Exodus 32 laws were given to Israel to help the people avoid idolatry. Therefore, these 'additional precepts' are not necessarily binding upon Christians. The pre-Exodus

3.   For a much fuller exposition of what follows, including a treatment that covers a much wider time span including Aquinas, see my article 'The Old Testament', in J.W. Rogerson, C. Rowland and B. Lindars, *The Study and Use of the Bible* (The History of Christian Theology, 2; Basingstoke: Marshall Pickering; Grand Rapids: Eerdmans, 1988), pp. 1-150.

4.   The prohibition against eating pork means, according to *Barn.* 10.3, 'Thou shalt not join thyself to men who resemble swine'.

5.   See the section 'Of the law' in the *Apostolical Constitutions* (Ante-Nicene Christian Library, 17; Edinburgh, 1892), pp. 162-70.

32 laws are in a different category, and are instances of the natural law. Cyril of Alexandria bases a dispensational approach on the law in Lev. 19.23-25 which says that the fruit of a newly planted fruit tree must not be eaten the first three years, that in the fourth year it is to be offered to God and that only in the fifth year can it be eaten generally. The three forbidden years are likened to the period of Moses, Joshua and the Judges, with the fourth year representing the purification of the law by the prophets, before the law of Christ can be enjoyed by all.[6] This, then, is a seemingly negative view of the Old Testament law.

The classificatory approach divided the Old Testament law into three types: ceremonial, civil and moral. A classical statement of this approach is found in the Articles of Religion in the Book of Common Prayer (article 7) which declare that ceremonial laws are not binding on Christians, and that civil laws are not necessarily binding. Only moral laws are binding.[7] However, this assumes that it is possible to distinguish between ceremonial and moral laws, and it can be shown that this was not always straightforward, by referring to the Sabbath commandment. The main reformers (Luther and Calvin) seem to have regarded the Sabbath commandment as ceremonial, and, therefore, as not binding upon Christians. It was up to individual believers or churches to decide which day should be the Lord's Day.[8] Tyndale is quoted as holding that even a Lord's Day was not necessary if the people could be taught without it.[9] On the other hand, groups that took the Sabbath commandment to be a moral commandment wished to apply it literally. This early seventh-day sabbatarianism was vigorously suppressed by the authorities in Reformation England.[10]

The purpose of this very selective sketch of some attitudes to using the Old Testament law has been to discourage the idea that one uses the Old Testament by referring to a passage and then applying it to today's world. This procedure can only work on the basis of a highly selective reading of the text, and which fastens on materials that can command some moral respect today, as opposed to the great quantity of material that offends the moral sensitivity of contemporary readers. Such an approach is not a responsible use of the Bible.

I turn now to some positive suggestions, fully aware that they reflect my own interest, and that they represent only one possible approach to the place of the Old Testament in Christian morality. The starting-point is a book recommended by my

---

6. A. Kerrigan, *St. Cyril of Alexandria: Interpreter of the Old Testament* (AnBib, 2; Rome: Institutum Pontificio Biblicum, 1952), pp. 170ff.

7. 'Although the Law given from God by Moses, as touching Ceremonies and Rites, do not bind Christian men, nor the Civil precepts thereof ought of necessity to be received in any commonwealth; yet notwithstanding, no Christian man whatsoever is free from the obedience of the Commandments which are called Moral'.

8. See D.S. Katz, *Sabbath and Sectarianism in Seventeenth-Century England* (Leiden: E.J. Brill, 1988), p. 4. Calvin, apparently, made a point of playing bowls on Sunday, while Luther is quoted as ordering people to work, ride or feast on Sunday, if the day is 'made holy for the mere day's sake'.

9. Katz, *Sabbath*, p. 4.

10. Katz, *Sabbath*, pp. 9-20.

teacher in moral philosophy from student days, Dorothy Emmet, and entitled *The Two Moralities*.[11] In this work, A.D. Lindsay contrasts the morality that he calls the 'morality of my station' and the 'morality of grace'. These moralities correspond roughly to natural morality and to the challenge to act graciously implied in the teaching of the Sermon on the Mount. Lindsay argues that the former is enriched by the latter and that the 'morality of grace' depends upon sensitivity, imagination and creativity.

A passage that sums up this aspect of Lindsay's argument runs as follows:

> Grace is not a thing that can be measured or calculated. There is in it, indeed, a certain extravagance. That is surely the moral of the story of the woman with 'the alabaster cruse of exceeding precious ointment'. There ought to be in the highest kind of conduct a touch of recklessness, not caring, not counting the cost to ourselves. The morality of grace cannot be codified. There is always a touch of the infinite about it… In the morality of my station and its duties the station presents us with the duty, and we say 'Yes' or 'No', 'I will' or 'I will not'. We choose between obeying or disobeying a given command. In the morality of challenge or grace the situation says, 'Here is a mess, a crying evil, a need! What can you do about it?' We are asked not to say 'Yes' or 'No' or 'I will' or 'I will not', but to be inventive, to create, to discover something new. The difference between ordinary people and saints is not that saints fulfill the plain duties which ordinary men neglect: the things saints do have not usually occurred to ordinary people at all.[12]

The statement that the morality of grace cannot be codified, that it is reckless and has a touch of the infinite about it sheds interesting light upon passages from Deuteronomy. In its version of the law of release of slaves (15.12-18) Deuteronomy instructs the master whose slave is leaving him after six years to 'furnish him liberally out of your flock, out of your threshing floor, and out of your wine press'. The passage does not so much enjoin a duty, which would specify that he should be given, say, a sheep, a bushel of grain and a measure of wine. It commands the master to use his sensitivity and to act generously. 'You shall furnish him liberally out of your flock…' Yet this is more than simply an appeal to the master's humanity. It is grounded in God's graciousness:

> as the LORD your God has blessed you, you shall give to him. You shall remember that you were a slave in the land of Egypt, and the LORD your God redeemed you; therefore I command you this today. (Deut. 15.15-16)

We have here what I call an 'imperative of redemption', which is to be expressed in what I call a 'structure of grace'.

An 'imperative of redemption' is a reason for commanding a particular action that is grounded in what God has graciously done in redemption. In the case of the release of slaves it has particular resonance, because the slave is in exactly the same position as the whole people was, before God acted to deliver them. But as a motive clause for justifying particular moral responses from Israel it has a much

---

11. A.D. Lindsay, *The Two Moralities: Our Duty to God and to Society* (London: Eyre & Spottiswoode, 1940).

12. Lindsay, *The Two Moralities*, pp. 48-49.

wider application, and it is found not only in Deuteronomy, but in the so-called Book of the Covenant (Exod. 21.1–23.19; see especially 22.21 [Heb. 20] and 23.9) and in Leviticus (see Lev. 19.34, 36; 22.33; 25.42, 55; 26.45). A 'structure of grace' is a social arrangement that is meant to work our graciousness in practical terms, so that both those who administer it and those who benefit are aware of the graciousness implied. Further, the aim of a 'structure of grace' is to enable beneficiaries to become independent citizens, using their freedom to the glory of God. In the case of the release of slaves in Deuteronomy 15, and the liquidation of debts and the restoration of land in the Jubilee year (Lev. 25), the aim is to restore the independence of those who through no fault of their own have lost their possessions and their freedom.

A second point in Lindsay's *The Two Moralities* which sheds light on the moral content of the Old Testament is his belief that the 'morality of my station' needs to be influenced by the 'morality of grace', so that the former develops new insights under the influence of the latter, insights that can be accepted by all, whether or not they acknowledge the existence of a 'morality of grace'. Now a number of Old Testament studies have been moving in the direction of showing how theologically driven tendencies shaped the moral content of the Old Testament and made it increasingly reflect God's graciousness. E. Otto's recent *Theologische Ethik des Alten Testaments* does this in exemplary fashion.[13]

Otto has written a series of articles comparing legal drafting techniques in the ancient Near East with those in the Old Testament. There are many similarities; but the differences lie in the way in which the Old Testament brings together secular laws and theological principles in order to make the laws as a whole a practical expression of the implications of the compassion of God. Of the Book of the Covenant, Otto writes:

> In the Book of the Covenant the individual is addressed and confronted with JHWH as the compassionate one… Thus, the individual must practise solidarity not because the king commands it, but because God is in solidarity with humankind.[14]

The pressure of divine compassion upon the 'secular' morality of the laws in Deuteronomy is particularly striking. In Deuteronomy, obligations to help each other that are elsewhere considered to be the duty of the family (in a narrow and in an extended sense) are extended to the entire nation. The entire nation is a nation of brothers (and sisters, we would need to add from today's perspective), so that each Israelite has the duty to act towards his fellow-Israelite as towards a brother in his immediate family. This *Bruderethos* (brother-ethic), as it has been called, is particularly striking in passages such as Deut. 15.7-9 (where readers who rely upon English translations should avoid gender-free renderings such as in the NRSV, where the force of the repeated word for 'brother' in the Hebrew is lost). But Deuteronomy goes even further than extending family obligations to the whole people.

13. E. Otto, *Theologische Ethik des Alten Testaments* (Stuttgart: W. Kohlhammer, 1994).
14. Otto, *Ethik*, p. 10 (author's translation).

It includes even enemies under the heading of the brother. This is seen if Exod. 23.4-5, 'If you meet your enemy's ox or his ass going astray, you shall bring it back to him', is compared with its revised version in Deut. 22.1, 'You shall not see your brother's ox or his sheep go astray, and withhold your help from them; you shall take them back to your brother'. In the deuteronomic version of this law, there are no enemies in Judah; only brothers. It has also been pointed out how Deuteronomy extends to women several of the protective measures that, in the Book of the Covenant apply only to men. Thus, in Exod. 21.1-6 only male slaves can be released after serving for six years. Exodus 21.7 explicitly says that a female slave 'shall not go out as the male slaves do'. However, in Deut. 15.12 both male and female slaves get their freedom after six years; and although the words 'or a Hebrew woman' in Deut. 15.12 look like a gloss that does not alter the exclusively masculine singular grammar of the remainder of the passage, there can be no doubt that the text as we have it means to extend to women slaves the right of release after six years. Another example is at Deut. 24.18 where the rule about restoring by nightfall a man's garment taken as a pledge (Exod. 22.26 [Heb 25] and cf. Deut. 24.12-13) is applied to a widow, whose garment may not be taken at all as a pledge.

The collections of laws in the Old Testament could not, and were never intended, to regulate the whole of ancient Israel's life.[15] This is not only clear when comparisons are made with collections such as the Laws of Hammurabi, but is evident from an examination of the laws themselves. There are no laws dealing, for example, with how men and women marry and divorce. Yet the existence of such laws or social customs is taken for granted in Deut. 24.1-4, which prohibits a divorced and remarried woman from returning to her first husband, and by Deut. 22.13-21, which protects a newly married woman from the charge that she was not a virgin when she married.

The laws in the Old Testament are a selection of laws that must have existed in ancient Israel, and the purpose of the selection was to make a theological statement about the character of God and of the divine requirements for Israelite society. This is probably why the Book of the Covenant begins with detailed laws about the freeing of slaves. Slaves hardly deserved such a prominent position in the laws if one reflects on their powerless and insignificant position in ancient Israel; but the laws are not just secular laws. They are God's laws to Israel, and the release of slaves is put first in the Book of the Covenant because it is not God's will that there should be slaves in Israel.

I am not suggesting that the laws contained in the Old Testament were not intended to be observed or put into practice. I am suggesting that the reason why they were selected and included in the Old Testament was in order to be illustrative of the character of God rather than to provide a comprehensive legislative programme for Israel. It may also be that some of the laws were too idealistic to be put into practice, for example, the laws of the Jubilee in Leviticus 25. If that is so, then their value lies in the area of theology rather than law.

15.   See, further, J.W. Rogerson and P.R. Davies, *The Old Testament World* (Cambridge: Cambridge University Press, 1989), pp. 233-35.

How does what has been said above affect the use of the Old Testament in contemporary Christian morality? I can only give a personal view, as follows. First, there are undoubtedly imperatives in the Old Testament that have a validity that transcends time and culture. Thus, the commands not to murder, commit adultery, lie or steal make universal claims upon human behaviour. Traditional moral theology has grounded these imperatives in natural law or natural morality. However, moral absolutes have to be applied to specific circumstances, and in situations of life or death, decisions have to be made that might entail lying to a sick person about his or her condition, or a mother stealing food to feed her young child. The Old Testament is not unaware of the dilemma about applying commands to specific circumstances, and provides, for example, for ways in which someone who has accidentally taken another's life may escape the penalty prescribed for murder (cf. Exod. 21.13; Num. 35.9-28).[16] Wrong acts do not cease to be wrong because it may be possible, exceptionally, to justify them in certain circumstances. That such dilemmas have to be faced is an indication that moral principles sometimes, or even often, have to be applied in a situation where a choice has to be made between two evils.

The second point is that there are many moral teachings that cannot be taken over from the Old Testament and applied to today's world. This is not a new idea in Christian teaching, as the beginning of this article indicated. What will be new is the way that this position is justified today. Thus, some laws are simply offensive to modern readers, such as that which prescribes the death penalty for striking one's parents (Exod. 21.15), while others simply cannot be applied because the situations that they envisage no longer exist. Slavery is illegal in today's world, thus making obsolete all the Old Testament provision for the release of slaves. Again, few readers, in the West at any rate, are subsistence farmers like the majority of the population in ancient Israel; and if farmers today want to help the poor it will not be by letting them glean in the fields at harvest time (cf. Ruth 2.2). How many modern Western readers of the Bible would know what to do with ears of barley or a sheaf of wheat (cf. Deut. 24.19)?

Thirdly, it may be possible to read some laws at the level of the spirit rather than the letter, and to see them as providing pointers to what to do in the modern world. Thus, while the Jubilee laws are largely irrelevant to an industrialized society when read at the level of the letter, the principle that they enunciate, that of freeing people from indebtedness so that they can take full responsibility for themselves, may have something to say to a world where the indebtedness of the two-thirds world to the first world may hinder the former from putting into place the economic measures needed for their specific circumstances. Again, regarding the laws about slavery, it will be possible to ask whether there are modern forms of slavery that exist in societies that have outlawed the institution.

16. There is, in fact, much more dialogue in the Old Testament about the application of moral principles than is often realized. See my article on 'Discourse Ethics and Biblical Ethics' in the proceedings of the symposium on Ethics and the Bible at Sheffield in April 1995: J.W. Rogerson, M. Davies and M.D. Carroll R. (eds.), *The Bible and Ethics: The Second Sheffield Colloquium* (JSOTSup, 207; Sheffield: Sheffield Academic Press, 1995), pp. 17-26.

However, and fourthly, the main contribution of the Old Testament to Christian morality may be by way of example rather than precept. If the Old Testament allows us a glimpse of a process in which imperatives of redemption led to the formulation of structures of grace, its challenge to us may well be that we should be asking what imperatives of redemption make claims upon us today, in response to which we then ask what arrangements should or could be made to express them in appropriate structures of grace.

Some imperatives of redemption may be suggested by the Old Testament itself, such as the repeated motive clause that God freed the Israelites from slavery in Egypt. For although modern readers will hardly consider themselves to be the descendants of freed slaves, the principle enunciated in the language of the exodus deliverance is clear enough: God is a God of liberation, including physical, political and economic liberation. Thus, any form of enforced dependence, whether of individuals upon individuals, or groups upon individuals or other groups, or of nations upon nations, is unacceptable to God. Christian morality will also draw upon the New Testament for imperatives of redemption, such as the declaration of Paul in Gal. 3.27-28. But it may also be the case that imperatives of redemption are suggested by the needs of those we encounter as, to quote Lindsay again, 'the situation says, "Here is a mess, a crying evil, a need! What can you do about it?"'[17] and we respond with generosity and creativity. In today's world the voices that call out to us will include not only the poor and powerless, but the unborn, and the other species with whom we share the planet.

What the appropriate 'structures of grace' might be will be a matter for experts in economic and social affairs. As Lindsay's book makes clear, and as Christian moral theory has always recognized, ethics is not just a religious, or Christian, concern. It is the point at which Christians meet those of other faiths or of no faith but who share a concern for peace and justice, and an equitable economic order. If Christians have a distinctive contribution to make it is by way of insights arising from the biblical witness to the liberating and sacrificial love of God; and it is in this regard that we can learn from the Old Testament how attempts were made to fashion structures that would enable ancient Israel to articulate its experience of God's graciousness.

17. Lindsay, *The Two Moralities*, p. 49.

Chapter 3

THE OLD TESTAMENT AND CHRISTIAN ETHICS

1. *Old Testament or Jewish Bible?*

In the past twenty years there has been a move in British and North American scholarship to use the term 'Hebrew Bible' (less often, 'Jewish Bible' or 'Jewish scriptures') in place of 'Old Testament'. The question affects ethics, as will be shown shortly. The reason for the move has been a wish to be sensitive to Judaism, and to avoid the impression, undoubtedly created in many people's minds by the term 'Old Testament', that the books designated by this name are inferior to or superseded by those known as the New Testament. In addition, there has been the feeling in some quarters that the Christian term 'Old Testament' is inappropriate in academia.

It is easier to be sympathetic to the reasons for the move than to feel that the underlying problem has been satisfactorily dealt with. The terms 'Jewish Bible' and 'Jewish scriptures' most naturally refer to texts held sacred by and used distinctively within Judaism. They are legitimate designations in that context. 'Hebrew Bible' is more problematic, because, on analogy with 'English Bible', it most naturally refers to the Bible in Hebrew, although few students who take courses in 'Hebrew Bible' in universities and colleges actually read it in that language. There is the further problem that 'Hebrew Bible' and 'Old Testament' are not synonymous. For the majority of Christians for most of the history of the church, 'Old Testament' has designated not only the twenty-four books of the Bible in Hebrew, but has also included the thirteen to sixteen books that Protestants call the Apocrypha but which are scripture for the Roman Catholic and Orthodox churches.[1] A partial compromise would be for 'Jewish Bible/scriptures' to be used in the context of Judaism and 'Old Testament' in the context of Christianity.

The matter is particularly relevant for ethics, because the two faiths have developed markedly different approaches to using the texts that they have in common in their scriptures. In Judaism the scriptures reveal God's explicit guidance for the regulation of every facet of the daily life of the faithful believer. This belief has two implications. First, because the laws actually contained in the scriptures deal with only very limited areas of life, Jews believe that God revealed two laws to Moses on Mt Sinai—a written law and an oral law. The former is found in the Jewish scriptures, and pre-eminently in the first five books (the Torah). The second was

---

1. For more details see J.W. Rogerson, *An Introduction to the Bible* (London: Penguin Books, 1999), Chapter 1.

passed down by word of mouth from Moses to Joshua to the prophets, and eventually to the rabbis of the era after the fall of Jerusalem in 70 CE, who began to write it down in the Mishnah (early third century CE) the Tosephta (fourth century CE) and the Babylonian and Jerusalem Talmuds (fourth to ninth centuries CE).[2] This leads to the second implication, which is that there has been, and continues to be, a process of legal and scriptural interpretation within Judaism designed to discover God's will for every detail of daily life. Further, although there have been, and continue to be, great authorities on how to interpret the laws, the field is not occupied merely by experts. In orthodox Judaism, all devout believers are students of the laws, and have devoted many hours of their lives to studying not only the scriptures but the dozens of volumes which contain the oral law.

Within Christianity, a quite different path was taken; and it is clear that the question of the extent to which Christians, and in particular Christians who were not Jews, should obey the laws of the Old Testament deeply divided the early church and left its mark on the New Testament. The matter was made more difficult by the fact that church and synagogue congregations were often rivals in areas such as Syria and Asia Minor. The letters of Paul indicate that there were conflicts between those who believed that Christ's death and resurrection had 'fulfilled' the law and removed from Christians the obligation of strict observance of it, and 'Judaizers' in the church, who took strict observance to be part of Christian discipleship. The Pauline party came out on top, and in the Acts of the Apostles, a book representing the Pauline viewpoint, a 'Council of Jerusalem' is described, which decided that non-Jewish Christians should observe only the following Old Testament laws: to abstain from eating meat that had been sacrificed to idols (not an explicitly Old Testament law but an interpretation of the prohibition of idolatry in the Ten Commandments), to avoid blood (i.e. to eat only 'kosher' meat) and to avoid unchastity (Acts 15.1-29, especially vv. 28-29). Whether or not there was a Council of Jerusalem, the point is that Acts 15 expresses a view about Christian obligation that was held in at least some Pauline churches.[3] As this chapter will indicate later, this 'minimalist' view of Christian obligation to the Old Testament laws contrasts sharply with some Reformation and modern reformed views that as much of the Old Testament as possible should be legislated upon contemporary societies.

2. *Problems of the Moral Content of the Old Testament*

Popular misconceptions about the Old Testament, such as that its God is a God of wrath, spill over into its moral tone, with passages being cited such as those about dashing the heads of babies against rocks (Ps. 137.9) or the demand of 'an eye for an eye' (Exod. 21.24). There is no denying that the Old Testament contains material that is offensive to modern readers, and that some of its leading characters

---

2. See E.E. Urbach, *The Sages—Their Concepts and Beliefs* (trans. I. Abrahams; Jerusalem: Magnes Press, 1975 [Hebrew original *Hazal: Pirqe Emunot veDe'ot* (Jerusalem: Magnes Press, 1971)]), Chapter 7 ('The Written Law and the Oral Law').

3. For a recent discussion see C.K. Barrett, *A Critical and Exegetical Commentary on the Acts of the Apostles* (Edinburgh: T. & T. Clark, 1998), II, pp. xv-xxviii, 706-45.

behave in ways that are illegal as well as offensive in a modern society. For example, Jacob (Gen. 29.21-30) and Elkanah (the father of Samuel, 1 Sam. 1.2) have two wives, a reminder that ancient Israelite society was polygamous. Joshua, at God's command, kills the entire population of conquered towns (Josh. 6.21), something that would be regarded as a war crime today. David commits adultery with the wife of one of his soldiers who is away fighting, and then arranges for the man to be killed in battle when it is discovered that he has made the woman pregnant (2 Sam. 11). David does not go uncensored (see 2 Sam. 12.1-15), yet he is described elsewhere as a man after God's own heart (1 Sam. 13.14) and as one whose heart was wholly true to God (1 Kgs 15.3).

For much of Christian history, these and other difficulties were explained and justified in various ways. The inhabitants of cities destroyed by Joshua were said to be wicked people who deserved to be punished; and in any case, if God commanded something it must be right—not, incidentally, the view of the author of Gen. 18.22-33, who argued that God must act in accordance with what is just.[4] The actions of David were justified on the basis of the distinction between what he did in his official capacity as a king, where he was blameless, and what he did as a private individual, where he was morally culpable. Although this is not an arbitrary distinction—an army officer acting in accordance with proper 'rules of engagement' will not be held guilty of murder if he orders his men to shoot at an enemy, whereas a civilian who tells an accomplice to shoot a member of the public will be accused of murder—it is unlikely to convince modern readers that David can be held up as a moral example in the ways that the Old Testament does. Indeed, one of the factors that led to the rise of modern critical study of the Bible was the refusal of scholars to go on justifying the questionable moral behaviour of Old Testament characters.

This is not the only problem, however. Some of the actual laws contained in the Old Testament are illegal in modern society. For example, the death penalty is prescribed not only for homicide (Exod. 21.12) but also for striking one's father or mother, stealing a man (i.e. depriving him of his freedom), cursing one's parents, sacrificing to any god other than the God of Israel and apostasy (Exod. 21.15-17; 22.20; Deut. 13.6-11). Also to be put to death are a stubborn and rebellious son, a woman found not to be a virgin on her first night of marriage, a man and woman caught in the act of adultery, a man and woman who commit incest and a man who has intercourse with a male as with a woman (Deut. 21.18-21; 22.13-21, 22-24; Lev. 20.11-13).

There is evidence that the death penalty was not being enforced in Judaism for at least some of these offences by the end of the first century CE;[5] but one of the implications of the presence of laws such as those listed immediately above is that any use of the Old Testament in ethics which simply quotes a passage and seeks to

---

4. See the use of these arguments and the general defence of the Bible against the charge of 'contradictions to morality' in T.H. Horne, *An Introduction to the Critical Study and Knowledge of the Holy Scriptures* (London, 10th edn, 1856), pp. 597-612.

5. See Urbach, *The Sages*, pp. 430-36 (Hebrew, pp. 380-84).

apply it directly to modern society must confine itself to those laws which are not yet illegal in modern society, and must explain why these laws continue to be applicable today when others are so much at odds with modern ethical sensitivity.

3. *How the Old Testament Has Been Used in Christian Ethics*

One striking feature of the New Testament is how little reference it makes to the Old Testament in regard to conduct and morality.[6] Jesus is presented as someone who rejects the common interpretation of the law about not working on the sabbath (Mk 2.23-28; 3.1-6) and who radicalizes the law in such a way that it can hardly be observed (e.g. Mt. 5.27 'every one who looks at a woman lustfully has already committed adultery with her in his heart'). Paul summarizes some of the Ten Commandments and 'any other commandment' under the heading of loving one's neighbour (Rom. 13.8-10). It is also arguable that in sending back the slave Onesimus to his master Philemon (if this is what the letter to Philemon is about), Paul is ignoring the stipulation in Deut. 23.15-16 that 'you shall not give up to his master a slave who has escaped from his master to you'.

The absence of reference to the Old Testament law continues with the texts known as the Apostolic Fathers. The *Didache*, which aims to guide its readers in the way of righteousness, has hardly any reference to the Old Testament, while *The Shepherd of Hermes*, which sets out twelve commandments for Christian living, has only one commandment which could be derived from the Old Testament, that on divorce. However, the author of *The Shepherd* is probably dependent on Matthew's gospel in this instance. *The Epistle of Barnabas* explicitly rejects the Old Testament sacrificial system, quoting Isa. 1.11-14 and Jer. 7.22 (famous prophetic critiques of sacrifice) in support (*Barn.* 2.5-6). It spiritualizes ordinances such as those about clean and unclean foods (these laws actually refer to different types of person whose company should be avoided), and it declares that Old Testament laws about the Sabbath are not to be taken literally by Christians (*Barn.* 10.1-9; 15.1-9).

When the Old Testament begins to be taken more seriously, it is on the basis of a kind of dispensationalism. The *Apostolical Constitutions* (probably dating from the fourth century and compiled in Syria) distinguishes between laws given before the incident of the Golden Calf and those given after it (Exod. 32; see *Apostolic Constitutions* VI, chs. 19–30). The laws and sacrifices prescribed after the Golden Calf incident are designed to correct Israel's apostasy and are not binding on Christians. The laws given prior to this incident include the Ten Commandments (which become increasingly important for the Church) and laws of which many begin with the word 'if'. These laws must be taken seriously by Christians; but they are not necessarily prescriptions. For example, Exod. 20.24 does not say 'make an altar of earth'; it says 'if you make an altar, make it of earth'.

---

6.   For what follows see my article, 'The Old Testament' in J.W. Rogerson, C. Rowland and B. Lindars, *The Study and Use of the Bible* (The History of Christian Theology, 1; Basingstoke: Marshall Pickering; Grand Rapids: Eerdmans, 1988), pp. 1-150.

Sophistication in handling the Old Testament is increasingly evident as it wins back the ground that it appears to have lost, at any rate in moral issues, in the early church. Aquinas was influenced by the Jewish scholar Maimonides' masterpiece *The Guide of the Perplexed* (c. 1190) and by its argument that the Old Testament laws could be defended rationally as instruments designed to keep the Israelites from paganism and to promote their physical health. Like others before him, Aquinas distinguished Old Testament laws that were moral from those that were ceremonial and judicial. The moral laws contained the obligations of natural law, and were therefore binding upon all humans. The ceremonial and judicial laws were applications of natural law directed to the specific circumstances of ancient Israel. In the form that they took in the Old Testament they were not, therefore, universally binding. Indeed, even the supreme expressions of the moral law in the Ten Commandments, immutable as they were, needed to be interpreted in order to be applied; and it was permissible for the sabbath law to be broken if one was acting in the interests of human welfare.[7]

The distinction between moral laws and ceremonial and judicial (or civil) laws was taken up with the Reformation, and stated, for example, in the seventh of the Thirty-Nine Articles of Religion of the Church of England. The article states that, of the 'Law given from God by Moses', those 'touching Ceremonies and Rites, do not bind Christian men, nor the Civil precepts thereof ought of necessity to be received in any commonwealth'. Only the moral commandments were necessarily binding. However, it was not always easy to decide which commandments were moral and which were ceremonial and civil. The main reformers, Luther, Calvin and Tyndale, apparently took the view that the sabbath commandment was ceremonial and therefore not binding upon Christians. In the view of Calvin and Tyndale it was up to a local congregation or community to decide which day should be the Lord's Day (it did not have to be Sunday), while Luther objected to any ecclesiastical authority that declared a day such as Sunday to be holy, and he regarded such a declaration as an affront to Christian liberty.[8]

If it is a surprise that such radical attitudes to the Old Testament law should have been followed, in certain areas of Protestantism, by the development of strict sabbatarianism, the reason is that some strands of the Reformation believed that as much of the Old Testament as possible should be legislated upon Christian nations. Representative of this view is Martin Bucer's *De regno Christi* (*On the Kingdom of Christ*), written shortly before Bucer's death in 1551 and dedicated to Edward VI of England.

Bucer accepted that Christians were not bound by the civil and ceremonial laws of Moses; but he also argued that:

> since there can be no laws more honorable, righteous, and wholesome than those which God, himself, who is eternal wisdom and goodness, enacted, if only they are applied under God's judgement to our own affairs and activities, I do not see why

---

7.   See Rogerson, 'The Old Testament', p. 71.

8.   D.S. Katz, *Sabbath and Sectarianism in Seventeenth-Century England* (Brill's Studies in Intellectual History, 10; Leiden: E.J. Brill, 1988), p. 4.

> Christians, in matters which pertain to their own doings should not follow the laws
> of God more than those of any men.[9]

In practice this meant that the king, like David, Solomon, Asa, Hezekiah, Josiah
and Nehemiah, should regulate the life and attitudes of the people through education, decrees and the administration of justice. Bucer advocated the death penalty
for blasphemy, violation of the sabbath, adultery, rape and certain types of false
testimony.

Examples of the differing ways in which the Old Testament has been used in
ethics could be multiplied. Although they do not necessarily inform us about how
the Old Testament can or should be used today, they indicate that there has been a
good deal of variation and of hermeneutical sophistication in such use. Anyone
who gives the impression that to use the Old Testament simply involves taking a
passage and applying it straightforwardly to today's world, and that this procedure
upholds biblical principles, is flying in the face of history.

4. *Contemporary Uses of the Old Testament in Christian Ethics*

Contemporary uses can broadly be divided into 'conservative' and 'liberal'
approaches, with considerable diversity within each division. Walter C. Kaiser's
Toward Old Testament Ethics is a learned attempt to defend the moral integrity of
the Old Testament and to advocate the view that its commandments are the
revealed will of God.[10] Thus he tackles head-on the moral deficiencies of some Old
Testament characters and laws that were pointed out in 'Problems of the Moral
Content' above, and seeks to blunt the criticism that these deficiencies provokes.
He uses, for example, the distinction between people acting in their capacity as
holding an office, and people acting as private individuals. His particular view of
the Bible and of God leads him to conclude that, in some cases, our conviction that
some of God's commands are immoral rests upon 'a deficiency in our view of
things and our ability to properly [*sic*] define terms or grasp the whole of the subject'.[11] Kaiser recognizes that Old Testament laws cannot necessarily be plucked
from their context and applied directly to today's world, and he sets out some
'Principles for Moral Interpretation of the Old Testament', which are ways of
getting at universal moral statements behind Old Testament laws that are situated in
Hebrew language and culture. At the same time, he argues that God's will as
revealed in the Old Testament for all sexual relationships is monogamous hetero-
sexual marriage (Gen. 2.24) in spite of the evidence that Old Testament society was
polygamous. Kaiser's book is a scholarly attempt to defend 'biblical principles'
against modern secular attitudes, yet it acknowledges the force of modern secular
attitudes by conceding that Old Testament morality has to be defended against the
charge of immorality.

---

9.   M. Bucer, *De regno Christi* (Library of Christian Classics, 19; London: SCM Press, 1959),
p. 319.

10.   W.C. Kaiser, *Toward Old Testament Ethics* (Grand Rapids: Zondervan, 1983).

11.   Kaiser, *Toward Old Testament Ethics*, p. 269.

A quite different 'conservative' approach is that of Christopher Wright, whose work is characterized and to some extent shaped by awareness of the history of how the Old Testament has been used in ethics.[12] Wright argues that Israel is God's paradigm of what a nation ought to be. This enables him to take full account of the historical and cultural conditions in which ancient Israel existed and to contrast Israel with its neighbours so as to point out striking differences which ultimately indicate the moral character of God.

The application of Old Testament laws is seen as a sophisticated process in which laws must be understood in their Old Testament context so that their primary objective can be discerned. Once this has been found, it needs to be reformulated in terms of modern circumstances, also taking into account the fact that, in ancient Israel as well as in modern society, moral decisions were not and are not made in neutral circumstances, but in circumstances where the choice will be between two evils. Wright asks, when interpreting and applying an Old Testament law, 'What is the balance of creation ideals and fallen realities, of justice and compassion, in this law?'[13]

Two aspects of Wright's work are problematical. First, as a 'conservative' scholar he accords a much higher literal historical value to the Old Testament than most critical scholars would. Secondly, in his reconstructions of Israel as a paradigm in contrast to Canaanite society, he is too dependent on Norman Gottwald's pioneering work in *The Tribes of Yahweh*.[14] Few scholars would now accept that it is possible to know anything about ancient Israel in the period 1250 to 1050 BCE. On the other hand, Wright's general position is similar to that of scholars who approach Old Testament ethics and their application to today's world from 'liberal' historical-critical standpoints.

This position sees the value of the Old Testament in terms of example rather than precept. It holds that within the Old Testament there are attempts to define and legislate compassion towards the poor and the oppressed, as well as towards the environment and the non-human inhabitants of the earth. These attempts cannot be directly applied to today's industrialized world, since they deal with the problems of a society based upon subsistence agriculture; but they stress the importance of justice and solidarity, including solidarity with the natural environment, and are a challenge to today's world to work out these values under modern conditions.

A notable example of an historical-critical presentation of this position is in Eckart Otto's *Theologische Ethik des Alten Testaments*, which concentrates on major collections of laws in the Old Testament, such as the Book of the Covenant (Exod. 21.1–23.19) and Deuteronomy 12–26.[15] Otto sees these collections as attempts to bring originally secular moral precepts into the realm of Israel's religion, so that

---

12. C.J.H. Wright, *Walking in the Ways of the Lord: The Ethical Authority of the Old Testament* (Leicester: Apollos, 1995).

13. Wright, *Walking in the Ways of the Lord*, p. 145.

14. N.K. Gottwald, *The Tribes of Yahweh: A Sociology of the Religion of Liberated Israel, 1250–1050 B.C.E.* (London: SCM Press, 1980).

15. E. Otto, *Theologische Ethik des Alten Testaments* (Stuttgart: W. Kohlhammer, 1994).

they express, and are used to put into practice, God's solidarity with humankind and especially with the poor and oppressed.

Working along similar lines, I have drawn attention to the presence in the Old Testament of 'imperatives of redemption' and 'structures of grace'.[16] Imperatives of redemption are motive clauses, that is, statements which give the reason why God commands certain things. A frequently found motive clause is 'you shall remember that you were slaves in the land of Egypt, and the Lord your God redeemed you; therefore I command you this today' (Deut. 15.15). It is an imperative of redemption because it refers to God's freeing of Israel from slavery in Egypt. In turn, this action has certain implications for Old Testament morality. God did not liberate a people so that they could enslave or oppress each other. This leads to the enjoining of the 'structures of grace', which are administrative and practical arrangements designed to introduce graciousness and compassion into the details of everyday life. In Deut. 15.13-14 there is a 'structure of grace' in the form of a command that a released slave should receive from his master generous gifts of animals, grain and wine. The implication is that these will enable him to start life as a free man with better prospects of avoiding future slavery than if he were merely released penniless. Another 'structure of grace', in Exod. 23.12, makes the main beneficiaries of the command that no work should be done on the sabbath, the domesticated ox and ass and the slaves of a household.

If it is accepted that the Old Testament can best contribute to Christian ethics by example rather than precept, that is, by challenging modern society to imitate its principles in ways appropriate to today's world, three factors can be dealt with satisfactorily. First is the fact that the laws of the Old Testament cover only very limited areas of everyday life even in the context of ancient Israel. It was pointed out at the beginning of this chapter that orthodox Jews believe in an oral law which supplements the written law; and Roman Catholic moral theology has traditionally appealed to 'natural law' in order to supplement what is contained in the Bible. Any use of the Old Testament in terms of precepts, that is, applying Old Testament laws directly to modern society, is going to find itself restricted by the limited coverage of the Old Testament itself. Secondly, this restriction will be further limited by the fact that many Old Testament laws are either illegal or unacceptable in a modern society. The 'precept' approach limits itself in practice to the area of human sexuality and the family. The 'example' approach, fully recognizing the particularity and situatedness of many Old Testament laws, can address far wider areas of modern life, including matters of justice, the economy and the environment. Thirdly, the 'example' approach recognizes fully that morality and ethics are of concern to secular as well as religious interests. To the extent that some Old Testament laws have close parallels with, for example, the much older laws of Hammurabi, it can

---

16.　J.W. Rogerson, 'Christian Morality and the Old Testament', *HeyJ* 36 (1995), pp. 422-30; 'The Family and Structures of Grace in the Old Testament', in S.C. Barton (ed.), *The Family in Theological Perspective* (Edinburgh: T. & T. Clark, 1996), pp. 25-42 [Editor's note: these articles appear as Chapters 2 and 13 of the present volume, respectively].

be said that the Old Testament acknowledges and draws upon a 'natural morality'.[17] If contemporary Christian ethicists are to devise 'structures of grace', they will need the help and expertise of modern 'secular' experts in the fields of law and sociology. Yet the 'example' approach maintains that religion has a part to play in the shared religious and non-religious enterprise of morality and ethics by providing prophetic insights that can shape morality and deepen sensitivity.

5. *Further Considerations*

The Old Testament contains a good deal of evidence or moral debate that went on in ancient Israel. If this is noticed, the view that the Old Testament is primarily a source of commandments in the form 'thou shalt not' will be considerably modified. Secondly, recent developments in ethics and in particular the discourse or communicative ethics of Jürgen Habermas and his followers can shed new light on moral discourse in the Old Testament.[18]

Three stories about an ancestor (Abra[ha]m twice and Isaac once) saying that the man's wife is in fact his sister (Gen. 12.10-20; 20.1-18; 26.6-11) raise the question whether it is legitimate to deceive people in order to secure a more important end. In these stories, the purpose of the deceit is to save the life of a male ancestor, who believes that he will be killed by the foreign ruler in whose territory he finds himself so that the ruler can take the wife into his harem. These stories can also be seen in a new light in terms of discourse ethics, as will be argued shortly. The same dilemma is explored in 1 Sam. 20.1-34, where both Jonathan and David lie about the reason for David's non-appearance at Saul's new-moon festival. They know that Saul is likely to try to kill David if he is present. Thus a lesser evil—lying—is agreed upon in order to avoid a greater evil—attempted murder. That the lie will be wrong, even if necessary, is indicated by the fact that Jonathan will not volunteer the lie but tell it only if challenged by Saul about David's absence.

A different dilemma is explored in Exod. 1.15-20 where the two(!) midwives charged with killing the burgeoning number of Hebrew boys at birth on the orders of the pharaoh, refuse to carry out the orders. In order to justify themselves, they tell the lie that robust Hebrew women (unlike Egyptian women) give birth before the midwives get to them. The question of whether or not one should obey the unjust orders of those in authority is one that has become particularly acute in the modern world.

---

17. See N.H.G. Robinson, *The Groundwork of Christian Ethics* (London: Collins, 1971).

18. For the remainder of this section, see my articles 'Discourse and Biblical Ethics' in the proceedings of the symposium on Ethics and the Bible at Sheffield in April 1995: J.W. Rogerson, M. Davies, M.D. Carroll R. (eds.), *The Bible and Ethics: The Second Sheffield Colloquium* (JSOTSup, 207; Sheffield: Sheffield Academic Press, 1995), pp. 17-26; 'Old Testament Ethics', in A.D.H. Mayes (ed.), *Text in Context: Essays by Members of the Society for Old Testament Study* (Oxford: Oxford University Press, 2000), pp. 116-37 [Editor's note: the first essay appears as Chapter 6 of the present volume].

In Gen. 18.22-33, a long discussion (again illuminated by discourse ethics) is recorded between God and Abraham concerning whether God should destroy Sodom if even ten righteous people are found in the city. Two questions are raised. 'Shall not the judge of all the earth do right?', asks Abraham (Gen. 18.25). In other words, is there a notion of justice derived from 'natural morality' to which God should be subject? Secondly, is the just punishment of a wicked majority more important than the unjust punishment of a righteous minority, or vice versa? The passage implies the answer that it is more desirable to avoid wrongly punishing the innocent (which means that the wicked would go unpunished), if any can be found. It is also important to note that parts of the Old Testament attack the view that the universe is a moral universe, one in which virtue is rewarded and vice is punished. This attack is most explicitly mounted in Ecclesiastes and is based upon the author's observations of life. There are oppressed for whom there is no help against their oppressors (Eccl. 4.1), there is wickedness in the place where justice should be administered (3.16), there are people who accumulate wealth and honour but who do not live to enjoy them (6.2), there is a poor wise man whose wisdom delivered a city but whose deed is forgotten (9.14-16). There are wicked people who succeed in life and righteous ones who do not (7.15). At the very least, such observations indicate that there are realism, compassion and even despair at the heart of the Old Testament's wrestling with moral issues. In this regard, Ecclesiastes becomes one of the most appealing texts for modern readers.

Discourse, or communicative, ethics as worked out by Habermas is an attempt to define the conditions under which ethical norms could be agreed by all those who had a legitimate interest in a matter, without coercion. The approach is directed especially against ethical relativism, and Habermas lays particular stress upon willingness to be persuaded by the force of the better argument. The twin ideas of discourse and of willingness to be persuaded by the force of the better argument are clearly evident in Gen. 18.22-33. They are also apparent in Gen. 20.1-17, the second of the three stories in which an ancestor deceives his foreign host by saying that his wife is his sister. The foreign host is Abimelech, king of Gerar, and the narrative contains an interesting dialogue between Abimelech and God, who comes to the king in a dream. God warns Abimelech that he is a dead man because he has taken a married woman into his harem. Abimelech, in his reply, appeals to the force of the better argument:

> Lord, wilt thou slay an innocent people? Did he [Abraham] not himself say to me 'she is my sister'? And she herself said, 'He is my brother'. In the integrity of my heart and the innocence of my hands I have done this.

The narrator justifies God's warning by making God say that it is he who has prevented Abimelech from having intercourse with Sarah; but the boldness with which the narrator describes Abimelech's dialogue with God is evidence for moral agonizing in ancient Israel, and recognition of the importance of appeal to the force of the better argument.

6. *Conclusion*

According to popular perceptions, the Old Testament contains crude morality and operates mainly at the level of 'thou shalt not'. This chapter has not tried to evade any difficulties. It has tried to show, however, that throughout Christian history the Old Testament has been used in sophisticated ways in ethics and that modern research has revealed its moral sensitivities, the importance of dialogue, the appeal to the force of the better argument and its attempts to make the practical arrangements of society reflect and express God's compassion for and solidarity with the world and all its inhabitants. A full appreciation of the range of its ethical concerns guards against simplistic application and enlarges the challenges that it presents to modern readers, including ethicists.

Part II

THE CONTRIBUTION OF PHILOSOPHICAL ETHICS
TO THE STUDY OF OLD TESTAMENT ETHICS

Chapter 4

LIFE AND DEATH BETWEEN CREATION AND FALL:
SOME THEOLOGICAL REFLECTIONS ON LIFE ISSUES*

Theological reflections will be of interest only to those who accept that theological statements have some meaning. Thus, it is entirely proper that the present session should run in parallel with a session devoted to strictly medical matters. Also, I am aware of the fact that, in speaking on 'Life' issues to people outside the churches, it is necessary to appeal to reason, and to put forward arguments that will be convincing to people of any faith or no faith. I hope, therefore, that no one will say to me after this address 'this is all very well, but you cannot say this sort of thing to non-believers'. The purpose of this session is to address believers and anyone else who wishes to listen, because Christians are by no means agreed about what attitude they should take to 'Life' issues. My own church, the Church of England, which is in any case at best only a semi-literate body when it comes to Theology, has no agreed position. Further, it is necessary to establish what exactly theology can and cannot say on 'Life' issues, so that we do not get involved in what I call the Galileo syndrome. We all know the story of how the theologians of Galileo's day thought that they knew better than he did about the relative motions of the planets, and how he was forced to submit to what he knew to be false. It would be nice to think that Theology can provide infallible information on ethical and medical issues; the truth is that while Theology does indeed at some points find it necessary to challenge secular ideas, it does not belong to the nature of Theology to be able to tell us, for example, when life begins. Personally, I accept the view that life begins at fertilisation, and that it is impossible to draw a line somewhere within the continuum that stretches from that point to the time of death, and to say that, at this point life begins. But I hold this position not as a believer or a theologian, but as a rational human being. The life that is referred to when we say that life begins at fertilisation is not life as a theologian can talk about, for Theology cannot speak about life apart from God. What the theologian has to say, then, may strengthen us in our conviction that we are right to argue as we do about the beginning of life, but it cannot decide the matter once and for all.

Let me begin, then, by talking about creation. From the perspective of faith, belief in creation is not belief about the origins of the universe. It is not the deduction from the world that we perceive that it has design features, and must therefore have

*   This study was delivered as an address to the Life National Conference, 14-15 October 1987, Coventry. The presentational style of the original has been retained.

a designer. To believe in the world as created means that we choose to live in a manner fitting to the sort of place the world is; and the sort of place the world is can be described as follows. First, it is a place whose originator and sustainer is the God revealed supremely in Jesus Christ. Second, it is a place in which the human race occupies a position of great trust and responsibility, and is called upon to exercise stewardship in partnership with other living creatures. Third, it is a place in which one of the most important human activities is worship. Worship is important not because God requires or needs humans to sing his praises, but because worship nurtures our awareness of God's transcendence, strengthens the bond between individuals, and lifts us above our petty concerns to catch a vision of a world living in harmony, and united in the service of God the creator. To believe in the world as created, then, means to live in it under the lordship of God, and in the attempt, sustained by worship, to act in accordance with the stewardship that he has entrusted to us.

Underlying this belief is an answer to the question that the Psalmist posed in Ps. 8.4—'What is humankind?' And the answer is that humankind is only truly human when living in dependence upon God. Humanity is not a natural endowment, as though merely by being born of human parents we are humans, in the way that giraffes are giraffes because born of giraffes or elephants are elephants because born of elephants. The meaning of the phrase from Genesis 1 that God made humankind in his own image as male and female, is at least that God made humankind to live in relationship with himself, and that when humankind ceases to do this, although it may remain *homo sapiens*, it is no longer human in the sense intended by God. In the parable of the Prodigal Son the Father says of his son who went to the far country and then returned: 'This my son was dead and is alive again'. Similarly the human race is dead if it cuts itself from the source and purpose of its life; and this is why Theology can welcome but not confirm the view that life begins at fertilisation.

The answer of faith to the question 'What is humankind?' runs counter to the answer that has been given implicitly to the same question since that complex movement that we call the Enlightenment, an answer that affects much of our thinking and practice today. The Enlightenment brought about a change in the way that human beings saw the place of humanity in the world, and for what I am about to say I refer to such sources as Charles Taylor's book on Hegel, or the popular book by the German theologian W. Pannenberg, *Was ist der Mensch?*, as well as the more recent work of E. Meinberg, *Das Menschenbild der modernen Erziehungswissenschaft*. According to these authorities, the pre-Enlightenment view of the world placed humanity firmly and clearly within a proper hierarchy within the world. At the top was God, then came angels, and then came human beings, who were above the rest of the natural order. The Enlightenment, by its stress upon the importance of human reason as the touchstone for judging the truth of everything, put humanity at the top of the tree, and proceeded to judge everything, including the Bible and traditional theology by means of the categories of human reason. This process was not in itself necessarily bad. It was part of a moment in which advances were made in the process of understanding, controlling and exploiting the resources of the natural world for the benefit of humanity. It also liberated religion from superstition and uncritical acceptance of tradition. It inaugurated biblical criticism, and encouraged honest questioning and criticism of biblical narratives. It enabled the advances in medical science and practice to take place, which culminated in the discoveries and techniques from which we all benefit today. But there was a price to pay, and that price comes to the surface when we are confronted today by 'Life' issues.

The medical science that has banished diseases that until recently could destroy whole populations and can bring relief, where in earlier ages people suffered, is the same medical science that can abort fetuses on a large scale and can freeze and store embryos; and when there is argument about the rightness or otherwise of these practices, the hidden assumption is often that human beings have a right to do anything that will promote their better health or well-being, because the promotion of such health and well-being is the first priority of what it means to be human. The more I reflect upon these issues, the more I feel that, in the secular as well as the theological field, we must ask in such circumstances not so much the question 'What is life?' as the question 'What does it mean to be a human being?'. What answer is being given to the Palmist's question 'What is man?'.

The answer contained in the belief in creation that I have been outlining must, it seems to me, deny that the human race has an absolute right to do anything that will further the well-being of one or more of its individuals. If truly to be human is to be dependent upon God and to exercise a stewardship for the benefit of the whole created order, we cannot regard human lives as disposable items or even as scrap to be cannibalised for the benefit of other humans. If, in worship, we catch glimpses of the majesty of God and of our own nothingness—and compare the words of Psalm 8

> When I behold the heavens, the stars and moon which you have made…what is man that you have regard for him? (vv. 3-4 [Heb. 4-5])

we shall hardly find it easy to accept the Enlightenment view of humanity as the essentially rational being able to dispose for his own benefit whatever exists in the world. None of this, you will notice, helps us to answer the question 'When does life begin?' or 'At what point does a human being become a person?'. As I said earlier, these questions have to be tackled in other ways. However, belief in creation, in my view, forces us to ask and answer the question 'What does it mean to be a human being?' in such a way as to make it impossible for us to regard ourselves as the all-sufficient rational beings who can decide in our interests the issues of life and death.

This brings me to the point where I can say something about death from the point of view of belief in creation. Death is the event which unmasks the human pretence that we are what we are in isolation from God. Death is a reminder that, in one sense, we are no different from the rest of the created order. We are as much subject to the cycle of birth, life and death as any other created thing. We may be able to prolong life and to make it more comfortable, but at the end of the day we cannot prolong it indefinitely, and its occurrence is a reminder of the transient nature of our being. If we have any hope of existence beyond death, that hope does not depend upon ourselves, but upon God; and part of belief in a created world entails that the creativity that people have achieved in life is not lost, but in God's purposes is taken into a higher order of being. For this, however, we are entirely dependent upon God's creative action. Belief in the immortality of the soul, that is, the belief that at death some part of us lives on because that is the sort of beings we are, such belief is not part of Christian faith in createdness. It is an attempt to understand what it means to be human apart from God, and it tries to assert that, because we are human beings, we shall survive death. It is a manifestation of the human pride that refuses to accept that we are limited, transient beings, whose life, death and hope beyond death depend entirely upon God. From this standpoint, it seems clear to me that we are not the arbiters of death, and that no human should be in a position to decide the death of another person. To exercise such power is to place ourselves in the position of God, and to assume control over something which we have no right to deal with. This viewpoint does not tell us whether aborted fetuses are people whose deaths we decide to bring about. This matter has to be argued on other grounds. However, a consideration of the question of death in the light of the question 'What does it mean to be a human being?' can have the effect of placing the whole matter in a context where we can see the paradox in which beings whose own death will reveal the limitations of their status in the world take it upon themselves to decide upon life or death for others.

I now propose to insert two interludes into the argument. The first deals with the question: From where do we get the faith in creation that I have been talking about? The second draws attention to the work of a modern political philosopher at the heart of which is an answer to the question 'What does it mean to be a human being?' that I believe can be used to address people for whom theological arguments carry no weight. On the question: 'From where do we get our faith in creation?', I can only give a personal answer based upon the relational and confessional theology which I accept. For me, belief in creation is not something that can be grasped simply by looking at the world in which we live. As I look at that world, I see many beautiful and sublime things; but I also see much apparent disorder, wastage and cruelty—I shall be coming to these things when I speak later about fallenness—so that if I were left to deduce from the world as I see it whether it was the expression of a divine purpose, I would have to be an agnostic. For me, then, it is not a matter of first believing in a creator God and then believing that Jesus Christ is the son of God. For me, faith in God without Jesus is not possible. It is Jesus who makes faith in God possible, and I would agree with the statement attributed to Rudolf Bultmann that we should not so much say that Jesus is God as that God is Jesus—although such a statement, of course, needs a lot of glossing.

The life of Jesus was the supreme answer to the question 'What does it mean to be a human being?', and the answer lived out by Jesus was, that to be fully human, one has to lead a life of absolute dependence upon God which results in total self-giving for others; and that where necessary, that self-giving may involve laying down one's life, in the belief that God can and will vindicate that supreme sacrifice. The God whom Jesus discloses is a God who is in the midst of life, involved in its contradictions, and suffering the injustices inflicted by humans upon each other, in order to achieve the harmony and mutual love that ought to lie at the heart of true human existence. The same idea can be traced back in the Old Testament, through the sufferings of God in and with his people, to the creation stories in Genesis. These are to be read, not as quasi-scientific accounts of the origin of the universe in conflict with the theories of Darwin, but as expressing the deepest visions of Israel's sages about the purpose of creation, the nature of humanity, and their role in the world as intended by God. But the greatest interpreter of these chapters of Genesis was Jesus, because he lived out his life in absolute faith in createdness, including his willingness to offer his life for others even unto death. This is why I want to stress that, imperfect as our faith and lives will be in comparison with his, to believe that the world is created is not primarily to do something with our heads, but to do something with our lives, by living as those who accept a particular answer to the question 'What does it mean to be a human being?'.

In the second interlude I want to mention the theory of communicative inter-action which has been the mainspring since 1981 of the German political philoso-pher J. Habermas. Earlier in the address I mentioned the Enlightenment view of mankind as that of the rational being whose reason was the touchstone for deciding truth and values, and who had learned to understand, control and exploit the world of nature. It is well known, of course, that Hegel criticised this idea of man as pri-marily a reasoning being uninfluenced by other factors, and that Marx developed a critique that stressed the economic and environmental factors that make humans what they are, seen in secular terms. Habermas has reasserted the importance of human rationality, while at the same time criticising the Enlightenment view of humankind as primarily a reasoning creature. His definition of what it means to be human is interesting for at least two reasons: first, because of his criticism of the Enlightenment view which is still so pervasive, and secondly because his defini-tion is counter-factual, that is, it defines mankind as something that is not, in fact, achieved, with the result that there is almost a redemptive element in his philosophy.

I must make it clear that I have no idea, in spite of reading a great deal of Haber-mas, what his views on 'Life' issues are, and that I may well have used his ideas in ways of which he would not approve. Yet Theology has never flinched from seek-ing help from philosophers, as witness the part played by types of Platonism in the formulation of the classical creeds of the Church, or the part played by the inter-pretation of Aristotle in Thomas Aquinas's reformulation of Theology in the thir-teenth century. Habermas's definition of what it means to be human assumes that we are mutually interdependent beings, and that this interdependence is based upon our ability to communicate with each other and to pass on our cultural achieve-ments from one age to the next. Interdependence is also a powerful argument in the discussion of 'Life' issues. As Professor Zachary has argued so powerfully, even after birth, we are totally dependent upon our parents and immediate family for our existence for many years. During our lives, we cannot be fully human if we live in isolation from others, and as we enter into old age, our dependence upon others again increases until it may become total.

But in fact, in the real world, human beings often act in such a way as to be anything other than interdependent. Wars, violence, quarrels, isolation, ignorance and neglect all belie what we are supposed to be, and Habermas brings powerful tools to bear in order to analyse why this is so, indicating, among other things, the ever-growing complexity of our life-systems and the distortion of our means of communication and thus interdependence by propaganda, misrepresentation and pornography. At the end of it all, he makes a powerful plea that we should become what we are, namely, rational interdependent beings, and that we should unmask everything that degrades our humanity, whether that degradation comes from adherence to impersonal things such as 'market forces' or from policies aimed to enable one group to exercise power over another group.

In connection with 'Life' issues, Habermas seems to me to deserve study for the following reasons. First, because he opposes the Enlightenment stress on the supremacy of reason as a means of gaining mastery over the world, and secondly, because he calls for the use of rationality to restore the interdependence which he believes to be fundamental to what it means to be human. In 'Life' terms we could use his position to argue that, if interdependency is fundamental to being human, then that interdependency begins from the moment that a unique individual cell is formed, and begins its journey through the continuum that will ultimately end in death. Thirdly, we can meet the challenge that we should use rationality to enable us to become more fully what we are, by so ordering our society that we deal rationally with the problems that produce the demand for abortions. This would include an attack on the poverty, ignorance, permissiveness and violence that produce unwanted babies. To arrange for babies to be born and adopted is a rational solution that preserves the idea of interdependence.

Habermas's view that, in much practice, human beings are not what they should be ideally now leads to the next, and in some ways most difficult, part of my talk, that which deals with fallenness. To hold that the world and the human race are fallen is to assert something that can only be maintained by faith. Of course, you do not have to be a believer to be aware of the contradictions that exist in the world. Believers have no monopoly of insight when it comes to recognizing cruelty, discrimination, sexism, racism, abuse of power, marginalisation, alienation etc. Also, you do not have to be a theologian to be aware of 'nature red in tooth and claw' alongside all that is beautiful and sublime in the world of nature. Where faith differs from other standpoints is in the way it puts these contradictions into context. A materialist can say that these contradictions as far as they affect the human world, are the result of economic conditions which, if changed, will lead to the elimination of the contradictions. Someone who believes in the progress of the human race may see the contradictions as inevitable growing pains or teething troubles which we shall one day rise above and leave behind. Theologians, too, have had their theories about the nature of the contradictions. For many centuries, a rebellion of the angels which spread to the human race was blamed for the human condition. The theme of original sin explained the corporate, shared dimension of fallenness as a taint conveyed by the reproductive process! A more liberal view would assert that the contradictions are the inevitable price we pay for the freedom which God has given to the human race.

tself into the structures and fabric of our common life, so that we may well have the kind of jobs in which we are required not to choose between good and evil, but to choose between evil and evil as we seek to serve others or make decisions that will affect others.

To believe in fallenness and at the same time to believe in createdness means that we have to hold on to ideals in a world in which it may often be impossible to practice those ideals. Non-violence, for example, is an ideal that is fundamentally grounded in the example of Jesus. Yet to practice it in the world in which we find ourselves may be to leave defenceless those who are at the mercy of naked power. On the other hand, if we abandon non-violence for the sake of defending the defenceless, we must avoid believing that the violence which we use is thereby somehow justified and ceases to be an evil. We need a frame of reference which allows us to hold our ideals clearly before us, even when circumstances do not allow us to practise them; and when we deny these ideals, as we may have to, we must never justify the fact that we have done so. We must recognise, rather, that we are enmeshed in networks of wrongdoing and compromise, which are part of what it means to be human in a fallen world, and that our only hope comes from belief in the createdness which has its source in the life and example of Jesus Christ.

What does this imply for 'Life' issues? In the first place, the fact that we need a medical profession at all is a constant reminder of one of the contradictions that is, for the theologian, part of fallenness. In a perfect world, there would be no illness. The fact of illness reveals the paradox that God's world is imperfect, and that the work of healing is human cooperation with God in order to act against this imperfection. But more importantly, just as belief in createdness enables us to reflect on the meaning of life and death, so belief in fallenness enables us to reflect upon life and death. In a fallen world, life has a tendency to be devalued, while death becomes that which must at all costs be avoided. This paradox results from the way in which power is exercised. A dictator, or a powerful ruling class, can happily engage in the enlargement of their power in a way that requires the sacrifice of the lives of many of their subjects. At the same time, we have seen in the twentieth century, and still see, the spectacle of elderly dictators hanging grimly on to life in order to prolong their power to the last possible moment. Or, life is devalued and death is respected by the stratagem of denying that people of other countries are really human beings at all, and that it is justified to kill any numbers of an enemy if this will prevent the deaths of one's own people. There is not much difference between this position and the view that argues that unborn children are not really human beings, and that the ending of their 'lives' can be justified by the enhancement of life that will result to those who have reached maturity.

And yet, at this point, I want to argue that those of us who take the pro-life position may have more in common with our opponents than we realise, and that this be of significance. People would not seek abortions were it not for the permissiveness or the pornography or the ignorance or the poverty or the violence of the world in which we live. At least some, or perhaps many, of the women who seek abortions are victims of the structures into which evil has insinuated itself, rather than simply irresponsible people who should have known better. Again, if their

My own view of the matter is that we cannot find a satisfactory
the contradictions that we perceive in the world, and that, in any ca
tianity offers is not an intellectual solution to the problem of evil, b
to live in the hope and faith that, in Jesus Christ, God has robbed e
to say the last and decisive word in the world. In this regard, the
series of pictures which indicate the struggle between God and evi
who believe in God can expect to fare. In the life of Jesus, we see
self-giving love is rejected by the vested interests of an established
leaders of the people, and even adapted for their own selfish purpc
stood closest to Jesus:

> Lord, let one of us sit at your right hand and the other at your left
> (Mk 10.37)

In his darkest hour, those men who had been closest to him left
one denied that he had ever known him. That is the dark side. Bu
that, after the resurrection, almost all of these same men, not to n
and women who had never known him in the flesh, laid dowr
course of their witness to his transforming love.

It is the same in the Old Testament. To take only one or two
Israelites had been delivered from the Egyptians at the Red
Golden Calf and worshipped that in place of the God who had
slavery. It was not the children or the grandchildren of the pe
rescued from slavery who did this, but the rescued slaves the
after David had rescued his people from the Philistines and ha
he abused his privilege as God's anointed king by committir
wife of one of his soldiers, and by having that same husband
he failed in his ruse to disguise the fact that, he, David, had m
nant. That is the dark side. But the bright side is that ancient
of the day, unable to defeat God's purposes, and that prop
claimed the truth in the face of the abusers of power and th
mass of the people.

When I say that fallenness is something that only faith can
that we accept in faith the invitation to live in what we believ
the expectation that we may be misunderstood, disadvantage
killed because we are his servants. We accept the intellectua
in an all-loving and powerful God, while aware of the ma
seem to count against this belief. We accept that love is s
forgiveness is stronger than anger, and that hope is stronger
around us there is so much to count against these convicti
delight and hope the great visions in the Bible of a restored
down with the wolf, the lion eating straw like the ox, the litt
and the lion together, without being able to understand hc
transformation if it really is God's world. We observe that
total of individual evil wills, including our own, but that ev

reason for seeking an abortion is the real possibility that they will produce a handicapped child, they may be victims of the defects in the world which makes necessary a medical profession. Their plight is similar to the dilemma that is produced by the ideal of non-violence in a fallen world. How can one uphold the ideal of protecting life at all costs, when it may be begotten by someone living in poverty, ignorance or violence, or as a result of genetic disorders, where no adequate support or provision exists if the birth is allowed to continue? Although I do not condone what I am about to say, I can understand that, in such a situation, a doctor might regard it as his or her duty to recommend an abortion out of compassion. Of course, this is treating the symptom rather than the cause; but I have had the satisfaction on the campus at Sheffield, of actually getting pro- and anti- 'Life' supporters to talk and listen to one another rather than shouting at one another, by establishing that there can be common ground between them, and that part of the reason for their disagreement is the different ways in which they are trying to act compassionately in situations that arise from the structures of evil and compromise in which we have to live.

This brings me to my conclusion. I have tried to argue in this session that the task of theology is not to provide supernatural answers to questions such as 'When does life begin?', but rather to articulate an understanding of the world from the standpoint of faith, within which believers, at any rate, will better understand what they are doing when they act in the pro-life cause. I have tried to show that, because we live in a fallen world, we shall find ourselves in situations in which it becomes difficult to uphold our ideals, and in which we may have more in common than we realise with those in the opposite camp. At the same time, a proper recognition, through faith, of what we are as human beings in relation to God, will assure us that we are not the disposers of life but its servants for God's sake. Worship will set the frailty of our humanity in the perspective of God's vastness, will help us to see the miracle of life, and encourage us at all costs and in spite of contradictions, to uphold its sanctity. To uphold this ideal may involve us in ridicule, misrepresentation or disadvantage. Such is the lot of those who seek to follow the path of God in a fallen world. The main task of theology is to expose the fallenness of the world and to proclaim the Kingdom of God. As part of this process, the question has to be addressed 'What does it mean to be a human being?' and the answer has to be given in terms of the life of Jesus Christ and all that follows from it. Part of the story of Jesus tells how his life as an infant was in danger from the power-fed suspicions of Herod the Great; and when I have done all the theologising that is possible I am still moved by this one simple fact: God became a human being in Jesus Christ and exposed himself to the hazards of living in a fallen world. He was once a defenceless unborn child as well as a defenceless born child. In that way, he set the sign of God's approval upon the very simplest form of human life that we know; and that is something that we can never ignore.

Chapter 5

'WHAT DOES IT MEAN TO BE HUMAN?':
THE CENTRAL QUESTION OF OLD TESTAMENT THEOLOGY?*

At the International Old Testament Congress in Salamanca in 1983, Erhard Gerstenberger put some straight and disturbing questions to the discipline as we know it in
the West in his lecture, 'The Relation of Old Testament Interpretation to Reality'.[1]
Having taught for six years in the south of Brazil, Gerstenberger interpreted his
invitation to address the Congress as a request to confront Western scholarship with
the insights and imperatives of Old Testament scholars working in Latin America.[2]
Beginning from the observation that

> Every exegete has his setting in life; the burning question is simply how the reality
> of life which has shaped him and of which he himself is a living part determines
> his outlook and way of thinking,

he posed the question:

> to what extent are the exegetical results of interpreters constrained by their time-
> conditioned circumstances and in what direction in the pursuit of our cooperative
> work as exegetes should we correct, extrapolate from or further develop these
> circumstances?[3]

In answering these questions, Gerstenberger left no doubt as to where his sympa-
thies lay. He argued in some detail that both the content of Western Old Testament
interpretation and the organization of its teaching and research were based on ideas
of power that were alien to the Old Testament itself. He did not deny, of course,
that the Old Testament concerns itself a good deal with kings, priests and other
forms of authority. But he threw down an uncompromising challenge in the following sentences:

> Are the Old Testament structures of power useful for us in any kind of form? After
> everything that we can learn from Jewish and Christian ethical tradition in the light
> of the whole of scripture, and after everything that we possess as information

---

* This study was delivered as a lecture given as the Presidential Address to the Society for
Old Testament Study, 4 January 1989. The presentational style of the original has been retained.
1. E. Gerstenberger, 'Der Realitätsbezug alttestamentlicher Exegese', in J.A. Emerton (ed.),
Congress Volume, Salamanca 1983 (VTSup, 36; Leiden: E.J. Brill, 1985), pp. 132-44.
2. Gerstenberger, 'Der Realitätsbezug alttestamentlicher Exegese', p. 132. (This and the
following quotes from Gerstenberger are the author's translations.)
3. Gerstenberger, 'Der Realitätsbezug alttestamentlicher Exegese', p. 132.

about the present-day world, we can only, in my view, describe the world situation in the following way. The traditional power and economic structures have already brought about the final catastrophe—in the form of mass poverty, destruction of the environment, sexism, racism, the arms race, wars and genocide. They have thus shown themselves to be in opposition to both God and humanity, and thus can no longer be considered as parameters for interpretation.[4]

Old Testament scholarship, in Gerstenberger's view, needed to take into account the fact that the reality of God in the Old Testament was a liberating reality, and that the world of the interpreter was one in which a majority of people lived in poverty so that a minority could enjoy affluence. Each interpreter needed to be aware of the understanding of reality that both informed his or her work and was implied in the text of the Old Testament.

The majority of people who hear or read a paper such as that of Gerstenberger react in one of two ways. Either they are hostile (and this was a noticeable reaction in the questions that followed the lecture in Salamanca), or they feel guilty, and ask themselves whether they should not, in fact, adopt liberation hermeneutics and abandon what they have up to now understood as the critical approach. Both reactions are understandable; but both seem to me to be inappropriate. On the one hand, any method that claims to be critical must be self-critical, and ought to welcome questions that probe the pre-understanding that we bring to texts.

On the other hand, it is not clear to me that the world of Old Testament interpretation is in fact one world, in which we are obliged to discover a hermeneutical method which must be applied to every situation in which the Old Testament is studied and taught. That there is a hermeneutic that is appropriate for Basic Communities in the churches of Latin America I do not doubt. Whether that hermeneutic is appropriate for non-confessional academic situations in the industrial West is a matter that needs to be considered carefully before any decision is reached.

Careful consideration is especially important in view of the fundamental changes that are taking place in Western society, and which are calling into question the place of the humanities within our society.[5] Whereas the voices from Latin America are urging us to disassociate ourselves from the power and economic structures of the industrial world if we wish to interpret the Old Testament authentically, the realities of our industrial society demand, at least from those of us in secular universities and secular polytechnics and colleges, that we justify our academic work in terms of its ability to attract private funding and to produce graduates who will have the skills to participate in the creation of material wealth.

It seems to me that if we are to come to terms with these seemingly diametrically opposed points of view—and to ignore them would be unwise, both academically and practically—we must look for analytical tools that will enable us to see more clearly the issues at stake, and will open up a dialogue that will hopefully resolve some of the tensions.

4. Gerstenberger, 'Der Realitätsbezug alttestamentlicher Exegese', p. 142.
5. See the analysis by J. Habermas in, 'Die Krise des Wohlfahrtsstaates und die Erschöpfung utopischer Energien', in *idem, Die neue Unübersichlichkeit* (Kleine Politischen Schriften, 5; Frankfurt am Main: Suhrkamp, 1985), pp. 141-66 (154-55).

As a starting point, I want to suggest that underlying the three positions that I have been talking about, that is, traditional critical academic Old Testament study, liberation hermeneutics and commercially orientated enterprise culture, is a view of what it means to be human; an answer, implicitly or explicitly to the question: What does it mean to be human?

Underlying traditional critical academic studies is what Eckhard Meinberg has described in his recent book, *Das Menschenbild der modernen Erziehungswissenschaft*, as 'der Verstandesmensche', a term that I shall use in German because I do not like its suggested English translation of 'rational man'.[6] According to this view, what distinguishes the human race from other creatures is its ability to discover, by means of reason, the 'laws' which lie behind the regularities of the natural world, and the ability to harness the potentialities of the natural world to the benefit of humanity. The *Verstandesmensch* must expose everything that is false or illusory and must oppose anything that threatens the unfettered use of reason in the search for truth. The unfettered search for truth is an essential safeguard for human freedom; that is to say, the *Verstandesmensch* cannot truly be itself if limits are placed upon the use of reason.

A quite different view of what it is to be human underlies liberation hermeneutics.[7] One must not, of course, overlook the theological basis of liberation theology, including its belief in God's identification with the poor and the oppressed. But, apart from its theological basis, liberation theology accepts the Marxist critique of the notion of the *Verstandesmensch*. It rejects the idea of a human reason which is exercised in isolation from economic and social conditions, and which is entirely interest-free. Liberation theologians insist time and again that exegesis is fundamentally shaped by the social conditions in which it is practiced, and that for them, the human race is a species in which a powerful minority enslaves the majority, thus calling forth the need to see God as the liberator of that majority from economic and social degradation. This sort of view clearly underlies what is expressed in the paper by Gerstenberger.

It is more difficult to articulate the view of humanity underlying what I have called commercially orientated enterprise culture. On the one hand, it shared with the *Verstandesmensch* view a stress on individual freedom and achievement; but it also has a strong anti-intellectual strain at two levels.[8] First, it blames intellectuals for the economic crisis of capitalism in the 1970s and 1980s, and prefers practice to theory, against the background of the regulating effects of market forces. Secondly, it desires social integration to be achieved by, among other things, conventional religion, and is thus hostile to anyone who calls into question, by the use of reason or research, the traditional fundamentals of religion. In Britain this last point is well illustrated by the provision, in the recent Education Reform Act, that religious

6.   E. Meinberg, *Das Menschenbild der modernen Erziehungswissenschaft* (Darmstadt: Wissenschaftliche Buchgesellschaft, 1988), pp. 27-38.
7.   See the influential *Pedagogy of the Oppressed* by Paulo Freire (trans. M.B. Ramos; Harmondsworth: Penguin Books, 1972).
8.   See Habermas, 'Die Krise des Wohlfahrtsstaates', p. 154.

instruction in schools should be 'broadly Christian', implicitly rejecting a non-traditionalist pluralist approach.

Now if what I am saying is correct, that Old Testament study as most of us know it depends on a view of what it is to be human that is being challenged by two other views, what is to be done? An obvious answer is that there needs to be a dialogue between the views, assuming that a forum can be found. Another question that arises is that of the place of the Old Testament itself in all of this. Is our interpretation of it entirely shaped by the circumstances in which we work and by the pre-understanding that we bring to it? Does the Old Testament affect its readers in any way, so that, on the one hand, Western critical scholars might find that they have much in common with interpreters in Latin America, and on the other hand, Western critical scholarship might be able to articulate a prophetic critique of their industrial society that will hope to make political opinion appreciative of Old Testament study?

These are obvious and important questions; but I do not propose to follow them up here. Instead I want to suggest that the recent work of the German political philosopher Jürgen Habermas can provide insights of value to Old Testament scholarship at many levels, which may well enable us to cope with the dilemmas that I have been outlining.

In what follows, I am not going to attempt to expound Habermas's system. His most important work, *Theorie des kommunikativen Handelns* (1981) runs to almost 1200 pages of philosophical and analytical German, to which must be added works such as *Der philosophische Diskurs der Moderne* (1985) and *Die neue Unüber-sichtlichkeit* (1985) which alone add another 700 pages to the task of anyone who tries to become familiar with the basic sources of Habermas's thought.[9] There are commentaries in English, of which the most recent, David Ingram's *Habermas and the Dialectic of Reason* (1987), is in many ways more difficult than Habermas himself.[10] For our purposes, the heart of what he has to say lies in the second 'Zwischenbetrachtung' of *Theorie des kommunikativen Handelns* entitled *System und Lebenswelt* (II, pp. 173-293); but before I comment on this section I want to indicate how I think that Habermas can help us.

In his *Zur Rekonstruktion des historischen Materialismus* (1976), Habermas considerably modified Marx's theory of the various levels of social reality—infrastructure, structure and superstructure—in which the economic factors which belong to the infrastructure affect the other levels, with religious beliefs belonging to the superstructure.[11] (Marx's view is used by Norman Gottwald in his reconstruction of the origins of Israel, and is partly responsible for his conclusion that Israelite belief

---

9. J. Habermas, *Theorie des kommunikativen Handelns* (2 vols.; Frankfurt am Main: Suhrkamp, 1981); *idem, Der philosophische Diskurs der Moderne* (Frankfurt am Main: Suhrkamp, 1985).

10. D. Ingram, *Habermas and the Dialectic of Reason* (New Haven: Yale University Press, 1987).

11. J. Habermas, *Zur Rekonstruktion des historischen Materialismus* (Frankfurt am Main: Suhrkamp, 3rd edn, 1982).

in its God was the *result* not the *cause* of the formation of a liberated, egalitarian tribal community in late Bronze Age Canaan.[12])

Habermas stresses the importance of two factors in social and economic change: first, the accumulation of technical knowledge and second, the development of new types of political organization which permit the more effective use of labour, but which must be given a rational justification if they are to succeed.

If we apply these ideas to the rise and fall of the united monarchy in ancient Israel, we can say that the military success and religio-political ambition of David enabled accumulated technical knowledge to be used to transform Israel. This technical knowledge extended into the areas of warfare, building and fortification, irrigation, agriculture and viticulture. The united monarchy also enabled labour to be made available on a larger scale than hitherto. This involved weakening the tribal system, by creating new agencies for coordinating the production of foodstuff agencies that replaced the traditional function of kin-based groups.

However, such a radical reordering of social life required a rational justification. This was sought by way of the theological legitimation of the Davidic dynasty; but this legitimation was not powerful enough to become part of the accepted agenda of the people as a whole. While the revolt of the northern tribes had as its immediate ground a protest against the social injustices of Solomon's reign, a deeper reason for the revolt was that the northern tribes possessed a rationalized view of their corporate identity that prevented acceptance of the Davidic legitimation. In the terms of Habermas's theory, this meant that a rationalization of the system of political integration did not succeed in becoming part of the communicative life-world of the northern tribes.

This introduction of some of Habermas's key technical terms makes it appropriate at this point to set out some of his leading ideas. In answer to the question, 'What does it mean to be human?', Habermas would maintain that what distinguishes human beings from other life forms is an interdependence based upon the ability to communicate with each other. Of course other species, for example bees and ants, are interdependent, and also apparently communicate with each other. Human communication, however, contains the potential to form abstract concepts, and, with the invention of writing, to pass on cultural and other knowledge in an objective form from one generation to the next. To be born as a human being means to take one's place within a network of shared meanings based upon a transmitted cultural heritage.

Habermas in fact rejects the idea of the *Verstandesmensch* as he rejects the philosophy of consciousness, that is, that predominant Western philosophical tradition that goes back through Heidegger, to Hegel and Kant and on to Descartes, and which defines philosophical activity as reflection upon human subjective awareness of the world.[13] Habermas substitutes for philosophy of consciousness what he calls a philosophy of communicative interaction, that is to say, reflection upon the means

---

12. N.K. Gottwald, *The Tribes of Yahweh: A Sociology of the Religion of Liberated Israel, 1250–1050 B.C.E.* (Maryknoll, NY: Orbis Books, 1979), pp. 631ff.

13. See Habermas, *Der philosophische Diskurs der Moderne*, for discussions of these thinkers.

by which humans articulate their interdependence, together with an examination of the way in which economic and other factors affect these communication processes.

To achieve his aim, Habermas uses the two notions of 'communicative life-world (*Lebenswelt*)' and 'system'.[14] To the communicative life-world belongs everything that is necessary for humans to communicate with each other in all the manifold circumstances of life. Habermas gives a trivial example of what he means, in order to show the complexity of the communicative life-world. The example is that of a senior member of a group of builders' labourers telling a young and newly arrived worker to run and get some beer for the rest of the group so that they can all have their breakfast. This situation implies the acceptance, by all concerned, of the right of the most senior to give these orders and the duty of the newest worker to comply, the existence in that part of Germany of the so-called second breakfast, and the fact that there is a place that sells beer that is open and is close enough for the junior worker to run there and back in a relatively short period of time. The negative of any one of these preconditions, for example, the information that the beer shop is closed that day, would vitiate the communicative action. Thus, the communicative life-world is in this case not just speech, but social authority, local custom, commercial practice and physical activity. It is not difficult to see how complex this theoretical notion of communicative life-world would be in practice if we could work out all its ramifications.

By system, Habermas means systems of social integration: marriage exchange, the exercise of power, the development of law, monetary exchange. It is his contention that social development is the result of uncoupling of the system from the communicative life-world, after which there is an increasingly complex dialectical relationship between the two.

In the simplest types of society, where the kinship group is the basic self-supporting economic unit, the system and the communicative life-world are united. If that group expands, or needs to cooperate with other groups, the system of social integration begins to be uncoupled from the communicative life-world. However, if social integration is achieved by marriage exchange, fictitious genealogies can restore the bond between system and communicative life-world. The system will be justified by the inclusion of the fictitious genealogies into the communicative life-world. The exercise of power does not lead to an uncoupling of system and communicative life-world so long as power is exercised within dominant lineages. Uncoupling takes place when the exercise of power is detached from the kinship system, and administration and law are formalized independently of kinship. Curiously enough, formalized law is a product of the communicative life-world in that it requires the formulation of abstract principles; but according to Habermas the uncoupling of system and communicative life-world is complete under a regime of formal law. This is presumably because the need for formal law is occasioned by the development within the communicative life-world of groups with divergent interests which cannot be reconciled by communicative interaction, and which thus

---

14. Habermas, *Theorie des kommunikativen Handelns*, II, pp. 171ff. For an exposition, see Ingram, *Habermas and the Dialectic of Reason*, pp. 115ff.

have to have recourse to law. All must accept this law. The development of monetary exchange indicates a further uncoupling of system and communicative life-world, especially where the control of monetary exchange is left to market forces. At this point, the system of social integration is almost independent from the communicative life-world, but can invade the domain of the communicative life-world by imposing financial restrictions upon some of its subsystems.

Within the communicative life-world, the effect of uncoupling from the system is to allow an ever-increasing diversity of communicative activity to develop. Culture is differentiated from society, and this allows important institutions to be freed from religious worldviews. In our own history, we can think of the secularization of schools and universities in the past century. Individuals gain greater freedom to be able to criticize and revise accepted traditions. Specialized disciplines develop in order to solve particular problems or to deal with complex pieces of cultural information—such as the Old Testament, I would add.

All this is an unfolding of the potential that is within the human ability to engage in communicative interaction; yet there is no doubt that the uncoupling of system from communicative life-world which makes possible this unfolding of human potential exacts its price. There arise conflicts of interest, a lack of common purpose and identity, the restriction of communicative activity by the invasion of system, especially the system of monetary exchange, and interference with communicative interaction by means of propaganda and misinformation.

The solution of this paradox lies in a proper analysis of the tensions between system and communicative life-world, to enable humanity to become more effectively what it is, namely, a community of interdependent beings sharing the potential for communicative interaction.

In the hope that this very inadequate outline has given some inkling of what Habermas is trying to do, I shall try to address it to the Old Testament and to some of the problems from which I began.

The Old Testament, taken as a whole, is arguably very concerned with the question of communicative interaction, what hinders it and what can restore it. The foundation stories, set in beginning time, picture a scene of perfect intercommunication between the man and the woman without rivalry, between the humans and the other living creatures, and between the humans and God. This is shattered by the human desire to become like God. Communicative harmony breaks down as Adam and Eve accuse each other of disobeying God, Cain murders and denies responsibility for his brother Abel, and Lamech boasts about the scale of retribution that he has exacted. The story of the tower of Babel marks a further breakdown in the human ability to communicate, to be followed by God's intention, in calling Abraham, to bring blessing to *all* the families of the earth.

The freeing of the Hebrews from slavery in Egypt is a story with strong communicative potential: those whom God has freed may not enslave each other or turn their brothers aside in time of need—a powerful principle even if it is not wholly extended to non-Israelites. The covenant—whenever it was established (I am speaking essentially synchronically)—is an elaborate communicative apparatus designed to integrate Israel's life into the worship and service of a God who demands exclusive loyalty so that human interdependence will not be compromised by the misuse of power. The sacrificial and penitential systems are means of restoring broken communication.

The conflicts between prophetic groups and power-exploiting kings can be read as the attempt of the prophets to counteract a disregard of human interdependence; and it is interesting that prophetic visions of a recreated world seem to stress communicative inter-action. The nations that flow to Zion in Isa. 2.2-4 wish to be taught God's ways. The law and word of God will go forth out of Zion, and implements of war will be turned into tools of agricultural cooperation. When God establishes the New Covenant described in Jeremiah 31 there will be no need for people to teach each other to 'Know the Lord'. All will know him.

What exactly am I doing here? As far as I can work it out, it is something as follows. I have outlined Habermas's theory of communicative interaction because it seems to throw much light upon the development of human society and the problems that we face currently in the world. At the heart of Habermas's position is a premise that is essentially speculative. We cannot prove that what makes us human is our ability to live in interdependence based upon communicative interaction; nor can we prove that it is our obligation as humans to work for a world in which our intercommunication is as perfect as we can make it. None of this can be proved; but it is also the case that the Old Testament can be read, without distortion, in such a way as to support this basic assumption, except with the difference that it looks to God as the only agency that can accomplish the goal of an ideal communicative world. Why it is possible to read the Old Testament in this way is not something that I have time to discuss here. But if there is truth in my contention, then I suggest that the time is right for an interpretation of the Old Testament to be worked out along those lines, not just for the sake of the specialized study of the Old Testament, but also as a contribution to the wider discussion of the question, 'What does it mean to be human?', which is taking place in philosophical and political circles. No notice may be taken in these circles of Old Testament specialists; yet the Old Testament is a collection of texts that still commands attention and excites interest outside of scholarship and the churches, and it would do no harm to show that, while there are legitimate specialisms within Old Testament study that can only be the preserve of experts, there is also a way in which a scholarly and non-politicized reading of it can play an important role in contemporary discussions about the goals and priorities of our society.

The other point that I want to make concerns the way we think about the discipline of Old Testament study. Reading Habermas has made me aware that my own work on the history of scholarship has been largely inspired by the *Verstandesmensch* model, and that I have overlooked factors which are suggested by a philosophy of communicative interaction.[15] In my work on de Wette, about whom I am writing a critical biography, I have concentrated principally on the intellectual background to de Wette's early critical work, and believe that I can demonstrate

---

15. See my *Old Testament Criticism in the Nineteenth Century: England and Germany* (London: SPCK, 1984).

that his epoch-making *Beiträge zur Einleitung in das Alte Testament* of 1806–1807 can be perfectly understood in terms of the work on mythology that was being undertaken in literary and philosophical circles by Karl Philipp Moritz and F.W.J. Schelling.

None of this is wrong; yet it is all at the level of intellectual influences, and what I have overlooked is the communicative interaction aspect. De Wette was able to write as he did in 1804–1807 because critical scholarship had developed as a specialist discipline, free, at any rate in Jena, from ecclesiastical constraints that could prevent the criticism of traditional opinions. At the same time, poetry and literature were so much a part of the intellectual scene that it was not surprising that they played such a large part in shaping de Wette's pre-understanding.[16] For most of his time in Berlin, from 1810 to 1819, de Wette had little contact with organized religion and continued to produce radical writings; however in Basel, where he went unwillingly because no other jobs were offered to him (he had been sacked from Berlin in 1819 on political grounds and the Prussian government had done its best to frustrate his further employment in Germany), he was expected to play an important part in church life, and was in fact later ordained. De Wette did indeed become less certain about some of his younger radical views during his time in Basel; but he accepted many of the radical arguments of Strauss's *Life of Jesus* in 1835 and appears to have become more conservative in Basel only because of the need to adapt some of his works for use by the church and schools of Basel. In other words, we see him in Basel participating in more ecclesiastical communicative sub-groups than he had done before, with a consequent effect upon some of his writings.

Turning to the modern situation, the persistence of fundamentalism is almost certainly due to the fact that it is an essential part of the communicative system of certain religious sub-cultures. When students from these sub-cultures come to study the Bible at a university, they can adapt, to some extent, to the conventions of the communicative system in whose context they have to do their studies; but this system is only a small part of their communicative life-world compared with what is provided by their religious affiliation. It should come as no surprise that their contact with academic study either makes them give up religion, or returns them to their religious group only marginally affected by their studies.

It is easy for some scholars to dismiss fundamentalists as misfits on whom academic study is wasted. Their existence, however, challenges academics to think more deeply about the communicative life-world in which academic study is located. This life-world has become a highly specialized subculture whose relationship to the outside world is not only questioned by fundamentalism, but by liberation hermeneutics and the enterprise culture. Yet, if what is being maintained in this lecture is correct, the Old Testament has something vitally important to say to the question that is basic to liberation hermeneutics and enterprise culture: What is humanity?

---

16.   See the comprehensive account in F. Strich, *Die Mythologie in der deutschen Literatur von Klopstock bis Wagner* (2 vols.; repr. [of 1910 edn]; Bern and Munich: Francke Verlag, 1970).

It may not be an exaggeration to say that the future existence of Old Testament study depends upon how it reacts to the questions that are being put to it by liberation hermeneutics and the enterprise culture. Yet what is really at stake is not the existence of Old Testament study as an academic sub-culture; the real issue is whether Old Testament scholars, without sacrificing any of their intellectual integrity, can make the Old Testament speak to the fundamental question of today: What does it mean to be human? In the past, theology has never ignored the help offered by philosophy in the working-out of its proclamation. Neo-Platonism, Aristotelianism, Kantianism, speculative idealism and existentialism have all been help-mates in the task. In my view, the political philosophy articulated by Habermas can not only help us today to understand better what we are about. It can help us to expound the Old Testament as a set of documents that address fundamental contemporary questions about the nature and destiny of the human race.

Chapter 6

DISCOURSE AND BIBLICAL ETHICS

The discourse ethics to be employed in this paper is that outlined and defended by Jürgen Habermas;[1] the biblical material will be taken from the Old Testament.

Discourse ethics arises from Habermas's movement away from an (individualistic) philosophy of consciousness to a (collective) philosophy of communicative action; from practical reason to the logical implicit in communicative action.[2] Discourse ethics enables Habermas to propound a type of ethics that is universalistic, collective and cognitive, in opposition to approaches that are relativistic, individualistic and emotive. His starting-point is the fact of language and communication, and that in everyday life we take for granted a whole series of conventions without which inter-personal communication would be impossible. Fundamental to such conventions is the notion of truth, in the sense that in dealings with each other we take it for granted that we can by argument persuade others or be ourselves persuaded that something is right. This activity is collective in the sense that it involves at least two people, universalistic in the sense that we believe that we can persuade or be persuaded by people from different cultures or backgrounds from our own, and cognitive in the sense that the outcome of such discussions is knowledge. Habermas believes that relativists are guilty of a performative contradiction. In order to maintain their view that truth or ethics are relative to a given group or culture, relativists depend upon the universalistic possibility of convincing others of the truth of their position by argument; but if the relativism that they advocate

---

1.   Inconsistently, I shall refer to discourse ethics as singular and biblical ethics as plural. For Habermas's expositions and elaborations see 'Diskursethik—Notizen zu einem Begründungsprogramm', in *idem, Moralbewußtsein und kommunikatives Handeln* (Frankfurt am Main: Suhrkamp, 1983; 3rd edn, 1988), pp. 53-125; 'Moralbewußtein und kommunikatives Handeln', in *Moralbewußtsein*, pp. 127-206; *Erläuterungen zur Diskursethik* (Frankfurt am Main: Suhrkamp, 1991; 2nd edn, 1992). Discussions in English include D.M. Rasmussen, *Reading Habermas* (Oxford: Basil Blackwell, 1990), pp. 56-74; S.K. White, *The Recent Work of Jürgen Habermas* (Cambridge: Cambridge University Press, 1988), pp. 69-89. German discussions include F.S. Fiorenza, 'Die Kirche als Interpretationsgemeinschaft: Politische Theologie zwischen Diskursethik und hermeneutischer Rekonstruktion', in E. Arens (ed.), *Habermas und die Theologie* (Düsseldorf: Patmos Verlag, 1989), pp. 115-44; W. Lesch, 'Theologische Ethik als Handlungstheorie', in E. Arens (ed.), *Gottesrede-Glaubenspraxis. Perspektiven theologischer Handlungstheorie* (Darmstadt: Wissenschaftliche Buchgesellschaft, 1994), pp. 89-109.

2.   The major work that marks the shift is Habermas's *Theorie des kommunikativen Handelns* (2 vols.; Frankfurt am Main: Suhrkamp, 1981).

is true, there are no such universal grounds on which they could base their assertions.[3]

As applied to ethics, Habermas's approach distinguishes between the structure of ethics and its content, and is concerned mainly with the former. Discourse ethics provides in the first instance an enabling framework called by Habermas the *Universalisierungsgrundsatz* (U) which states that

> every valid norm must fulfill the condition that the foreseeable consequences and side-effects which foreseeably result from its general application in order to satisfy the interests of all, can be accepted by all those concerned without compulsion, and can be preferred to the consequences of all known possible alternative arrangements.[4]

This is supplemented by the *diskursethiker Grundsatz* (D) which states that

> only those norms can be considered valid that receive the acceptance of all involved as people who do or can take part in practical discourse.[5]

Several comments need to be made on these *Grundsätze*.

First, it is clear that discourse ethics does not provide norms and principles for applying these norms; it rather states the ideal conditions under which norms can be discovered and applied. Second, while aiming to provide a universalistic framework for ethics, discourse ethics allows that in a particular period or culture the agreed norms will be relative to those situations. This entails, third, what Habermas calls the in-built fallibility of discourse ethics; that is, the admission that inability to know or foresee all the consequences of applying a norm may lead to mistakes.[6] Fourth, discourse ethics is participatory in that it does not allow norms to be discovered or applied by individuals detached from the situations and people involved. Fifth, discourse ethics avoids the charge that can be brought against the Kantian categorical imperative, that it is egoistic and represents particular class or gender interests. Finally, although the word 'argument' does not appear in either 'U' or 'D' the norms are to be mutually established by argument, and it is important to know that Habermas includes under this term the exchange and evaluation of information, principles, terminology (including the revision of vocabulary or descriptions) and expert opinion.[7]

Discourse ethics is a determinedly post-metaphysical exercise, and Habermas is ever-ready to criticize 'platonic' or Kantian-type transcendental notions which lie

---

3. See, for example, Habermas's criticism along the lines of A. MacIntyre in *idem*, *Erläuterungen*, pp. 209-18.

4. Habermas, *Erläuterungen*, p. 134 (author's translation, omitting Habermas's emphases which are given in the German). There are several versions of U (cf. *idem*, *Moralbewußtsein*, p. 131), but what is given here is the fullest version that I have found. See also the further discussion in *idem*, *Erläuterungen*, pp. 137-39, where further possible refinements that have been proposed are considered.

5. Habermas, *Moralbewußtsein*, p. 103 (author's translation).

6. Habermas, *Erläuterungen*, pp. 165-66.

7. Habermas, *Erläuterungen*, p. 164.

behind ethical theories. At first sight, this is not a good starting-point for discussing biblical ethics, with their metaphysical commitment to God as the ultimate author and upholder of justice. But it has to be acknowledged that any modern reading of the Bible, including that by believers, inevitably criticizes biblical ethics from a modern ethical position, whether the reader is consciously aware of commitment to a particular ethical stance or not. This is true for the most obviously unacceptable statements in the Bible such as, 'Whoever curses father or mother shall be put to death' (Exod. 21.17).

But it is also true for what we might call biblical ethics as a whole; for biblical ethics presupposes a worldview that is not our own, and the history of Christian ethics is a series of attempts to harmonize biblical and Christian viewpoints with successive philosophical positions.[8] In examining biblical ethics from the standpoint of discourse ethics I shall discuss (1) categorical statements such as those in the Decalogue, (2) the discourse ethical implications of passages such as Gen. 18.22-33, (3) the problem of those unable to discuss, (4) the relation between ethics and laws and (5) sacrifice.

1.   In his recent *Erläuterungen zur Diskursethik* Habermas devotes a section to B. Gert's modern statement of the Ten Commandments, most of which have the form 'you shall not...'.[9] Habermas acknowledges that such statements seem to be at the heart of attempts to state moral obligations in a categorical way, and to support the deontological separation of the right from the good, and the deontological insistence that the primacy of such obligations is undermined if attempts are made to relate them to specific goods or goals. However, he criticizes this position as exhibiting what he calls an individualistically diminished moral category (*ein individualistisch verkürtzter Moralbegriff*) which results in a monological negative command addressed to an anonymous community.

From the point of view of discourse ethics, obligations cannot be imposed; they must be seen to be justified and must be capable of being willingly accepted. For example, the assertion, 'You shall not deceive anyone', does not take account of instances such as those where to deceive someone about the nature of an illness can arguably be justified if the deception is intended to aid a person's recovery. Habermas wants duties to be discussed and agreed, with the result that, in terms of discourse ethics, they will be stated positively not negatively. Thus the assertion, 'You shall not lie', should be positively formulated as,

> act in a manner directed towards understanding, and allow each person the communicative freedom to adopt a position with regard to claims of validity.[10]

As applied to biblical ethics this approach has two implications. First, we can see within the biblical tradition a tension between (usually) negative categorical statements and positive situated statements that rely on consent rather than imposition.

---

8.   Cf. N.H.G. Robinson, *The Groundwork of Christian Ethics* (London: Collins, 1971).
9.   Habermas, *Erläuterungen*, pp. 171-76.
10.   Habermas, *Erläuterungen*, p. 173 (author's translation).

Thus, as well as the negative categorical statement, 'You shall not murder' (Exod. 20.13), there is the more situated statement, following a categorical positive statement prescribing the death penalty for anyone who kills another:

> if it [the act of killing] was not premeditated, but came about by an act of God, then I will appoint for you a place to which the killer may flee. (Exod. 21.13)

As well as the categorical statements there is a statement that implies discussion, or recognition of the injustice of putting to death someone guilty of accidental as opposed to deliberate killing. These two types of law are usually described as apodictic and casuistic, and attempts have been made to relate them to different form-critical or liturgical backgrounds. Whatever the truth of these attempts, from an ethical point of view most readers, I would maintain, would find the passage in Exod. 21.13 preferable to the categorical statements, because it is more humane and implies agreement about how ethical principles are to be put into practice.

The second implication is that if we agree with Habermas that obligations should be established by agreement and not imposition (and we also see this in some cases exemplified in the Bible), then we shall have a useful procedure for trying to apply biblical ethics in modern society. The debates about abortion and euthanasia which are based upon Exod. 20.13 might be more constructive if opponents were required to consider the nature of the categorical statements to which they appeal. The same would be true of the categorical statements about homosexual actions in Leviticus 18 and 20. Further, an attempt to get agreement about whether, and if so why, adultery is wrong (cf. Exod. 20.14) would be preferable to attempts to impose the view that it is wrong upon a society that is encouraged by literature, films and the media to believe that adultery is trivial. Discourse ethics would require that the interests of all parties affected by adultery were considered, and its rightness or wrongness would be an agreed decision that was in the interests of all parties.

2. Discourse ethics is set in the framework of a discussion of norms by all affected parties. The Bible records no such discussions, although the book of Job contains a series of dialogues on the question of suffering. However, an interesting feature of the Bible is the extent to which individuals engage in dialogue with God, often about matters which impinge on justice.

An elaborate instance is found in Malachi, where God, speaking through the prophet, answers a series of statements or objections voiced by 'the people'. The climax of these questions comes in Mal. 2.17:

> You have wearied the LORD with your words. Yet you say, 'How have we wearied him?' By saying, 'All who do evil are good in the sight of the LORD, and he delights in them'. Or by asking, 'Where is the God of justice?'

This is a kind of dialogue where the shared assumption is that justice can be recognized independently of God, and that God has a duty to uphold it. God is, in effect, accused of acting unjustly, a charge to which he responds robustly in ch. 3, where he warns that he will send his messenger who will visibly enforce what is just.

Another instance of dialogue is in Gen. 18.22-33, where Abraham intercedes with God to spare the city of Sodom. The basis of Abraham's argument is that it would be unjust to destroy righteous people along with the wicked, and he bargains God down to agreeing that the city could be spared if there were ten righteous people in it. He asks, 'shall not the Judge of all the earth do what is just?' (Gen. 18.25). Here again the implication seems to be that what is just can be established independently of God, and that God as supreme judge must act justly. Further, in this passage justice is not simply an abstract notion. It is applied to particular circumstances, and it is argument that establishes what, in this case, it would mean to act justly, and in the interests of at least ten righteous people in Sodom (if they existed).

Passages such as Gen. 18.22-33 show that within the Old Testament there are conflicting ethical strands, some of which assert moral obligations or find no difficulty in the notion of corporate responsibility,[11] others of which imply that what is just in a given situation is to be established by dialogue, taking into account the interests of individuals. An approach via discourse ethics will identify with the latter strand, and will include among passages that accord with this approach texts not normally regarded as ethical, such as psalms and intercessory dialogues in which the speakers engage with God on the question of what is right and just.[12]

3.   Habermas's *diskursethiker Grundsatz* assumes that norms are to be established by those who can or do participate in practical discourse. What about those who cannot?[13] At the end of the *Erläuterungen* Habermas discusses the moral status of animals.[14] He rejects the view that our respect for animals can be grounded in an obligation not to make them suffer. He regards it as a paradox that, on the one hand, our conviction that they should not suffer is based upon a human understanding of suffering which is then applied to animals, while on the other hand, most humans have no qualms about killing animals in order to eat them; that is, the analogy with humans breaks down at this point. Discourse ethics understands the process of becoming an individual human as the discovery of the self as one becomes ever more integrated into a network of social reciprocities, in which the claims and needs of others are fully recognised.[15] Animals belong to the networks into which we integrate, and although our relationships with animals are always asymmetrical (we talk to them not vice versa) they become part of our social world in such a way that we accept that we have moral obligations to them (in discourse ethical terms) as we do to other humans. Habermas evidently has some sympathy with vegetarians and does not exclude the possibility that their view expresses a correct moral intuition.

11.   I have in mind passages such as Exod. 20.5 which speak of God visiting the sins of the fathers upon the children to the third or fourth generation.

12.   Examples would include Pss. 9 and 10 and similar complaints against the wicked, and the passages in Exodus and Numbers where Moses intercedes with God about the plight of the people.

13.   This question is raised by F.S. Fiorenza in his article cited in n. 1 above. Habermas has since addressed the question, as my discussion here shows.

14.   Habermas, *Erläuterungen*, pp. 219-26.

15.   See further Habermas, 'Individuierung durch Vergesellschaftung', in his *Nachmetaphysisches Denken* (Frankfurt am Main: Suhrkamp, 1988), pp. 187-91.

The point that I wish to take from this is that discourse ethics can envisage a role for those who engage in practical discourse as speaking for, or protecting those, who are excluded from the process. In certain types of society the disadvantaged will not only include animals, but the poor and oppressed; and this brings us to the heart of biblical ethics. The obligation of the king to uphold the rights of the poor and oppressed is well known in the Old Testament, as well as prophetic denunciations of the failure of kings to do this, and the belief that ultimately God will defend the defenceless in default of humans meeting their obligations.[16] Within the context of the Old Testament this complex of ideas is grounded in the exodus event, when God freed the Israelites from slavery in Egypt and formed a nation whose social arrangements were meant to embody the principle of freedom from oppression which found practical expression in the exodus.[17] From the perspective of discourse ethics (and this probably reflects what happened in ancient Israel) the story of the exodus became a powerful explanatory symbol for an Israelite conception of justice which transcended class interests and affirmed the interests of all who would be potentially affected by decisions taken in the name of the nation or sections of it. The *diskursethiker Grundsatz* (that every valid norm must have the agreement of all those involved as regards their interests) is in effect invoked by biblical authors who represent the prophets in particular as denouncing situations in which the agreement of those potentially affected by the behaviour of the rulers is certainly not present.

4.   The latter point leads to the question of the relation between ethics and law in the perspective of discourse ethics. This is a subject that Habermas has addressed in his most recent major book of over 700 pages, *Faktizität und Geltung*, and which, at the time of writing this paper, I have not studied sufficiently closely.[18] However, at various points in earlier writings Habermas speaks of the role of institutions in safeguarding and mediating ethical principles, and in enabling individuals to discover these in the process of socialisation. This suggests the following thoughts.

In the Old Testament there are collections of laws that can be described as utopian. These include sections of Deuteronomy and the Jubilee law in Leviticus 25. These collections require communicative action that places a high premium on the rectification of inequalities and disadvantages that result in some people becoming poor, homeless, debt-ridden and enslaved. Whether or not these laws were, or could have been, enforced, is a topic that has been much discussed; and it is easy to dismiss them as impracticable. However, these collections can be seen as an ideal statement of principles of social justice that would have been agreed to be in the

16.   Passages that can be cited include Ps. 72 and Ezek. 34.
17.   The issue is not whether, and if so in what way, the exodus happened, but how the exodus story was used to enjoin upon the Israelites the 'imitation of God' who had acted according to the story to free the people from oppression. In Exodus and Deuteronomy we repeatedly meet the motive clause which states that the Israelites must act in a certain way because they were once slaves in Egypt, and God redeemed them from there.
18.   Habermas, *Faktizität und Geltung: Beiträge zur Diskurstheorie des Rechts und des demokratischen Rechtsstaats* (Frankfurt am Main: Suhrkamp, 1992; rev. edn, 1994).

interests of all had such a discussion been able to take place. Their function is to encourage people to regard seriously the interests of all classes, to warn those who disregard the interests of others and to give hope to those whose interests are disregarded. They add what might be called a prophetic dimension to discourse ethics.

5. Is a prophetic dimension appropriate to discourse ethics? In a remarkable passage in the *Erläuterungen*, Habermas writes as follows:

> The validity of moral commands is linked to the condition that they will be generally obeyed as the basis for common behaviour. Only when this condition of general acceptance is fulfilled do the commandments express what everyone could wish. Only then do the moral commands lie in the common interest and make no claims on deeds of supererogation, because they are equally good for all. In this way the morals of reason set their seal on the abolition of sacrifice. Nevertheless those people deserve our admiration who follow, for example, the Christian commandment of love and make sacrifices in the interests of their neighbours that go beyond the equitable demands of morality; for deeds of supererogation can be understood as ventures in cases of a tragic situation or under barbaric living conditions, which call upon our moral indignation to combat fateful unjust suffering.[19]

If one were unfamiliar with Habermas's writings it could easily be concluded that he had seriously underestimated the amount of evil in the world, and was writing as though tragic situations or barbaric living conditions were the exception in today's world. In fact, inhumanity predominates in today's world just as it did in the world of ancient Israel. Wonderful as it would be if the ideal situation envisaged by discourse ethics were to exist so that there was indeed no need for sacrifices in pursuit of loving one's neighbour, we are far from this ideal and will probably never attain it. This counter-factuality does not invalidate discourse ethics, but rather points to what I call a prophetic factor.

The prophetic witness in the Old Testament (including parts of Leviticus and Deuteronomy) is uncompromising in its advocacy of social and ethical arrangements that are in the interests of all members of society, including the poor and the powerless. It is also often the case that the very survival of the nation is put into question because the people have acted unjustly;[20] and there are visions of a future just world in which the Israelite national interest is transcended to embrace the interests of all the nations and the interests of the natural order.[21] This witness runs far ahead of what rulers and people could either comprehend or were prepared to consider. The prophets often suffered persecution for their stand, and in the concept of a righteous remnant we have a glimpse of a small minority who were prepared to stand against the inhumanity of the larger society.

Thus within the Bible we not only see discussion taking place about what it would mean to act justly in a given situation (cf. Gen. 18.22-33), we see groups prepared to suffer for their commitment to justice and who believe that their

---

19. Habermas, *Erläuterungen*, pp. 136-37 (author's translation).
20. Cf. Amos 3.1-15; 7.19; 8.1–9.10.
21. Cf. Mic. 4.1-4; Ps. 96.

suffering will be a powerful means of helping others willingly to embrace the same vision.[22] Discourse ethics throws this factor into sharp relief and helps the Bible to add a new dimension to what Habermas includes under the category of the argumentation designed to bring universal agreement.

22. Cf. Isa. 53.1-12.

Chapter 7

ETHICAL EXPERIENCE IN THE OLD TESTAMENT:
LEGISLATIVE OR COMMUNICATIVE RATIONALITY?*

> Whoever strikes his father or his mother shall be put to death.
> Whoever steals a man, whether he sells him or is found in possession of him, shall
> be put to death.
> Whoever curses his father or his mother shall be put to death. (Exod. 21.15-17)

These commandments present the Old Testament at its most problematic for modern readers. We do not have a death penalty in Britain and when we did have one, at any rate in recent times, it did not apply to people who struck or cursed their parents. Embarrassment at these verses is not new, moreover. The Puritan commentator Matthew Poole noted the possibility that striking one's parents meant striking them fatally, and the mediaeval Jewish commentator Rashi, drawing on earlier Jewish tradition, maintained that what the law about striking covered was any striking that produced a wound.[1] The popular Reformed commentator J.F. Ostervald, concluded from these verses that striking and cursing parents were very serious offences indeed, but he stopped short of advocating the death penalty. Offenders should be very seriously punished by the magistrate, he maintained.[2]

These efforts at interpretations point to a paradox at the heart of traditional Christian use of the Old Testament for ethics. On the one hand the laws of Moses have been held to be the laws of God given to Moses. This is explicitly stated by the Article of Religion of the Church of England.[3] On the other hand it has been acknowledged that they are not necessarily binding on Christians. The Articles of Religion divide the laws into three categories—ceremonial, civil and moral—and declare that only the latter are binding on Christians. No guidance is offered on how to place particular laws in the appropriate categories, and the difficulty of

---

* This study was presented as the third of four Prideaux lectures delivered in the University of Exeter, February 1998. The presentational style of the original has been retained.

1. M. Poole, *Annotations on the Holy Bible* (London, 1685, reprint under the title *A Commentary on the Holy Bible* [Edinburgh: Banner of Truth Trust, 1962], to which reference is made here), I, p. 163; A.M. Silberman (ed.), *Pentateuch with Rashi's Commentary* (London: Shapiro, Valentine & Co., 1946), II (Exodus), p. 111, 'He is not…punishable with death except for a blow which causes a wound'.

2. J.F. Ostervald, *The Holy Bible…with Annotations…and Practical Observations* (London, 1783), on Exod. 21.12.

3. In Article 7 of the Thirty-Nine Articles.

doing this is illustrated by the fact that, in the sixteenth century, leading reformers such as Luther, Calvin and Tyndale regarded the Sabbath commandment as a ceremonial commandment, and therefore as not binding on Christians.[4]

Even the view that moral laws in the Old Testament are binding on Christians is problematic. Does the commandment 'You shall not kill' in Exod. 20.13 cover killing in warfare? If it does, then Christian nations supported by Christian leaders have broken the commandment on a grand scale. If it does not, and the commandment is an injunction to private individuals, what is the moral status of national heroes, such as William Tell, who delivered their people from killing tyrants such as Gessler? An approach to ethics in the Old Testament along the line of attempts to interpret or apply legislative commandments is full of pitfalls, and the aim of this third lecture is to explore a quite different approach, that of communicative or discourse ethics. I shall argue that discourse ethics enables us to consider a number of passages that are not normally invoked in the use of the Old Testament in ethics and that his approach offers a challenge to us as moral agents and as readers and users of the Old Testament.

What is discourse ethics? The outline of a complex philosophical matter that now follows must necessarily be superficial, and targeted to the subject of the lecture.[5] A good starting-point is the passage from Exod. 21.15-17 cited at the outset of the lecture. Why are these verses unacceptable to us today? The polite theological answer is that God accommodated them to the specific historical and cultural circumstances of ancient Israel. Another way of putting it is to say that they were relative to their time and situation, as all moral teaching is, including moral teaching of our own society and its embodiment in legislation. Who knows where moral teaching and legislation will have moved to in fifty years' time? Fifty years ago there still was a death penalty in Britain for homicide, and hire purchase legislation prevented a wife from signing a hire-purchase agreement. Only a husband could do that. But if moral teaching and its embodiment in legislation is constantly changing, does this mean that there are no universal moral principles on which such teaching and legislation can be or ought to be based? In some circles the answer is no. Ethical principles have been declared to be meaningless because incapable of verification, or as indicative simply of personal preferences.[6] More recently, stress has been placed upon the fact that moral philosophers and legislators are situated in particular cultural traditions and that their attempts to discover universal principles

4.   D.S. Katz, *Sabbath and Sectarianism in Seventeenth-Century England* (Leiden: E.J. Brill, 1988), p. 4.

5.   For further details see my article 'Discourse and Biblical Ethics' in the proceedings of the symposium on Ethics and the Bible at Sheffield in April 1995: J.W. Rogerson, M. Davies and M.D. Carroll R. (eds.), *The Bible and Ethics: The Second Sheffield Colloquium* (JSOTSup, 207; Sheffield: Sheffield Academic Press, 1995), pp. 17-26 [Editor's note: this essay is appears as Chapter 6 of the present volume]. See also S. Benhabib and F. Dallmayr (eds.), *The Communicative Ethics Controversy* (Cambridge, MA: MIT Press, 1991); S. Benhabib, *Situating the Self, Gender, Community and Postmodernism in Contemporary Ethics* (Cambridge: Polity Press, 1992).

6.   These issues are discussed, for example, in R.M. Hare's *The Language of Morals* (Oxford: Clarendon Press, 1952).

are comprised by their situatedness.[7] It is also possible to point to the overwhelmingly male, white, Western, privileged nature of ethicists and legislators.

In this situation where it is claimed that ethical statements at most express preferences and that all ethical systems are culturally determined, discourse ethics seeks to establish universal principles upon which ethics can be based. It does this by claiming that in language and communication there is a universal pragmatics, that is, a universal assumption that the purpose of language and communication is mutual understanding and an acceptance that in any discussion the force of the better argument will prevail. Anyone who tries to maintain that ethical principles are relative does so by relying on the force of the better argument. But this is a universal principle, and by using a universal principle to maintain a relativist view of what can be established, such a person is guilty of performative contradiction.[8]

By building, then, on the claimed universal principle that language and communication presuppose mutual understanding between people based on acceptance of the force of the latter argument, Jürgen Habermas has formulated a *Universalisierungsgrundsatz* for ethics as follows:

> to be valid a norm must fulfill the condition that the foreseeable consequences and side-effects which foreseeably result from its general application in order to satisfy the interests of all, can be accepted by all those concerned without compulsion, and can be preferred to the consequences of all known possible alternative arrangements.

This is supplemented by the *diskursethiker Grundsatz* that:

> only those norms can be considered valid that receive the acceptance of all involved as people who do or can take part in practical discourse.[9]

It is important to see what discourse ethics is and is not trying to achieve. It is not a method for deciding what is right in a particular ethical instance; it is not a way of saying that an ethical norm is decided by a majority vote; and it is not an attempt to resolve ethical dilemmas by working out a compromise between conflicting viewpoints. What it is, is a critical tool that can be applied to ethical norms, that claims that cross-cultural norms are in principle achievable, and which sets before moral agents and their societies the challenge of working towards 'ideal speech situations' in which the interests of people legitimately involved in particular issues are recognized and satisfied. To take one simple example, discourse ethics could not accept a situation such as *apartheid* as validly based because it excluded a majority whose legitimate interests were ignored. The same would have held if those adversely affected had been a small minority.

---

7. See A. MacIntyre, *After Virtue* (Notre Dame: University of Notre Dame Press, 1981).

8. See my article, 'Discourse Ethics and Biblical Ethics', where reference is made to J. Habermas, 'Diskursethik—Notizen zu einem Begründungsprogramm', in *idem*, *Moralbewußtsein und kommunikatives Handeln* (Frankfurt am Main: Suhrkamp, 1983; 3rd edn, 1988), pp. 53-125, and *idem*, *Erläuterungen zur Diskursethik* (Frankfurt am Main: Suhrkamp, 1991; 2nd edn, 1992).

9. See 'Discourse Ethics and Biblical Ethics', p. 18, for further details [Editor's note: p. 61 of the present volume].

One of Habermas's most persuasive interpreters, Seyla Benhabib, has pointed out, convincingly in my opinion, that discourse ethics conceals two principles, those of universal respect (for others) and egalitarian reciprocity—the willingness to see things from the perspective of the other person—and she follows this up with another observation that will be important towards the end of the lecture.[10] She addresses the objection to discourse ethics that could be brought by sado-masochists when discussing the maxim 'do not inflict unnecessary suffering'. Suppose they argue that *their* interests consist 'precisely in the opportunity to inflict and receive such suffering'?[11] Citing the principles of universal respect and egalitarian reciprocity she argues that to adopt the infliction of unnecessary suffering as a norm of action would be to undermine the very idea of a moral dialogue in the first place. Discourse ethics posits—counterfactually—a situation of moral relationships characterized by respect and reciprocity and she concludes:

> when we shift the burden of the moral test in communicative ethics from consensus to the idea of an ongoing moral conversation, we begin to ask not what all would or could agree to as a result of practical discourse to be morally permissible or impermissible, but what would be allowed and perhaps even necessary from the standpoint of continuing and sustaining the practice of the moral conversation among us. The emphasis now is less on *rational agreement*, but more on sustaining those normative practices and moral relationships within which reasoned agreement *as a way of life* can flourish and continue.[12]

What I propose to do now is to examine several texts from the viewpoint of Habermas's *diskursethiker Grundsatz*

> only those norms can be considered valid that receive the acceptance of all involved as people who do or can take part in practical discourse

supplemented by Seyla Benhabib's principles of universal respect and egalitarian reciprocity.

The first passage to be considered is Gen. 18.22-33, Abraham's intercession with God regarding the destruction of the city of Sodom. Abraham objects to God's intention to destroy the city, on the grounds that there might be fifty righteous people there, and that it would be unjust to slay the righteous with the wicked 'so that the righteous fare as the wicked' (18.25). 'Shall not the judge of all the earth do right?', asks Abraham. In the ensuing dialogue, Abraham bargains God down to agreeing not to destroy Sodom if ten righteous people are to be found in the city.

The first point that needs comment is the phrase 'Shall not the judge of all the earth do right?'. In the Hebrew there is a word-play upon the words 'judge' (*shophet*) and right (*mishpat*), nicely captured in de Wette's German translation as

---

10. S. Benhabib, 'Afterword: Communicative Ethics and Contemporary Controversies in Practical Philosophy', in Benhabib and Dallmayr (eds.), *The Communicative Ethics Controversy*, pp. 330-69.

11. Benhabib, 'Afterword', p. 342.

12. Benhabib, 'Afterword', p. 346.

'wird der Richter der ganzen Welt nicht Gerechtigkeit üben?'[13] and brought out even better by Jerome's 'qui judicas omnem terram, nequamquam facies judicium hoc'.[14] How is the Hebrew word *mishpat* to be understood here? Leaving aside the lexicographical possibilities it can be observed that for the writer of Gen. 18.22-33, *mishpat* was something independent of God which God was expected to uphold. Faced with the question 'Are things good because God commands them or does God command them because they are good?', the writer would presumably have opted for 'God commands things because they are good'. From the viewpoint of discourse ethics, *mishpat* could be interpreted as follows. For the divine action to be based upon a valid ethical norm it would need to be capable of receiving the acceptance of all involved who could take part in practical discourse. Now it is important to stress that we do not know what the outcome of such a discourse would have been. The innocent, if there were any, might well have said that they would be unjustly punished if the city were to be destroyed; but they might equally have said that their own destruction would be a small price to pay for ridding the earth of such a wicked city. But the wicked would also be entitled to represent their interests, and whereas they would be unlikely to agree that their destruction was a preferred option, we do not know how they would have been affected by the need to engage in dialogue with the innocent on this matter. It could possibly have led to their repentance, or to the repentance of some of them, at any rate. If, then, there is an objection on the part of the discourse ethics to what God is about to do, it is an objection based on the fact that the interests of at least one party, the innocent, have not been taken into account. Abraham represents those interests and conducts a dialogue with God from the standpoint of an ever-diminishing number of possible righteous people in the city of Sodom.

Secondly, it can be said that the dialogue is based upon universal respect and egalitarian reciprocity. The narrator goes out of his way to stress Abraham's respect for God: 'Behold, I have taken upon myself to speak to the Lord, I who am but dust and ashes' (v. 27); and again, 'Oh let not the Lord be angry and I will speak again but this once' (v. 32). And yet, from the point of view of the moral discourse, Abraham is an equal partner with God, thus illustrating egalitarian reciprocity. As to universal respect, Abraham does not allow the fact that Sodom has an evil reputation to divert him from trying to prevent a possible injustice.

Now I must make it clear that I am not suggesting that anything of what I have just said have occurred to or even have been understood by the writer of Gen. 18.22-39. Discourse ethics was formulated only in the 1980s! What I would claim, however, is that there is a universality about moral dilemmas and attempts to solve them by discussion that enables discourse ethics to highlight features of these processes that have previously been overlooked.

The next incident to be discussed is one which occurs in three related versions, namely, that of the dangers posed to Sarah (twice) and to Rebekah, when their

13. W.M.L. de Wette, *Die Heilige Schrift des Alten und Neuen Testaments* (Heidelberg, 3rd edn, 1839), p. 16.
14. *Biblia Sacra juxta vulgatam Clementinam* (Rome: Descleé, 1927), p. 16.

husbands try to pass them off as their sisters. The incident occurs at Gen. 12.10-20, 20.1-18 and 26.6-11, and I accept the view of John Van Seters that in their present form the three narratives are based one upon the other.[15] I shall comment on each in turn and how it handles the moral dilemma implicit in the incident.

In Gen. 12.10-20 Abram and Sarai go to Egypt because there is a famine in Canaan.[16] Abram, fearing that he will be killed by the Egyptians so that Sarai can become Pharaoh's wife on account of her great beauty, tells Sarai to say that she is Abram's sister. This is done and Sarai is taken by Pharaoh into his house; but the mischief is discovered when God afflicts Pharaoh with great plagues because Pharaoh has taken Sarai as his wife. There is no moral comment in the passage apart from Pharaoh's indignation that he has been punished by God for acting in good faith on the basis of Abram's deception.

In Gen. 20.1-18 the supposed danger to Abraham and Sarah is posed by Abimelech king of Gerar in the Negev, whence Abraham has journeyed. The action is described in one verse only: 'Abraham said of Sarah his wife, "She is my sister". And Abimelech king of Gerar sent and took Sarah' (20.2). Much of the remainder of the chapter consists of two dialogues: between Abimelech and God during a dream, and a face-to-face encounter between Abimelech and Abraham. The narrator informs us that Abimelech 'had not approached' Sarah and this sharpens Abimelech's dispute with God in reply to God's warning that Abimelech is a dead man for having taken another man's wife. In language reminiscent of Abraham's intercession on behalf of Sodom, Abimelech asks God 'Will you slay an innocent people?' (v. 4) and points out that Abraham had described Sarah as his sister and that Sarah had concurred by calling Abraham her brother. God defends himself by saying that he had prevented Abimelech from touching Sarah. Abimelech's language to Abraham is equally strong: 'You have done to me things that ought not to be done' (v. 9). Abraham justifies himself by saying that he did not expect that there would be any fear of God in Gerar, and he insists that he was telling the truth when he said that Sarah was his sister, because she was in fact his half-sister.

The moral unease of the writer of this chapter is plain. It is clear that he believes that both God and Abraham have acted unjustly—Abraham by deceiving Abimelech and God by punishing him by closing 'all the wombs of the house of Abimelech'. The narrator finds it necessary to justify Abraham—his deception is partly true—and to justify God—it is God who prevents Abimelech from having sexual relations with Sarah.

In Gen. 26.6-11 it is Isaac who says of Rebekah that she is his sister—there is no ground for this as she is the daughter of Isaac's cousin Bethuel[17]—and it is Abimelech king of the Philistines in Gerar in whose domain Isaac settles. Abimelech does not, however, take Rebekah to be his wife, and the true nature of the

---

15. J. Van Seters, *Abraham in History and Tradition* (New Haven: Yale University Press, 1975), pp. 167-91.

16. In the first version of the story, their names have not yet been changed to the more familiar Abraham and Sarah.

17. Gen. 24.24.

relationship between Isaac and Rebekah only becomes apparent when Abimelech sees Isaac doing something with Rebekah which the translations render with words such as 'sporting' (AV), 'fondling' (RSV), 'caressing' (NIV), 'laughing together' (NEB[!]) and 'making love' (GNB).[18] The discovery leads to an altercation between Abimelech and Isaac, and Isaac is accused of endangering Abimelech's people, since guilt, and by implication divine punishment, would have been brought upon the people if any of them had had intercourse with Rebekah. Isaac's only defense is that he thought that there would be a good chance that he would be killed if it had been known that Rebekah was his wife.

These narratives can be commented on from various moral perspectives. It can be noted, for example, that the narratives are uneasy about the idea that the end—the survival of Abra(ha)m and Isaac—justifies the means—the deceit about the true relationship between the men and the women. Further, anyone concerned with women's issues, men or women, will be embarrassed at the way in which the wife is exposed to danger in order to preserve the life of the husband.

From the standpoint of discourse ethics the objection can be made that the actions of Abra(ha)m and Isaac not only ignored the legitimate interests of their wives, but also the interests of the rulers and their subjects whom they exposed to actual or potential divine punishment. It is noteworthy that in the third version of the incident the interests of the ordinary people are explicitly represented by their ruler. It is also interesting that in two of the three versions there is an ethical dialogue between God, a ruler and an ancestor and that appeal is made implicitly to the force of the better argument. Thus, in his dialogue with God in 20.5, Abimelech points out that in the face of statements by both Abraham and Sarah that they were brother and sister, it was reasonable to conclude that Sarah was not married and that it was in order for him to take her as a wife.

The principles of universal respect and egalitarian reciprocity can also be invoked. There is no doubt intended irony in the narratives when the fears of Abra(ha)m and Isaac that they are about to settle among people who will kill them because they have beautiful wives, turn out to be unfounded. The narratives show, on the contrary, that the non-Hebrew peoples among whom the Hebrew ancestors move are capable of respecting foreigners as well as able to conduct ethical discussion in a rational way.

The third passage that I wish to consider (2 Sam. 14.1-11) is quite different. It is part of the subterfuge used by Joab to persuade David to restore Absalom to court after Absalom had been banished because he killed Amnon for raping his (Absalom's) sister Tamar. Joab persuades a wise woman from Tekoa to dress as a mourner and to ask David to adjudicate on a legal and moral matter. How she turns the discussion to Absalom's restoration will not concern us, nor is it necessary to discuss whether the incident is historical or not. The point is that the narrative presumably was a credible account for its presumed hearers/readers of the way in which cases were brought to and decided by kings or tribal chiefs or judges.

18.   The GNB appears to be the most convincing rendering in context, the NEB the least convincing.

The woman explains to David that her husband has died and that her two sons have had a quarrel in which one killed the other. The rest of the family is now demanding that the murderer should be put to death, one of the reasons being that the family would be guilty of not avenging the bloodshed if no action were taken. However, the execution of the son would leave the widow without a male heir and her husband's line would die out—a major disaster materially and psychologically. After persistent pleas by the woman, David agrees that the surviving son will not die. The woman insists that if any guilt is incurred by this action it will rest upon her family and not that of the king.

The incident is an example of legislative rationality in that the matter is resolved by a ruler whose decision is final. It is, however, a decision reached on the basis of dialogue, and an appeal not to abstract principles but to the interests of someone who could not participate in the dialogue, namely, the deceased husband. There is, therefore, an element of communicative ethics in the incident. From the point of view of the *diskursethiker Grundsatz*, however, the norm on which the decision is based is not valid because the interests of all those legitimately concerned are not represented. If the woman's relatives were afraid that failure to punish the murderer would result in possible divine retribution directed at the family, they would have genuine grounds for anxiety at the woman accepting this guilt on their behalf. It has to be stressed again that discourse ethics is not a method for guessing what the outcome of a dialogue between all the interested parties might have been. Discourse ethics is a claim that ethics can be universally grounded given certain conditions; and as applied to particular examples it points out how such examples fall short of the ideal. It can also show, however, that even within instances of decision making that fall short of the ideal there are implicit appeals to the force of the better argument and to the principles of universal respect and egalitarian reciprocity. In the case of 2 Sam. 14.1-11, the woman appeals to the king to see the issue from the perspective of her dead husband and appeals to what she hopes is the better argument, namely, that the safeguarding of her husband's interests is more important than the fears of her relatives that they may be held guilty for not punishing a murderer.

In the final part of this lecture I want to try to work out the implications of two other features of discourse ethics for reflecting on the ethical content of the Old Testament and its possible abiding significance. They are, first, the fact that in order to establish principles for morality that have universal validity, discourse ethics has to postulate, counter-factually, an ideal speech situation in which all the legitimate interests of those in a particular matter are not only represented, but are respected in a situation of non-coercion. The second feature is Seyla Benhabib's observation that what discourse ethics aims at is not consensus but the establishment of communities within which moral relationships based upon reasoned agreement become a way of life.

I cannot here engage in the considerable amount of discussion that has been generated by the utopianism of discourse ethics in positing ideal communicative situations.[19] My own view is that it is valuable to place ethical dilemmas alongside the formal demands of ideal communicative situations because this makes us aware of the provisionality of the solutions that are proposed. We live in a world where questions are being asked about the legitimate interests of unborn children, animals and the species that inhabit the natural world. Decisions that are made, for example, preferring human interests above those of the environment, are compromises. Set against the utopianism of the ideal speech situations of discourse ethics they prevent, or ought to prevent, anyone from supposing that such decisions are unequivocally right. They challenge us to sharpen our sense of universal respect and egalitarian reciprocity.

From an Old Testament perspective, the utopianism of discourse ethics closely resembles the utopian framework that brackets the Old Testament understanding of creation and which generates hopes for the future role of God which will eliminate all injustice from the world. Recent studies of the narrative framework of Genesis 1–11 have made it clear that the world of Genesis 1 is not the world of our experience.[20] The world of Genesis 1 is a vegetarian world in which the animals are also vegetarians (Gen. 1.30). This use of vegetarianism is a way of describing a world at peace with itself. The world of our experience comes into being only after the flood, and is a compromise creation in which animals and humans can eat meat (Gen. 9.3-6). When visions of a new creation are given, such as in Isa. 65.17-25, the vegetarian creation returns: the wolf and the lamb feed together and the lion eats straw like the ox. The biblical writers were probably able to believe that the creation had once been entirely vegetarian; we cannot do so. We can, however, agree with the biblical writers that moral life has to be lived in a world that is compromised. Taking the Old Testament as a whole we can say that even its most uncompromising demands, such as those in the Ten Commandments, have to be seen within the Old Testament perspective that the world is in need of transformation, and that that transformation is beyond human possibility.

The result of paying attention to the utopian aspects of discourse ethics and its Old Testament counterpart is to bring into the ethical limelight passages that would not normally be considered under this heading. An obvious example would be the oracle about the latter days found in both Isaiah 2 and Micah 4, and which I shall cite in its Micah form:

> It shall come to pass in the latter days that the mountain of the house of the LORD shall be established as the highest of the mountains, and shall be raised up above the hills; and the people shall flow to it, and many nations shall come and say: come, let us go up to the mountain of the LORD, to the house of the God of Jacob; that he may teach us his ways and we may walk in his paths. For out of Zion shall go forth the law, and the word of the LORD from Jerusalem. He shall judge between many peoples, and shall decide for strong nations afar off; and they shall beat their

19. See, e.g., K.-O. Apel, 'Is the Ethics of the Ideal Communication Community a Utopia? On the Relationship between Ethics, Utopia, and the Critique of Utopia', in Benhabib and Dallmayr (eds.), *The Communicative Ethics Controversy*, pp. 23-59.

20. See J. Rogerson, *Genesis 1–11* (OTG; Sheffield: Sheffield Academic Press, 1991).

swords into ploughshares, and their spears into pruning hooks; nation shall not lift up sword against nation, neither shall they learn war any more; but they shall sit every man under his vine and under his fig tree, and none shall make them afraid. (Mic. 4.1-4b)

There are in this passage many ingredients of an ideal speech situation. Having turned their implements of war into tools for providing food, the nations will live peaceably together, without fear or compulsion, and will be guided by moral principles that they can gladly accept. The passage is, of course, expressed in terms of ancient Israelite particularities, and especially in terms of the predominance of the national Israelite sanctuary. Yet this is not the historical temple in Jerusalem but a transformed temple, and one that has become central for 'many nations'.

In such passages as Ps. 96.10-13 objects from the natural world are included in the ideal speech communities as God's coming to judge the world with righteousness is greeted with rejoicing on the part of heaven and earth, the sea, the cultivated land and the trees of the wood. Such sentiments take on an added sharpness in an age in which human interests demand or cause the depletion of the ozone layer, the poisoning of land and sea, the covering of cultivated land with concrete and the wholesale destruction of forests.

But it is not enough simply to invoke utopian ideal speech situations as a method for establishing valid ethic norms. As Seya Benhabib points out, discourse ethics challenges us to establish communities in which moral relationships based upon reasoned agreement is a way of life. How is this to be done?

In the Old Testament it is attempted by prophets who insist that morality is not simply a private matter and that there must be public discussion about the moral values that affect the nation as a whole. A typical example of such insistence can be found in Amos 8.4-8:

> Hear this, you who trample upon the needy,
>   and bring the poor of the land to an end,
> saying, 'When will the new moon be over,
>   that we may sell grain,
> And the Sabbath,
>   that we may offer wheat for sale,
> that we may make the ephah small and the shekel great,
>   and deal deceitfully with false balances;
> that we may buy the poor for silver
>   and the needy for a pair of sandals,
> and sell the refuse of the wheat?'
>   The LORD has sworn by the pride of Jacob,
> 'Surely I will never forget any of their deeds.
> Shall not the land tremble on this account,
>   and every one mourn who dwells in it,
> and all of it rise like the Nile,
>   and be tossed about and sink again, like the Nile of Egypt?'

Needless to say, the prophetic view that moral injury to the poor and needy was a matter for public proclamation and divine condemnation was not popular. Amos is accused of conspiracy against Israel for saying that the nation's wickedness will result in its exile, while Micah bitterly attacks those who say to him, 'Do not preach —one should not preach of such things' (Mic. 2.6). Jeremiah also finds himself mocked and derided for speaking judgment in God's name.

In a remarkable passage, Habermas acknowledges that in the interim between the present situation when ideal speech communities do not exist and the counterfactual situation when everyone could accept that commandments expressed what everyone could wish, there is a need for sacrifice and for works of supererogation. He writes that

> those people deserve our admiration who follow, for example, the Christian commandment of love and make sacrifices in the interests of their neighbours that go beyond the equitable demands of morality; for deeds of supererogation can be understood as ventures in cases of a tragic situation or under barbaric living conditions, which call upon our moral indignation to combat fateful unjust suffering.[21]

Conclusion

To anyone not familiar with discourse ethics or the discussions surrounding it, the theory as I have tried to present and use may have sounded at best far-fetched and at worst unintelligible. Even if that is the case, I hope that the discussions of Abraham's intercession for Sodom, the incidents of Abra(ha)m and Isaac passing off their wives as their sisters, and the case made to David by the wise women of Tekoa have indicated that consideration of ethics in the Old Testament can and ought to be extended beyond its legislative commandments and their possible application to today's world.

It is significant that hard-line groups such as the Restoration movement, a group within fundamentalist Christianity which seeks to legislate as much of the Old Testament as possible upon today's world, confines this activity to the sphere of private morality.[22] Whatever else it does, as it seems to me, discourse ethics requires that morality is put at the top of the agenda of public affairs. To insist that a valid norm must be freely accepted by all those who have a legitimate interest is to abolish the distinction between public and private morality; and in this regard discourse ethics points to something that is at the heart of Old Testament ethics. The latter know nothing of a private sphere with which God is concerned, and a public sphere from which God is excluded. Of course, there were those—the ruling classes—who preferred to believe that God's justice had no place in the public sphere; and this led to confrontation.

I would want to maintain that part of the ethical value of the Old Testament for today's world is its insistence that morality applies as much to the public sphere as to the private sphere; and it challenges us to take that principle actively into the

---

21.   Habermas, *Erläuterungen*, pp. 136-37 (author's translation).

22.   For a thoughtful discussion of these tendencies see C.J.H. Wright, *Walking in the Ways of the Lord: The Ethical Authority of the Old Testament* (Leicester: Apollos, 1995), pp. 97-109.

public sphere even at the cost of ridicule or persecution. Zygmunt Bauman, in his *Modernity and the Holocaust* argues that

> the Holocaust was an outcome of a unique encounter between factors by themselves quite ordinary and common; and that the possibility of such an encounter could be blamed to a very large extent on the emancipation of the political state, with its monopoly of means of violence and its audacious engineering ambitions from social control—following the step-by-step dismantling of all non-political power resources and institutions of social control.[23]

23. Z. Bauman, *Modernity and the Holocaust* (Cambridge: Polity Press, 1989), p. xiii.

Part III

THE RELEVANCE OF THE OLD TESTAMENT
FOR MODERN SOCIAL ISSUES

Chapter 8

THE OLD TESTAMENT AND THE DEBATE ABOUT NUCLEAR DISARMAMENT*

> So Joshua defeated the whole land, the hill country and the Negeb and the lowland and the slopes, and all their kings; he left none remaining, but utterly destroyed all that breathed, as the LORD God of Israel commanded. (Josh. 10.40)

The idea that the Old Testament might be used to support unilateral nuclear disarmament will seem strange to many people. If they have any knowledge of the Old Testament at all they will probably think that its message can be summed up in the principle 'an eye for an eye and a tooth for a tooth'. They will not be surprised to find a passage such as that from Josh. 10.40 in the Old Testament. It will only be evidence that at best the Old Testament is fiawed, and at worst that it would seem to support both the possession and first use of weapons of mass destruction.

Clearly, the attitude to war found in parts of the Old Testament is a problem that has to be faced, and an attempt to do this will be made at the end; but before we retreat into the familiar practice of ruling out the Old Testament as a book about a God of hate, and try to concentrate on the New Testament as a book about peace and love, it is worth considering what, in fact, the Old Testament has to say. It is my conviction that it is more helpful in many respects than the New Testament on the issue of nuclear disarmament. I shall discuss its contribution under six headings.

1. *The Requirements of a Just Ruler, and the Power that He Should Use*

Where the Old Testament lays down requirements for the just ruler, it is made clear that he has the responsibility to protect and uphold the rights of the weak against the strong, and that he should use force to do so if necessary. The prayer about the ideal king in Psalm 72 contains the petitions:

> May he defend the cause of the poor of the people,
>   give deliverance to the needy,
>   and crush the oppressor!...
> May his foes bow down before him,
>   and his enemies lick the dust...

* This study was delivered as an address given at a night vigil organized by students of the University of Sheffield, Friday 16 March 1984. The presentational style of the original has been retained.

For he delivers the needy when he calls,
　　the poor and him who has no helper.
He has pity on the weak and the needy,
　　and saves the lives of the needy.
From oppression and violence he redeems their life;
　　and precious is their blood in his sight. (vv. 4, 9, 12-14)

Whether or not the Old Testament envisages passive and pacifist resistance on the part of individuals is an interesting question. One might argue, on the basis of what is said about the suffering servant of God, that the Old Testament does envisage such passive and pacifist resistance. Consider, for example, the following well-known verse from Isa. 53.7:

He was oppressed, and he was afflicted,
　　yet he opened not his mouth;
like a lamb that is led to the slaughter,
　　and like a sheep that before its shearers is dumb,
　　so he opened not his mouth.

This could well be an example, whatever else it is, of the endurance of innocent suffering such that the perpetrators or witnesses are forced later to confess that this suffering has led to healing and reconciliation for themselves:

he was wounded for our transgressions,
　　he was bruised for our iniquities;
upon him was the chastisement that made us whole,
　　and with his stripes we are healed. (Isa. 53.4)

However, I am not concerned in this essay so much with the individual or with small groups, although their importance can never be exaggerated. I am concerned with what the Old Testament says about those in authority, and it seems to be quite clear that such people have a duty to uphold justice and to protect the oppressed, and to use force if necessary. If this last statement is offensive to pacifists, it is also a reminder that the debate about unilateral disarmament is not simply a debate between pacifists and non-pacifists. It is also a debate between two groups who believe in the right and necessity in certain circumstances to use force, even though to resort to force is in itself an evil. Where these groups differ is that one group accepts the morality of the possession and use of weapons of mass destruction, whereas the other group believes that there are strict limits to the force that should be deployed. It is my belief that while the Old Testament requires rulers to restrain injustice and oppression by force if necessary, the Old Testament sets strict limits on the use of such power.

2. *The Ruler Is Subject to Divine and Moral Law*

There are two famous incidents in the Old Testament which show kings abusing their privileged power. The first is in the story of David (2 Sam. 10–12). While his army was besieging the capital of the Ammonites, David, at home in Jerusalem, saw another man's wife, made her pregnant, and tried to cover up the deed by recalling her husband from the battle. His assumption that the man would have intercourse with his wife was a false assumption, since the rules of war required abstinence from marital intercourse while the battle was in progress. Uriah thus refused to sleep with his wife, and David finally solved the problem by arranging for Uriah to be put in the fiercest part of the battle line, and for the troops with him to withdraw suddenly. The ploy succeeded and Uriah fell in battle. For the prophet Nathan, however, David had committed not only adultery but murder, and he passed judgment upon David for committing these crimes. The second incident is in 1 Kings 21, and is the story of king Ahab acquiring Naboth's vineyard by deceit and treachery, which involved having Naboth executed on a charge of which he was innocent. Again, in this case, there is prophetic denunciation of a king who thought to act above the law.

It could be said that these two examples refer to the private and not the public lives of the kings in question; but the Old Testament itself seems not to draw a distinction between what kings do in public and in private. The crimes of David, even though he repents, involve him, his family, and his people in the traumas of dissent and rebellion. There is an Old Testament conception which has been called 'ruler responsibility', according to which a ruler's subjects will be caught up in the consequences of the ruler's misdeeds. Although this conception is based upon ideas of corporate solidarity that may be stronger in ancient times compared with today, who can deny the validity of the insight that subjects cannot in many cases escape from the consequences of decisions made by their rulers, even in so-called democratic societies? In the modern world, the decision of rulers to manufacture and if necessary employ nuclear weapons would undoubtedly have dire consequences for their subjects.

It is also the case that part of the prophetic tradition condemns excesses in the misuse of power in war. The oracles against the nations in the opening chapters of Amos contain clear condemnations of war atrocities:

> For three transgressions of Damascus,
>   and for four, I will not revoke the punishment;
> because they have threshed Gilead
>   with threshing sledges of iron...
> For three transgressions of Gaza,
>   and for four, I will not revoke the punishment;
> because they carried into exile a whole people
>   to deliver them up to Edom...
> For three transgressions of Edom,
>   and for four, I will not revoke the punishment;
> because he pursued his brother with the sword,
>   and cast off all pity.
> For three transgressions of the Ammonites,
>   and for four, I will not revoke the punishment;...
> because they have ripped up women with child in Gilead,
>   that they might enlarge their border. (Amos 1.3, 6, 11, 13)

In the light of the condemnations of the abuse of power by David and Ahab, the concept of 'ruler responsibility' and the condemnations of 'war crimes' it can be reasonably asserted that if the Old Testament envisages a legitimate use of force and power, it sees strict limits to such uses. The responsibilities of rulers are further underlined by the Old Testament view of humankind as a responsible steward in God's world, responsible to God for its proper use.

3. *Humankind as God's Steward of the World, Responsible to God*

The interpretation of the opening chapter of Genesis is not easy; yet in recent studies several lines have converged together. The language of Gen. 1.26-27

> Then God said, 'Let us make man in our image, after our likeness; and let them have dominion over the fish of the sea, and over the birds of the air, and over the cattle, and over all the earth, and over every creeping thing that creeps upon the earth'.

has been set in the context of the divine royal court. The 'we' language is the language of divine royalty addressed to the court, and in the formula of giving humankind dominion over the created order there is being given to humankind not carte blanche for the human race to do what it likes, but a divine royal commission to rule the earth as God's stewards. One study of the meaning of the 'image of God' has interpreted the phrase in the light of the practice of conquerors setting up statues of themselves throughout their conquered territories, to indicate their lordship over the territory. The practice is not unknown to us—how many statues of Queen Victoria are still to be found all over the former British Empire? On this interpretation of humankind being the 'image of God', the human race is, as it were, set up to show and perform the sovereignty of God in the world. The tragedy is, and the Old Testament is unsurpassed in indicating this, that the human race will have none of the service of God which is perfect freedom. Not only does the story in Genesis 3, in which Adam and Eve disobey God because they have been told that if they do so they will be like God, knowing good and evil, express humankind's desire to be sole rulers of the universe without God; stories such as the Tower of Babel record humankind's desire to usurp God's place in the world. In the story of the Tower of Babel the result is confusion, and the division of humans from each other by the barriers of language and thus race.

If, according to the Old Testament, humankind is in the world to care responsibly for it in accordance with God's will, it follows that rulers have a particular responsibility. Power lies in their hands in a way that it does not with the rest of us. This was true in Old Testament times as well as now, even though Old Testament kings did not have the power to destroy the world completely. The Old Testament image for the ruler acting responsibly before God in leading and supporting the people is that of the shepherd. We have to ask whether it is a proper use of power given to rulers who are God's stewards that they should possess weapons that can destroy the whole human race and the world with it, and that in order to possess these weapons they can see resources diverted from the conquest of poverty, ignorance and disease. It might be objected that to talk thus about rulers is to ignore the existence of leaders whose beliefs are totally materialistic or in opposition to any idea of God. What is remarkable about the Old Testament is that its writers were well aware of the fact that most of the world rulers knew nothing of the God of Israel and his demands. Israel was constantly being harassed by the great empires of the day. The writers of the Old Testament need no lectures from us about the harsh realities of war, occupation and exile. This makes their witness even more remarkable, and leads to the next point.

4. *The Nation Is Not Sacrosanct if It Ignores God's Laws*

One of the most remarkable things about the Old Testament is the amount of prophetic teaching that it contains threatening the nation with oblivion if it does not turn or return to God. As early as the story of the loss of the ark and the overwhelming defeat of the Israelites by the Philistines in 1 Samuel 4, the theme can be seen that God will not overlook the wickedness of his own people, and if necessary will make them lose their independence. The book of Amos threatens:

> I will take you into exile beyond Damascus, says the LORD, whose name is the
> God of hosts. (Amos 5.27)

The book of Micah proclaims that:

> Zion shall be plowed as a field,
> Jerusalem shall become a heap of ruins,
>   and the mountain of the house a wooded height. (Mic. 3.12)

and the burden of the preaching of Jeremiah is that God is fighting against Jerusalem, that he will surely give it into the hands of the Babylonians, and that the only hope of safety is surrender (see, e.g., Jer. 38). Of all parts of the Old Testament, these may be the most difficult for us to appreciate, precisely because we have enjoyed freedom from foreign domination for centuries, as has our principal ally the United States. For us, the loss of independence and our domination by a foreign power is such a terrifying idea that we can easily be persuaded that any means would be justified to prevent such an occurrence. One of the strongest appeals made by the pro-nuclear lobby is to this sense of how appalling it would be for us to lose our independence, and that only nuclear weapons will guarantee our independence. For the writers of the Old Testament, matters were quite different. They were not starry eyed about the Egyptians, the Assyrians or the Babylonians, as many CND supporters are supposed to be starry eyed about the Russians. The description of the 'foe from the north' being brought by God upon his people, as found in Jeremiah can hardly be more terrifying:

> A lion has gone up from his thicket,
>   a destroyer of nations has set out;
>   he has gone forth from his place
> to make your land a waste;
>   your cities will be ruins

without inhabitant.
For this gird you with sackcloth,
lament and wail. (Jer. 4.7-8)

The reason why the prophets could write and speak like this is that terrifying as the human foe might be, God was to be feared even more. Further, the God of the prophets was not only the one who could punish but the one who could restore, and who could use even the most bitter exile as the occasion for his people to gain new strength and to learn new truths.

The challenge of the Old Testament in this matter can be summed up as follows. If God is God, then he will be with his people even if they experience, as did the Israelites, occupation, exile and oppression. Powerful empires do not have the final word, and they are not to be feared rather than God. Any nation that is prepared to act immorally in order to safeguard its existence is in grave peril.

5. *Times and Circumstances Change, and the Right Word for Today Must Be Sought*

It can be urged against me that I have been selective in what I have written; that I have ignored incidents such as Isaiah's support for the resistance of King Hezekiah to the Assyrian invasion of Judah in 701 BCE. This particular incident is interesting precisely because it is in contrast to what I have said, and it enables an Old Testament comment to be made about an issue that is often raised. It is often said that it was right for Britain to declare war on Nazi Germany, and that it would have been wrong for a maniac such as Hitler, with his programme of mass extermination of Jews, Poles, Russians and Gypsies, to have gone unpunished. The further point is then often made that there is a parallel between the 1930s and the post-war situation; that because we were not sufficiently militarily prepared to resist Hitler, therefore we should be fully prepared to fight the Russians today.

I have a certain amount of sympathy for the view that it was right to declare war on Hitler, although I do not believe that it was right to oppose him by the indiscriminate bombing of civilian targets, culminating in the use of atomic bombs in Japan. All my own earliest childhood memories are of the London blitz, of night after night in air raid shelters, of evacuations to parts of the country where the sympathy of local people soon evaporated so that it was necessary to return to the ordeal of the bombing. I can still remember what a shock it was, on being evacuated, to go three whole days without hearing an air raid siren. In Germany, boys of my own age must have experienced the same dread for no better reason than that they were innocently caught up into the horrors of 'total war'. I have a certain sympathy for the view that in the immediate post-war situation the nuclear deterrent actually worked, and helped to preserve the peace. But the support which Isaiah gave to Hezekiah in 701 BCE to resist the Assyrians was completely reversed by Jeremiah a little over a hundred years later, when, as already stated, he proclaimed the imminent fall of Jerusalem and the exile of its people. Similarly, what was right for 1930 and for 1950 is not necessarily right for 1980. Today we are in a quite new situation compared with earlier years. We have proliferated nuclear weapons to the point of insanity, and we have accordingly increased the proportion of our resources devoted to their manufacture. We have brought the possible accidental destruction of ourselves and our planet to a few minutes to midnight. What may once have been right does not in changed circumstances remain right. The Old Testament writers knew this better than we do.

6. *The Old Testament Attitude to War*

If I have been successful in indicating that the Old Testament expects power to be exercised responsibly, as a trust from God, who is to be feared more than the mighty empires and in whose hand lies the ultimate destiny of the nations, I still have to deal with its attribution to God of the command to destroy utterly whole populations. There is no point in denying that on occasions, the Israelites showed no mercy to their enemies because they believed that God wished the enemies to be 'devoted' to him, in accordance with the ideas of war then prevalent. As the narratives describing these slaughters were passed down from generation to generation, they received a new interpretation that refiected the changed perception of God brought about by the prophetic witness, which, as we have seen, was strong in its denunciation of abuses of power. As received by later generations, the narratives expressed the view that Israel's misfortunes had resulted from the people's disobedience to God, a disobedience which resulted from following the gods of the people who shared the land with the Israelites. In many cases, compromises with other gods had led to just those denials of rights and the support of the poor so close to the heart of Old Testament religion at its best. The narratives about Israel completely destroying an enemy, or not doing so, as the case might be, became a way not of glorifying war, but of urging upon the people the need for utter loyalty to the God of Israel and his laws, to the exclusion of compromise with the debased values of the gods of Israel's neighbours. Passages such as the one at the head of this essay should not be read at their face value, nor taken to be in any way representative of the distinctive witness of the Old Testament. The Old Testament is not a collection of dubious teachings about a primitive tribal god. It is a witness to the faith of people whose belief in the reality of God was such that they could envisage the destruction of their own country if that country put its own interests above those of God and of humanity. It is the expression of future hopes of people who believed that there could be universal peace and harmony among nations only under the rule of God and of his laws. In our own thinking about the nuclear issues of today, can we afford to ignore such faith and such hope?

Chapter 9

USING THE BIBLE IN THE DEBATE ABOUT ABORTION

'Go buy the book and then go by the book' is a successful slogan used by the United Bible Societies to promote the circulation and reading of the Bible. Excellent though the slogan is, it fails to indicate that 'going by the book' is not always a straightforward matter. In the probably apocryphal story about a person who was seeking guidance from the Bible and who turned up in succession a passage about Judas hanging himself and the command, 'Go and do thou likewise', we see the dangers of random text selection at their greatest. Unfortunately, this does not prevent people from plucking texts out of their context, and applying them to contemporary social issues without regard to what these texts meant in their original setting, and whether they can be legitimately applied to the modern world.

Fortunately, in the case of the debate about abortion, there are no texts that can be simply applied to the matter. The Bible does not directly mention abortion anywhere. However, this does not prevent the misuse of passages that are thought to indicate a pro-life stance in the Bible, and there is a danger that over-zealous advocates of the pro-life viewpoint may damage their cause by using the Bible in ways likely to be repugnant to people who are not hard-line fundamentalists. Examples of this misuse will be provided later. In the first instance, it will be useful to outline what is known about pregnancy and birth practices in biblical times.

In the standard versions of the Bible, it is often stated that a woman conceived.[1] Of course, this does not relate in any way to the modern medical understanding of conception. The biblical writers knew nothing about fertilization, but they knew about women's periods (which made women 'unclean' while they lasted)[2] and about the best times for achieving pregnancy through sexual intercourse. Strictly speaking, the Hebrew and Greek phrases translated as '(she) conceived' ought to be rendered 'became pregnant'.

This is, in fact the rendering found in *The Translator's New Testament* for Mt. 1.23: 'A maiden will become pregnant and bear a son, and they will name him Emmanuel'.[3] The signs of the onset of pregnancy having been recognized, precautions were to taken to prevent injury to the unborn child that might arise through the mother attempting heavy manual jobs. The evidence for this is not in the Bible,

---

1. Gen. 4.1 and some 30 other occurrences in a non-metaphorical sense.
2. Cf. 2 Sam. 11.4-5.
3. *The Translator's New Testament* (London: British & Foreign Bible Society, 1973), p. 2.

but in later Jewish writings.[4] If it is fair to reckon back from these to biblical times, we can also say that many superstitions would be affected by the eating and living habits of the mother.[5] What is not clear is whether the unborn child was thought of as a person.

The Old Testament gives several passages in which the growth of the unborn child is described. Unfortunately for our purposes, these passages are in poetry, and we cannot be sure whether they represent what the biblical writers actually thought was happening inside the womb. Job 10.10 asks the rhetorical question: 'Didst thou not pour me out like milk and curdle me like cheese?'. It continues: 'Thou didst clothe me with skin and flesh and knit me together with bones and sinews'.

The reference to curdling may reflect the fact that as a result of miscarriages and premature births, the biblical writers were aware of the difference between the fetus in an undeveloped state, and in a state where the outward form of the child was already complete.[6]

The other main passage which speaks of the growth of the child in the womb is found in Ps. 139.13-16:

> For thou didst form my inward parts,
>   thou didst knit me together in my mother's womb.
> I praise thee, for thou art fearful and wonderful.
>   Wonderful are thy works!
>   Thou knowest me right well;
> My frame was not hidden from thee,
>   when I was made in secret,
>   intricately wrought in the depths of the earth.
> Thy eyes beheld my unformed substance;
>   in thy book were written, every one of them,
>   the days that were formed for me, when as yet there was none of them.

In this passage, the stress is again upon the growth of the child from something formless (v. 16) to something developed and complete. It is clear that the psalmist, like Job, believed that God was intimately involved in this process of growth and development. Whether this point is of relevance to the modern debate about abortion must be considered later.

Before the proper time for birth, 'natural abortions' could occur, and Job, lamenting the fact that he was born at all asks, 'Why was I not as a hidden untimely birth, as infants that never see the light?'.[7] The addition of the word 'hidden' to the Hebrew word translated 'untimely birth' most likely indicates that such 'untimely births' were immediately disposed of, and not shown to family or neighbours.

---

4. S. Krauss, *Talmudische Archälogie* (GGJ, 3; repr. [of 1911 edn]; Hildesheim: G. Olms, 1966), II, pp. 3ff. and p. 424 nn. 1ff.

5. Krauss, *Talmudische Archälogie*.

6. The Hebrew word *golem*, which occurs in the Bible only at Ps. 139.16 but which is attested in Post-Biblical Hebrew, means 'a rolled up, shapeless mass, whence...lump, a shapeless or lifeless substance' according to M. Jastrow, *A Dictionary of the Targumim, the Talmud Babli and Yerushalmi, and the Midrashic Literature* (repr., New York: Pardes Publishing House, 1950), I, p. 222.

7. Job 3.16. The word rendered 'untimely birth' is related to the verb 'to fall'.

For birth itself, it is likely that the mother adopted a squatting position, and that the infant was received onto the knees of the midwife.[8] Thus Job complained, 'Why did the knees receive me? Exodus 1.16 mentions a birthstool—possibly something on which the mother sat, with an opening to enable the child to pass from the womb and to be taken by the midwife.[9]

That abortion was known, practised and punished in the ancient Near East is evident from the Middle Assyrian Laws, where we read:

> If a woman has had a miscarriage by her own act, when they have presented her (and) convicted her, they shall impale her on stakes without burying her. If she died in having the miscarriage, they shall impale her on stakes without burying her. If someone hid that woman when she had the miscarriage (without) informing (the king)...[10]

The text breaks off, but it is a safe deduction that the laws prescribed penalties for those who aided abortions.

It is difficult to know what to conclude from the complete silence of biblical law on the subject. Arguments from silence are always open to being stood on their head. However, the view that will be taken here is that the silence indicates that abortion was not commonly practised, if at all, in ancient Israel. This tentative conclusion can be justified by the following considerations.

(a) It is known that exposure of unwanted female children took place. This is clear from Ezek. 16.4, where God speaks of finding Jerusalem as one might find an exposed infant girl:

> Your navel string was not cut, nor were you washed with water to cleanse you, nor rubbed with salt, nor swathed with bands. No eye pitied you, to do any of these things to you out of compassion for you, but you were cast out on the open field, for you were abhorred, on the day that you were born.

Since it is clear that male children were much to be desired in ancient Israel,[11] it is likely that pregnancies were not interfered with, lest a male child be lost. Exposure of unwanted children, almost certainly females, although no doubt regarded as a serious crime (in fact, Old Testament law is silent in this matter also), had the advantages of preventing the danger of death that might occur to the mother because of the abortion, and of keeping the options open in case a male child was to be born.

---

8.   See the article by J.S. Licht, 'Ledah (giving birth)', in *Encyclopaedia Biblica* (Jerusalem: Bialik Institute, 1962), IV, pp. 431-35 (Hebrew).

9.   See Licht, 'Ledah'. The information, in Gen. 50.23, that Joseph's sons were born upon his knees may denote that the father assisted with the birth, or that after the birth he took them onto his knees as a sign of welcoming into the family.

10.   See T.J. Meek, 'The Middle Assyrian Laws', in J.B. Pritchard (ed.), *Ancient Near Eastern Texts Relating to the Old Testament* (Princeton, NJ: Princeton University Press, 2nd edn, 1955), p. 185. G.R. Driver and J.C. Miles, *The Babylonian Laws* (Oxford: Clarendon Press, 1952), I, p. 367, assume that abortion was practised in Babylon as well as Assyria.

11.   Ps. 127.4, 'Like arrows in the hand of a warrior are the sons of one's youth'.

(b) Old Testament penalties for adultery, fornication and incest were extremely severe, usually involving the death penalty. The husband had far-reaching powers if he even *suspected* adultery on the part of his wife,[12] and thus it may well be that few situations existed outside wedlock in which an abortion would be necessary. It is true that the Old Testament contains a word (*mamzer*) usually translated 'bastard' at one of its two occurrences, Deut. 23.2: 'No bastard shall enter the assembly of the LORD'. However, the meaning of the word is disputed. A majority viewpoint is that it refers to a child born of an incestuous union. If this is correct, then we must suppose that if the death penalty was enforced for incest, this was delayed until the birth of the child. If we could be sure that the *mamzer* was a child from an incestuous relationship who had been allowed to be born before his parents were executed, this would be of considerable importance for the discussion about abortion. However, in the light of the uncertainties involved, the point can not be pressed.[13]

A passage that has attracted some attention, since it appears to bear upon how the unborn child was regarded in the Old Testament, is in Exod. 21.22-24. The law envisages a pregnant woman getting hurt in a fight between two men (perhaps she goes to the aid of her husband), and having a miscarriage as a result. If 'harm' follows, the penalty is in accordance with *talion*—life for life, eye for eye, etc. If there is no harm, the man causing the injury is fined. Unfortunately, it is not clear whether the 'harm' refers to harm done to the woman or to her prematurely born child. The most natural interpretation is that the harm refers to the woman. It would be a very harsh law indeed that put to death a man who unintentionally caused a miscarriage early in a woman's pregnancy. Presumably, the antagonist would take particular care if the woman's pregnancy was obviously well advanced. However, distinguished advocacy has been put forward on behalf of the view that the guilty man will be punished for injury caused to the *prematurely born child*, and if this is the correct interpretation, it suggests that unborn children were highly regarded in ancient Israel.[14]

The discussion so far has shown what ought to be obvious in any case, but what is, in fact, overlooked time and again, that the Bible presupposes a social and cultural situation totally different from that which obtains today. If I am correct in assuming that abortion is not prohibited in the Bible because it was not commonly practised, this only goes to point up the difference between ancient Hebrew and Jewish society where children were generally desired, and our own over-populated world where abortions can be numbered in millions. Faced with this cultural difference, a possible conclusion could be drawn that the Bible has no place in the modern discussion, and is best left out. This is not a view that I share; but at the same time, I must also say that I find it difficult to agree with some of the arguments commonly

12.   See Num. 5.11-31.

13.   See S. Loewenstamm, '*Mamzer*', in *Encyclopaedia Biblica*, V, pp. 2-3. If *mamzer* does not mean the offspring of an incestuous union, it may denote a child of a mixed marriage. For the death penalty for incest see Lev. 18.6-18.

14.   See J. Weingreen, 'The Concepts of Retaliation and Compensation in Biblical Law', *Proceedings of the Royal Irish Academy* 76 (1976), pp. 1-11 (Section C, No. 1).

put forward in support of the pro-life position on the basis of the Bible. These will now be considered.

It is often asserted that the Bible as a whole has a strong pro-life orientation, and that it forbids the taking of life. Two texts in particular are cited: 'Whoever sheds the blood of man, by man shall his blood be shed; for God made man in his own image' (Gen. 9.6) and, 'You shall not kill' (Exod. 20.13). It is not my intention to deny the importance of these passages. However, the argument that the Bible is pro-life will hardly satisfy the uncommitted, if no attempt is made to deal with those parts of the Old Testament in which God commands the killing of men, women and children. Thus, we read in Josh. 10.40 that Joshua 'utterly destroyed all that breathes, as the LORD God of Israel commanded'. Again, in 1 Sam. 15.2, God commands Saul to smite the Amalekites: 'Do not spare them, but kill both man and woman, infant and suckling...' No doubt it can be said that the Amalekites were being punished because they opposed the Israelites on their way out of Egypt; but sensitive modern readers can be forgiven for doubting whether they should take any notice of a book which contains such crude notions of corporate responsibility, even if our modern so-called civilized society has perfected violent forms of retaliation that do not discriminate between the innocent and the guilty.

My own approach to passages such as those in Josh. 10.40 and 1 Sam. 15.2 is that we must recognize frankly that the conventions of ancient war did allow for whole communities to be 'devoted' to the god, and thus to be completely wiped out. The belief of Israelites, in the early stages of their history, that their God wished them to 'devote' people to him was sincere, but mistaken. On the other hand, it is clear from recent scholarship that the passages which speak of this wholesale slaughter reached their present form during or after the exile (sixth century BCE). In their final form, they were not intended primarily to be commands to exterminate enemies, but rather to be object lessons about the ills that befell the Israelites when they turned to the gods of the peoples alongside whom they lived.

Another common appeal from the Bible in support of the pro-life position urges that according to the Bible, human life begins at conception.[15] There are several difficulties here. First, it has already been pointed out that the Bible knows nothing of conception in the modern medical sense. Second, we cannot be *certain* that the life of the unborn child was regarded as sacrosanct in the Bible. We *can* be sure that at least the writer of Job and the author of Psalm 139 believed that God was intimately involved in the growth of the unborn child, and it would not be unreasonable to appeal to this fact in the abortion debate. Indeed, this sense of God's involvement in the process of growth seems to be taken to the point where it is asserted that he is responsible also for the handicaps with which people are born. Thus, in Exod. 4.11, the rhetorical question is addressed to Moses:

> Who has made man's mouth?
> Who makes him dumb, or deaf, or seeing, or blind?
> Is it not I, the LORD?

---

15. Thus, *Abortion: A Matter of Life and Death* (Belfast: n.p., 1981), section one, para. B.

Yet this last point only reveals another difficulty. Ignoring the fact that people who are not hard-line fundamentalists will find it difficult to take literally statements about God's *direct* participation in the growth of unborn children, there is no doubt that they will find repugnant the assertion that God is responsible for the handicaps of handicapped children. Are we to suppose that thalidomide victims were somehow God's intended results? Why did Jesus combat evil in the form of physical handicap, and regard it as part of the kingdom of Satan?[16] If doctors and surgeons work to help handicapped people overcome their handicaps, are they defying the will of God? Further, if unborn children begin to develop in the wrong parts of the mother's body, thus necessitating a termination of pregnancy in the sense defined by Mr. Norris, is not this an interference in the activity of God who has supposedly placed the child where it is?

Another line of approach appeals to texts in which individuals are named who are called before birth. Among these are Jeremiah in Jer. 1.5, the prince of the five names in Isa. 9.1-6, and our Lord in Mt. 1.21. In the Old Testament examples, we must be clear what can and what cannot be proved. Even if it is accepted that Jeremiah and the prince were 'people' before their birth in God's sight, it does not follow that this is true of all mankind. We have noted that the Old Testament writers were familiar with so-called natural abortions. In these cases, had God named or called them before their birth? If so, why did they not live? If not, can we assert that every person is known to God before his birth?

The case of our Lord is different, and deserves much deeper reflection than I am capable of here. The idea that our Lord, once conceived, could have been aborted, will surely be repugnant to many Christians. But there is the further point that Christians believe that in his Incarnation, our Lord was fully identifying himself with our humanity. Many Christians will therefore conclude that just as it is repugnant to think of aborting our Lord, so it ought to be repugnant to think of aborting any member of that human race with which our Lord has fully identified himself.

This brings us to the point where we must consider one of the most frequently used biblical ideas, that of mankind being created in the image of God. We have already seen that the creation of man in the image of God forms the motive clause for the prohibition about shedding man's blood. However, what use can be made of the notion, as it appears in the Bible, for the abortion debate is not clear, certainly to me. Recent scholarly attempts to understand what was meant by the writer of Gen. 1.27 have been expressed in relational rather than ontological terms. The 'image' has been taken to indicate man's stewardship over the world, as God's representative in it.[17] Or it has been interpreted as indicating man's unique ability within the created order to hear and respond to the voice of God.[18] Even if we assume that the 'image' is asserting something ontological about mankind, what we do not know is

16. Cf. Lk. 13.16.

17. See H.W. Wolff, *Anthropology of the Old Testament* (trans. M. Kohl; London: SCM Press, 1974), pp. 159-65.

18. See the important Excursus on Gen. 1.26-27 in C. Westermann, *Genesis* (BKAT, I/1; Neukirchen–Vluyn: Neukirchener Verlag, 1968), pp. 203-14.

whether the 'image' (whatever it is) is present from the moment of conception, or whether, in Old Testament terms, it is there only after the 'unformed substance' has reached its definite human form. In all honesty, I could not totally disregard the argument that accepted that the 'image of God' in man was vital in the abortion debate, but which held that the 'image' was not present before a certain point in the unborn child's development, and that abortions up to that point were in order. I do not agree with this point of view, but in fairness, I must say that nothing in the Bible clearly shows that the image of God is 'present' from the moment of conception.

It is now time to turn from these largely negative observations. They have been deliberately presented because I think that the abortion issue is too important to be argued about in terms more suitable to a biblical and theological kindergarten. If the Bible can be used at all to support the pro-life position, it be used in a manner calculated to gain the respect, if not the agreement, of intelligent people who desire more than literalist text-quoting.

What follows is divided into three sections. The first section is about the Bible, based upon the view that the main purpose of the Bible is to express the witness to faith in God of the people of the Old and New Testaments, so that we might come to faith. The second section assumes that as well as being a 'life' issue (in the sense defined), it is also a rights issue.

In Gerhard Ebeling's *The Nature of Faith* the following definition of the Bible is found:

> The Bible bears witness to a proclamation that has taken place and is the impulse for a proclamation which is to take place.[19]

This definition recognizes that the Bible was produced in specific historical and cultural circumstances, while allowing that the Bible is more than a guide to ancient history or ancient religion. It emphasizes that the Bible is a proclamation—in the Old Testament the proclamation that God is for his people; in the New Testament a proclamation that God is for all mankind in Jesus Christ. The main purpose of the Bible is to help us to respond to God who is the subject and the object of the proclamation. If we respond in faith, we shall find a new orientation for our lives, which we may wish to express in one or more of the biblical affirmations: 'Jesus is Lord', 'God has made him both Lord and Christ, this Jesus (who was) crucified', 'If anyone is in Christ, there is a new creation'.

To respond in faith to the proclamation contained in the Bible does not give access to information concerning the 'nuts and bolts of life'. A Christian does not possess superior knowledge about matters of medicine, science or morals, compared with non-Christians, but he finds himself confronted by the imperatives of the biblical proclamation about God: 'You must love your neighbor as yourself.'; 'If anyone says "I love God", and hates his brother, he is a liar.'; 'There is neither Jew nor Greek, there is neither slave nor free, there is neither male nor female, for you are all one in Christ Jesus.'

Within the Bible itself, the effect of these imperatives upon social attitudes and

---

19. G. Ebeling, *The Nature of Faith* (trans. R.G. Smith; London: Fontana, 1966), p. 183.

actions can be clearly seen. In the version of the Ten Commandments in Deut. 5.6-21, the exodus from Egypt is given as the reason why a man's servants and animals must be allowed to rest on the sabbath day. God had graciously delivered his people from bondage; they must graciously allow their servants to rest. The same motive clause is found in passages which command that provision should be made for the sojourner, the fatherless and the widow (Deut. 24.19-22).

A most instructive passage is that relating to the release of slaves in Deut. 15.12-18. If this is compared with Exod. 21.11, it will be seen immediately that Deuteronomy treats women slaves on an equal footing with male slaves, while Exodus 21 discriminates against women slaves. In fact the words 'or a Hebrew woman' are clearly a later addition to Deut. 15.12, as even the reader of an English version such as the RSV can see (this is obscured in NEB and GNB). That the reference to the woman is a later addition is, however, most significant. It indicates a development within the biblical tradition, as a result of which the implications of God's having redeemed the Israelites from slavery in Egypt are extended to include women slaves as well as men slaves. In other words, the imperative based upon God's redeeming action is given a wider application.

This brings us to the heart of what I take to be proper use of the Bible in social and moral questions. It is to discover the imperatives which arise from the proclamation of God's redemption, and to apply those imperatives to the situations in which we find ourselves. In the parable of the Good Samaritan, Jesus did not define who was meant by 'the neighbour'. He left us a story that is quite frightening in the way in which it makes clear our responsibility to regard as our neighbour anyone, friend or foe, whom we perceive to be in need. It took Christian civilisation nearly 1800 years to implement the full implications that there is neither slave nor free in Christ Jesus, and to abolish slavery.

This is not to say that the Bible is devoid of commandments and instructions laid upon Christians; far from it. The Ten Commandments, in their Old Testament formulation and in their New Testament distillation into love for God and for one's neighbour, still represent the core of the obedience to God of those who have come to faith in him. But it must never be forgotten that in using the Bible, Christians have traditionally been concerned with the spirit rather than the letter, and have not hesitated to pick and choose what they held to be binding upon them. In Acts 15, the apostolic Church required only four things of Gentiles who had become Christians: abstention from food offered to idols, from fornication, from meat not ritually killed, and from eating blood. The demand that they should be required to observe the Mosaic law was rejected.[20] Again, in the 39 articles, only those laws of the Old Testament deemed to be moral (as opposed to Old Testament civil laws or laws concerned with rites and ceremonies) are held to be binding upon Christians.[21]

The way forward in using the Bible in the abortion debate seems to involve exploring the demands of the biblical imperatives of salvation, rather than in searching for texts that can be literally applied in the debate.

20. Acts 15, esp. vv. 5, 20, 28-29.
21. Article VII, 'Of the Old Testament'.

This brings us to the second section, which concerns us with the sense in which we should regard abortion as a 'life' issue. The two main definitions of 'life' that are relevant are life understood in biological terms, and life understood in relational terms. The first definition is implied in the charge sometimes made against pro-life supporters, that they ought to have the same concern for the animals whose meat they consume, as for the unborn children whose lives they seek to protect. While there is much to be said to support vegetarianism, including the fact that it enables us to respect the rights of animals, it has to be emphasized that what pro-life supporters are mainly concerned to protect are potential human beings whose destiny it is not merely to exist biologically, but to share human relationships, and to love and to be loved. In this connection, the imperative of salvation that 'life depends upon love' becomes important.

At the heart of the Christian proclamation is the belief that it is the love of God which makes possible the Christian life. Perhaps the passage that comes nearest to saying this explicitly is Gal. 2.20: '...the life I now live in the flesh I live by faith in the Son of God, who loved me and gave himself for me'. But the notion is implicit in many parts of the Bible. The life which Israel enjoyed in the presence of God was made possible only by his love, even if that love was repeatedly cast back into his face: 'When Israel was a child, I loved him, and out of Egypt I called my son' (Hos. 11.1). In the New Testament, it was the fact that the Good Samaritan in the parable was 'moved with compassion' that saved from certain death the man who had been robbed and beaten. In the parable of the Prodigal Son it was the love of the father that made possible the renewed life of the son who had been 'dead, and is alive again' (Lk. 15.24). The very possibility of Christian life depends on the fact that God commends his love towards us 'in that while we were yet sinners Christ died for us' (Rom. 5.8).

The link between life and love is also apparent in non-religious contexts. Loneliness and isolation are not things that can be easily borne. Often, even the affection of a cat or a dog can help to enrich the life of a lonely person. The relationships that may develop between a kidnapped hostage and his kidnappers may be the best hope for the saving of his life. The more that people respond to each other as persons, the less easy it becomes to think of killing. In the case of handicapped children, the love of those who care for them can enrich their lives; and the response of the handicapped is itself ennobling to others.

If it is true that life depends upon love, it also seems to be true that disregard for life militates against love. It takes hardness and callousness to carry through the sort of destruction of human life that this century has perfected. It is rumoured that first World War generals who were sensitive about the level of casualties among their men were distrusted by the General Staff. In order to carry out mass killings, it is often necessary to present the intended victims as less than human. Jews become 'vermin', and brave soldiers on the other side become the 'enemy' whose lives are as expendable as those of our own side are meant to be precious.

If, at the heart of the gospel, it is the love of God which makes life in a relational sense possible, the Christian is called to resist any degradation of the life of any human being, friend or foe, who is potentially a son or daughter of God, and thus a sister or brother.

In the case of unborn children, it now seems to be clear that from the moment of fertilization, that 'programming' is present in the fertilized ovum which makes it unique, and which determines the physical and mental characteristics that will accompany it through life; that will find expression and develop and change in the individual through the stages of childhood, adolescence, adulthood and old age. Any attempt to draw a line and to say that prior to a particular point in time an unborn child is not a person or a human being worthy of respect and protection, is arbitrary. It is sometimes said that the difference between an unborn child and a newly born one is that the latter is no longer totally dependent upon its mother. But a newly born child is as helpless and dependent on its mother as a child in the womb; and this condition continues for a number of years. This is a powerful argument against drawing an arbitrary line, but it is an argument from the biological, not the relational. If we consider this latter angle, we have to accept that our natural behaviour towards unborn children implies that we regard them, relationally, as deserving of the utmost that our love and loyalty can offer. Parents want the best for them. Nurseries are newly decorated; clothes in appropriate colours are purchased or made at home. Cots are provided. The survival of the unborn child into life and beyond relies utterly on the love and care that are lavished upon it. It is sadly true that by no means every unborn or newly born child enjoys this degree of love and care; but where such love and care are absent in societies where communal action can be taken to remedy the situation, the fact that these attempts are made to remedy the situation indicates that the kind of world in which people wish to live is one in which love and care to the tiny and defenceless is the ideal.

Can we, at one and the same time, be under the imperative of love, and be satisfied with a society that denies to the unborn the possibility of living? What sort of a society is it that leaves it to small voluntary agencies to try to persuade mothers who are bearing 'unwanted' children to let those children live, while there are many families in which love will make a full life possible for 'unwanted' and 'rejected' children? It is no part of this essay to adopt a superior moral attitude towards mothers who find themselves bearing unwanted children. What a Christian society ought to do, however, is to stress that the love of God stretching out to the unwanted and the unworthy is at the heart of the gospel, and that the practical application of this imperative in all its ramifications is a task laid upon the Church.

This leads us to the third section, which is about rights. One of the paradoxes of the present century is that, on the one hand, it has seen more brutal destruction of human lives than in any previous century; but second, it has seen a remarkable growth of sensitivity to the rights of minorities and the defenceless. The Bible has much to say about minorities and the defenceless, under the imperative that 'the strong must defend the weak'.

There are many passages, especially in the Old Testament, where this imperative is asserted explicitly. Of the ideal king in Psalm 72 it is prayed:

> May he defend the cause of the poor of the people,
>> give deliverance to the needy, and crush the oppressor! (v. 4)

The shepherds (i.e. the rulers) in Ezekiel 34 are condemned because they have not cared for the weak:

> The weak you have not strengthened, the sick you have not bound up, the strayed you have not brought back, the lost you have not sought... (v. 4)

In Psalm 82, God appears to condemn the divine beings whom he had set over the foreign nations, to see that justice prevailed among them:

> How long will you judge unjustly
>> and show partiality to the wicked?
> Give justice to the weak and fatherless;
>> maintain the right of the afflicted and the destitute.
> Rescue the weak and the needy;
>> deliver them from the hand of the wicked. (vv. 2-4)

In applying this imperative to our present world, we must include the unborn among the weak and defenceless. They cannot speak for themselves, and because they cannot be seen in everyday life, their uniqueness as individuals is overlooked. They are as much in need of defence as are people who are wrongly imprisoned and are as easily eradicated from our consciences.

The main burden of this essay is that the use of the Bible is not a matter of selecting texts and of trying to apply them as though they were legislation for modern situations. The point that has been stressed is that the Bible's primary function is to bring us to faith and to keep us in faith. The faith which we confess is faith in a God who responds to human need, who justifies the unrighteous and who seeks the outcast. The Bible lays upon us imperatives that derive from the heart of our salvation, and our task is to work out those imperatives in the situation in which we find ourselves.

Abortion has always been a feature within human society. Probably for much of human history, it was practised on a small scale and was based upon ignorance of the precise medical and scientific facts of the beginnings of life.[22] Today, we know that from the earliest moments of life, a unique individual is present in the womb. But also today, we have become tolerant of the destruction and cheapening of human lives in many ways (including plans for future so-called nuclear defence) and we have developed techniques for the relatively safe and convenient termination of pregnancies on a large scale. The Bible does not address itself directly to this latter problem. What it does is to challenge us to include unborn children along with the defenceless and minorities whose task it is for the strong to defend. What it does is to ask us whether at one and the same time we can assert our faith in a God who seeks the unworthy and the unwanted, and be indifferent to the fact that thousands of unwanted unborn children have their individuality terminated. The

---

22. For ancient knowledge of the medical facts see the articles 'Abtreibung' and 'Embryologie', in *RAC*, I, pp. 55-60, and IV, pp. 1228-44, respectively.

Bible does not provide us with 'knock down' arguments that take from us the responsibility of being informed and of entering into dialogue with those who find abortion unobjectionable. The debate about abortion is a debate about an issue which demands of Christians that they think deeply about what the heart of Christian faith is, and how that faith is to be expressed in a world that appears to know little of the true spirit of Jesus Christ.

Chapter 10

THE USE OF THE OLD TESTAMENT, WITH REFERENCE TO WORK AND UNEMPLOYMENT*

One of the most urgent needs at the present time is for the development of a way of using the Bible that will enable it to be applied convincingly to modern social problems. In Britain there is an awakening in many church circles of a desire for church leaders to speak out on social issues, and to give guidance to church members. Nor is it simple national or parochial concerns that are responsible for this renewal of a social conscience in the churches. Such facts as the difference in wealth between countries north and south, the challenge of famine in parts of Africa and the proportion of the world's resources that is being devoted to armaments have played their part in challenging Christians to think again about what they mean when they claim that they are living in God's world.

Christians who look to their leaders for guidance expect that guidance to be based in part upon the Bible. In practice, however, church leaders and their social responsibility committees are better at analysing problems than suggesting solutions based upon explicitly biblical or theological principles.[1] Where the Bible is appealed to, the hidden assumption is often 'the Bible says so-and-so, but this is out of line with contemporary standards. We must try to set aside what the Bible seems to say, and we must find a way of making it agree with what we want to say'.[2]

This caricature of the use of the Bible is written, not in a spirit of superiority, but in a spirit of humility. If responsible church leaders and bodies do not know how to use the Bible, biblical scholars are partly to blame. We must admit that, until comparatively recently, we have not been prepared to acknowledge that the use of the Bible in social and moral questions was an admissible subject within professional biblical scholarship. Now that some recognition is beginning to dawn, we find ourselves woefully inadequate to take up the challenge.

---

*   This study was delivered as a paper presented to the Scripture, Theology and Society Group, Oxford, April 1986. The presentational style of the original has been retained.

1.   This is made particularly clear in the work of two of my research students, Angela M. Johnson, who successfully presented an MPhil thesis in 1985 on 'The Use of the Bible in the Debate about Homosexual Relationships', and Kenneth R. Brown, who is completing an MPhil thesis on 'The Use of the Bible in the Statements of the Department of Social Responsibility of the Methodist Church'.

2.   See Johnson, 'The Use of the Bible in the Debate about Homosexual Relationships', *passim*.

The aim of the present essay is to propose a model for using the Old Testament, with regard to the specific issue of work and unemployment. This issue has been chosen deliberately because of the totally different conditions that obtained in Old Testament times with regard to work and unemployment, compared with the problems in today's industrialised world (there would, of course, be a closer 'fit' between the Old Testament and modern simple agricultural societies). It would have been easier to write an essay about politics in the Old Testament, understood as the use of power in relationships with other countries. In this respect, ancient Israel stood close to those modern countries which, situated on land masses and surrounded by other countries, have had to come to terms with their neighbours whether this involved peaceful cooperation, dominating their neighbours or being dominated by them. Some of the issues here have been explored in W. McKane's study *Prophets and Wise Men*.[3]

1. *Work and Unemployment in Modern Industrial Society*

The recent interest in church circles in this matter is the result of the growth of mass unemployment, and the prospect that there will not be a return to full employment as it was known in the 1950s and 1960s. When I trained for the ministry in the late 1950s and early 1960s, I assumed, together with the ecclesiastical and theological climate of that time, that my ministry would be directed to people at home and in their leisure. Industrial missions were regarded with curiosity by some, and with hostility by others, and many were agreed that money would be better spent on parish ministry rather than on industrial missions. I make this observation in order to emphasise the fundamental point that the churches' newly found interest in work and unemployment, though welcome, is misconceived in the sense that the basic issue is not that of work versus no work. The basic issues are: What is man? What sort of a society is one in which the claim of God upon it is recognised? How should such a society express its understanding of man in the way it orders its economic affairs?[4]

If we examine the situation of full employment as we used to know it, we shall see that from the standpoint of the Old Testament, it implies a view of man and society that must be subjected to severe criticism. Full employment depended upon large-scale industries such as coal mining, steel manufacture, textile weaving, ship building, and car manufacture, together with the support industries that provided materials and machinery. Yet these industries were in different ways the product of the industrial revolution, and they implied a view of man that was hardly biblical.

In the first instance, man was not valued as a creative and unique person in his own right; workers were part of a system, and the purpose of the system was to generate wealth. Man was thus viewed as a means to an end, the production of wealth, and not an end in himself. Of course, there were employers, especially in

---

3. W. McKane, *Prophets and Wise Men* (SBT, 44; London: SCM Press, 1965 [repr. 1983]).

4. For a fundamental discussion of the question 'what is man?', see W. Pannenberg, *Was ist der Mensch?: Die Anthropologie der Gegenwart im Lichte der Technologie* (Göttingen: Vandenhoeck & Ruprecht, 1968), p. 3.

the late nineteenth century, who had the interests of their workers at heart, but they do not alter the fact that workers were valued only for what they could contribute to the generating of wealth.

Secondly, the type of work, and the conditions in which people worked were such as to cause dehumanisation, conflict and alienation. The performance of repetitive tasks for hours on end was not only dehumanising, but has been argued to be destructive of a positive and creative use of leisure time. Conflicts between workers and management, and between workers and workers, meant that the workplace was a particularly apt place for human fallenness to find expression. Situations were created in which survival depended upon the practice of such 'virtues' as deceit, dishonesty, crafty laziness, as well as those corporate 'virtues' of the schoolroom and the shop floor, such as lying to cover up for a colleague and sending to Coventry anyone who placed respect for individual conscience above the herd instinct. Alienation resulted from the unfair distribution of the wealth generated. Many dedicated and skilled workers toiled for a lifetime, and at the end of it had little material wealth to show for all that they had put into their work. In contrast, employers, executives and managers, who were not necessarily more able and hard working, although it is acknowledged that they bore responsibility, enjoyed rewards out of proportion to what they put in.[5]

In what has been just written, the past tense had been used, as though the dehumanising, conflict and alienation are past and done away with. Hopefully, their worst manifestations are no longer with us. Basically, however, nothing has changed. The advent of mass unemployment and the weakening of trade unions have given employers the power to put workers under new pressures, with consequent alienation and conflict. This can be seen in what have become the new large-scale employers, such as the National Health Service, where work such as laundering and catering has been put out to private contractors, and low-paid workers, often women, have had to accept less favourable conditions of employment. The criterion of generation of wealth as a way of according value to a person or an activity has, if anything, become more strident. The education system at every level is now judged in terms of its ability to produce employees who will generate wealth. In universities, the Arts and Humanities are having to defend their right to be there at all, and in some circles they are seen merely as contributing to what people will do with their leisure.

If this sketch of employment has been presented in essentially pessimistic terms, this is because it is important to emphasize that when we turn to unemployment we are not turning from light to darkness. If full employment, from an Old Testament point of view to the outlined shortly, has dark sides to it, those same dark sides are taken over into unemployment. In the first place, the valuation of people in terms of their economic productivity continues. The unemployed are looked down on, and in many cases look down on themselves, because they have failed the test that confers value upon a person—the ability to get wealth. This often leads, secondly, to

---

5.   See the section 'Die Entfremdung von der Arbeit', in R. Kramer, *Arbeit* (Göttingen: Vandenhoeck & Ruprecht, 1982), pp. 50-57.

alienation, in that the unemployed cannot afford to do the things that their wage-earning friends do, and such friendships often break up under the strain. Dehumanising is a further result, brought about by personal demoralisation which is made worse by social attitudes that see unemployed people as 'failures'. In recent discussions about work and unemployment much has been said about the need to define, or redefine what we mean by 'work', so that we can include under the term a whole variety of voluntary, unpaid activities. Again, it has been stressed that the work of women, especially mothers and housewives, has been totally undervalued and insufficiently recognised. I fully support these sentiments, yet, important as these issues are, they ignore the fundamental issues if all that they seek to obtain is some better tuning in the material way in which we accord value to persons.[6]

2. *Work and Unemployment in the Old Testament*

This will be a short section with two aims. The first will be to indicate that work in Old Testament times was utterly different from the situation produced in the industrial nations by the industrial revolution. This will lead secondly, to the third section of this essay, which is to discuss and develop a model for applying the insights of the Old Testament to the contemporary situation.

Old Testament society was basically an agricultural society in which extended families, living in villages, farmed land that was owned by the heads of the families. The main crops were barley and wheat, and the fruits included olives, figs, dates and grapes. Sheep and goats were kept for their wool and milk and oxen and asses were the chief beasts of burden. Because of the widely differing types of land and climate in the land of ancient Israel, there were some variations on this pattern. The lowlands of Judah (*Shephelah*) were extensively given over to vines and fig sycamores, and were possibly managed by the royal household (see 1 Chron. 27.28), while in parts of the Judean wilderness sheep husbandry was possible on a large scale (1 Sam. 25). It is also the case that reorganisation under David and Solomon led to the extension of royal ownership and employment (see 1 Chron. 27.26-31, if this late source gives authentic information about David). Solomon certainly imposed heavy burdens in the form of levies of both goods and manpower. However, in spite of political change, and the existence of guilds of craftsmen, Israel remained basically a land of peasant farmers, with elaborate laws to prevent the alienation of the land. The attempt by King Ahab to seize by trickery a piece of land belonging to Naboth met with strong prophetic denunciation (see 1 Kgs 21).[7]

There were no large-scale employers of labour in ancient Israel. The royal household employed stewards, agents, workers and mercenary soldiers, but of their conditions of service the Old Testament says nothing. Most families worked their land simply to support themselves. Where the Old Testament condemns abuses these concern the alienation from their land of peasants who fell victims to the acquisi-

6.   Kramer, *Arbeit*, pp. 73-75, summaries the social problems of the unemployed.

7.   See my *New Atlas of the Bible* (London: Macdonald, 1985), *passim*, for details of the regional variations and land use in Old Testament times.

tiveness of wealthy landowners.[8] There were always slaves, and classes of the poor such as unsupported widows and orphans. Israelite landholders were expected to provide subsistence for the poor, and to treat slaves humanely. The fact is that there is practically no point of contact between the workaday world of Old Testament times and our modern industrial and post-industrial situation. What then, if anything, can the Old Testament say to the modern situation?

3. *A Model for Using the Old Testament*

Up to now, the usual model that has been used for biblical and theological reflection on work and unemployment has been a creation model.[9] On the basis of the creation narratives in Genesis, the following points have been made. (1) Work is part of what it means to be human, because Adam is put into the Garden of Eden to look after it *before* the 'fall'. (2) Man is made in God's image, and God is described as having 'worked' in creating the world. (3) 'Image of God' language is language about stewardship. Mankind is therefore responsible to God for the proper use of the world's resources. This implies that there must be no exploitation in general, and certainly not of other human beings in particular.[10] (4) 'Image of God' language also implies that mankind's humanity is not something that is possessed 'naturally', as though mankind continues to be 'human' even if God is rejected or ignored.[11] Part of what it means to be human is to accept human dependence upon God. Any other way of valuing human beings is a rejection of both God and the humanity of mankind.

It will not be denied here that a creation model is capable of yielding valuable insights. In particular, it has the power to challenge the valuation of mankind in economic terms, and it can assemble a strong case for an 'ecological theology' which would entail the stewardship of the world's resources in ways different from the practice of modern industrial society.

However, the creation model will not be used in this essay, and this for two reasons. First, the appeal to Genesis 1–2 leaves the theologian open to the charge that these chapters merely reflect the folk beliefs of an agricultural society and cannot be taken seriously in the modern situation. I am not suggesting that this charge is either compelling or incapable of being refuted; but we must never forget that, rightly or wrongly, Genesis 1–2 are still tarnished by association with the Darwinian controversy, and that anyone who appeals to them runs the risk of being thought to appeal to witnesses whose credibility has been damaged. The second reason for not appealing to the creation narratives is that the toil associated with work is directly ascribed in Gen. 3.17-19 to Adam's disobedience of the divine command.

---

8. See Isa. 5.8-10, Mic. 2.1-2 and B. Lang, 'The Social Organisation of Peasant Poverty in Biblical Israel', *JSOT* 24 (1982), pp. 47-63.

9. See the summary of Catholic teaching on work in Kramer, *Arbeit*, pp. 37-49, and the Protestant contribution in H. Mogge (ed.), *Arbeitsethik und Arbeitswirklichkeit* (Frankfurt: Haag & Herchen Verlag, 1984), pp. 64-70.

10. See Kramer, *Arbeit*, pp. 9-11.

11. K. Barth, *Die Kirchliche Dogmatik* (Zürich: Evangelischer Verlag, 1948), II/1, pp. 206ff.

We are in danger of proving too much if we refer to this text. All the undesirable features of work which were outlined in section 1 could be said to be part of the divine will as a punishment for human disobedience.

The model that is proposed here is based upon Israel's election, and the implications of this election for the sort of people Israel is to be. Whatever the origin and date of the ideas of election and covenant in ancient Israel's history, they constitute two of the most fundamental themes of the Old Testament taken as a whole. The 'centre' of the Old Testament had been summed up in the phrase: Yahweh the God of Israel, Israel the people of Yahweh.[12] Interpreted, this phrase is a reminder that Israel associated the name Yahweh with the Exodus deliverance; the deliverance constituted a claim by Yahweh upon his people to live by fashioning what I call 'structures of grace', whose purpose was to make effective in Israelite society the implications of God's gracious dealings with his people. This will be spelled out in more detail shortly. For the moment, I want to observe that what appeals to me about this model is that it is based upon an actual attempt, even if it failed in ancient Israel, to challenge the norms of the pagan world by advocating a type of society in which the fundamental basis for its ordering was the belief that God set infinite value upon that society and its members.

Perhaps it is accidental that the Exodus story in the Old Testament begins with the enslavement and forced labour of the Israelites in Egypt. Whether accidental or not, the story introduces us to a people that is valued not in terms of itself, but as means to an end, the accomplishment of the building projects of the Pharaoh. Indeed, it is not too much to suppose that the Israelite labour gangs had a much worse time of it than people working in the mass unemployment industries of mining, steel-making and textiles in the nineteenth century.

At the heart of Old Testament proclamation is the belief that God altered the status of the Israelites from people who were valued in economic terms to a people with value that derived from the unmerited graciousness of God:

> The Lord your God has chosen you to be a people for his own possession, out of all the peoples that are on the face of the earth. It was not because you were more in number than any other people that the Lord set his love upon you and chose you ...but it is because the Lord loves you, and is keeping the oath which he swore to your fathers... (Deut. 7.6-7)

This special status that God conferred upon Israel out of his graciousness has implications. Above all, Israel is expected to develop what I call 'structures of grace', which are meant to reflect at the level of the ordering of society the graciousness that God has bestowed upon Israel. The most common motive clause in Deuteronomy, that is, the reason for a commandment being enjoined upon Israel, had to do with God's graciousness in freeing Israel from slavery:

> You shall remember that you were a slave in the land of Egypt, and the Lord your God redeemed you; therefore I command you this today. (Deut. 15.15)

12. J. Wellhausen, *Israelitische und Jüdische Geschichte* (repr., Berlin: W. de Gruyter, 1958), p. 23.

Some instances of how 'structures of grace' are to work are now given from Deuteronomy 22.

Verses 1-4 deal with the responsibility towards one's neighbour's property. A person who sees his neighbour's ox or ass wandering astray must take them back to the neighbour. If it is not known whose the animals are, the finder must look after them until the owner seeks them out. It is noteworthy that the Hebrew verb translated 'withhold your help' in the RSV (Deut. 22.1) means literally 'hide yourself'. There is no question of turning a blind eye; the commandment is inescapable. Neither does it allow room for the sort of calculating that so often impairs or prevents action. How much would it cost to feed the animals of the unknown neighbour? Would he be expected to reimburse these costs if and when he turned up? Whose would the animals be if he did not turn up? Or is there a period of time, say, three years, after which the finder could claim ownership even if the original owner appeared? None of these questions are considered, because grace is not calculating but vulnerable, and begins by placing value upon people and animals in their own right.

Verses 6-7 decree that if a person discovers a bird's nest, its eggs or its young may be taken, but not the mother bird. No doubt this is offensive to our modern ideas of conservation that would discourage tampering with the nest at all. This perceived difference between the biblical injunction and our modern attitude enables me to emphasize that, at this stage, I am not suggesting that these Old Testament 'structures of grace' can or should be legislated into our modern industrial society. What 'structures of grace' should be like for our society is for experts to work out, once the principles have been got right.

Verse 10 forbids ploughing with an ox and an ass yoked together. Although it is possible to exercise much ingenuity on this verse, the common sense interpretation should not be ruled out, that because the animals are of very unequal strength they must not be made to do joint work.

These examples of 'structures of grace' may appear to be trivial; but they have been chosen precisely because they seem to take the idea of the gracious ordering of life into what might be regarded as trivial areas. There is no difficulty in finding other instances that are much more central.

Whatever the date and historicity of the book of Ruth, it is arguable that the story shows us 'structures of grace' at work in enabling Naomi and her foreign daughter-in-law to gain security and re-integration into society. However heroic Ruth's determination to remain with her mother-in-law might have been, it would not have met with success if the social practices mentioned in the story had been different. If there had been no law allowing the poor to glean in the fields during the harvest, Ruth would not have been able to provide for herself and her mother. If the law about gleaning had applied only to Israelites and had excluded foreigners, the result would have been the same. If there had been no law which enabled Boaz to marry Ruth so that the latter's children would be reckoned also to Naomi's family, the restoration of Naomi would not have been possible. The story of the book of Ruth is the story of God's graciousness in restoring Naomi from a position of utter hopelessness in a foreign land to a position of acceptance and security among her own people. However, this restoration was made possible not only by the risks that Ruth and Boaz were prepared to take, but by the 'structures of grace' in the context of which their action was set, and which also shaped the response of the majority of the people in the story.

To conclude this section, the election model can be summarised as follows. It begins with God's grace in intervening in a divided world to establish a people whose value depends entirely upon God's unmerited love. But a people so constituted stands under an imperative of redemption to devise 'structures of grace' that will translate into everyday life the unique status of a people valued not in economic terms, but in terms of its divine calling.

4. *Application of the Model to the Modern Situation*

In ancient Israel the model outlined above failed. It failed because it did not suit the way in which the powerful wished to exercise their power. There was probably also an inability of the people to live up to the demands of being a people of the gracious covenant. The paradox between the demands of the gracious covenant and the failure of ancient Israel's rulers and people is one of the features of the Old Testament that makes it such a remarkable set of writings, as well as the occasion of the prophetic calls for social justice.

Can a failed model, and one of which it has been said that it implies the need for a theocracy, be seriously applied in modern industrial society? It can if the modest claim is made for it that its purpose is to provide a framework of thought and values in terms of which our common life is to be ordered. From a Christian point of view the model is reinforced by the fact that through the Incarnation, God has bestowed a dignity upon the human race as a whole, and in the Passion of Jesus had shown each individual to be of such value to him that he gave that which was most costly to him. But if the New Testament gives the election model a universality that the Old Testament lacks, it is the Old Testament that points the way in providing a challenge to those who accept God's claim upon them to translate this claim into 'structures of grace'.

Anyone who takes seriously those parts of the Old Testament that have been discussed in this essay ought to find it impossible to accept any form of society in which, whether in work or not, people are defined in economic terms, and are set in structures which give occasion for conflict, alienation and the inequitable distribution of material rewards. If Theology is to have an authentic voice in today's world, it must demand that we seek for 'structures of grace' that will express the value which God sets upon human societies and human lives. What those structures might be like, and how power would be exercised in and through them is for experts to work out who are convinced of the framework in which they are thinking and working. It is possible to point to many ideas that have been discussed recently: the development of cooperatives, a national wage, the sort of benevolent employer/employee relationships that are being pioneered in Japan.[13]

---

13. Various possible strategies are outlined in Kramer, *Arbeit*, Chapters 8-11.

The Old Testament does not provide us with a blueprint for ordering industrial society. What it does is to claim that power must be exercised in such a way that society is an expression of the value that God in his grace places upon humanity in a world that is marred and deformed by mankind's determination to usurp the place of God. It also shows us that, at their best, ordinary Israelites tried to practise the mutual help and support implicit in the idea of a people valued in terms of God's grace. Our future survival depends not only on discovering the right structures in terms of which to organise our common life. These structures must be part of an ideology that appeals to what is best in mankind. A spiritual renewal is not only desirable; it is absolutely essential.

Chapter 11

Welfare: Some Theoretical Reflections[*]

The aim of this paper is to reflect on recent discussions about the organisation of welfare in Britain and elsewhere, in the light of social action and systems theory. Hopefully, this will inform our discussion of welfare in the Old Testament and whether and how what is contained in the Old Testament can be applied to modern societies.

My starting point is M.J. Bayley's occasional paper entitled 'Welfare—A Moral Issue?'. Bayley outlines two major current views, the 'Welfare State' view and the view of the 'New Right'. He traces the former from its beginnings early in the twentieth century to its classical expression in the Beveridge Report of 1942. He points out that the report was an immediate best-seller (How many of us have read it? I certainly have not) and describes why: 'It expressed the aspirations of the nation. It was not something imposed, it expressed something which society wanted'.[1]

He adds that it was also a response to an external threat (the Second World War) but I am not sure that this is either accurate or relevant. It is, however, important for Bayley's thesis (which is too simplistic) that the war created a sense of solidarity out of which the Welfare State grew, and that this solidarity has now broken down.

For his account of 'New Right' thinking on welfare provision Bayley relies mainly on Lord Harris of High Cross's article 'The Morality of the Market' of 1985. Harris's main complaint is that:

> Every avoidable extension to government coercion violates freedom of choice and must tend to diminish the significance of the individual, the family, and every form of voluntary endeavour... Moral growth and personal fulfilment require the widest possible freedom for individuals to make their own choices and to accept responsibility for their own decisions... It is no substitute for adult individuals to be wrapped in cotton wool that may keep them safe...but only at the expense of enlarging their dependence on others.[2]

There is considerable rhetorical power in these observations, especially in the closing sentence. The Welfare State has produced what is called welfare dependency,

---

[*]   This study was delivered as a paper at the Scripture, Theology and Society Group, Oxford, April 1990. The presentational style of the original has been retained.

1.   M.J. Bayley, *Welfare: A Moral Issue* (Sheffield: Diocese of Sheffield Social Responsibility Committee, 1989), pp. 32-33.

2.   Bayley, *Welfare*, p. 48

variously described as the welfare-dependency trap and 'transmitted deprivation'.[3] This is to be observed in a group which includes the elderly, families of immigrants, and working-class families in areas of high unemployment. There is no doubt that welfare provision for this group is a considerable factor in Britain's economic performance. 'New Right' thinking believes that only a market economy with minimal state coercion can provide the context in which welfare-dependent groups will be able to make their own choice and have the opportunity to escape from the dependency trap.

In what follows, I now intend to reflect upon the problem of welfare provision from the standpoint of social action and systems theory.[4] A system is a self-referential institution within society, related to and interlinked with other institutions.[5] The economy is one such system, with its self-referential unit of value (money) and distinctive sub-systems such as banks, credit houses, stock exchanges and so on. Welfare provision is similarly a system with specific types of professional training and institutions. It has subsystems that specialize in the handicapped, the elderly, young offenders, etc.

The important question is, how do systems relate to each other in a society? Münch provides a number of conceivable constellations, of which the following selection may be relevant:

1. The subsystems are strongly developed, but the mediating systems are poorly developed: the result is conflict.
2. One subsystem is strongly developed, but the others and the mediating systems are poorly developed: the result is the dominance of that one subsystem over others.
3. All subsystems are poorly developed, but the mediating systems are more strongly developed: the result is an undeveloped but integrated action system.

Münch comments on mediating systems as follows:

4. Exchange produces open and unstable integration.
5. Authority causes integration which is compulsively enforced domination.
6. Communal association leads to a conformist and immobile integration.
7. Discourse implies integration through reconciliation.
8. The combination of exchange, authority, communal association and discourse...is the main precondition for the inter-penetration of strongly developed subsystems.[6]

Taking this framework to the two views presented by Bayley we can make the following points:

---

3. R. Segalman, *The Swiss Way of Welfare* (New York: Praeger, 1986), p. 21.
4. See R. Münch, 'Parsonian Theory Today: In Search of a New Synthesis', in A. Giddens *et al.*, *Social Theory Today* (Cambridge: Polity Press, 1987), pp. 116-55.
5. N. Luhmann, *Soziale Systeme* (Frankfurt am Main: Suhrkamp Verlag, 2nd edn, 1988).
6. Münch, 'Parsonian Theory Today', p. 127.

1. Since the inception of the Welfare State the mediating system between it and the economy has been poorly developed. This has resulted in firstly, conflict and secondly, the dominance of the economy as conflict weakened welfare provision.
2. The failure of the Welfare State to achieve what was expected lies at least as much in the failure of the mediating system as in the welfare system itself.
3. To posit the all-sufficiency of one system (the economy) is to fall short of the ideal set out in point 8, where exchange, authority, communal association and discourse all have a part to play.
4. It has to be accepted that welfare provision is a system dependent upon other systems, and that integration with them will have to include a recognition of the importance of exchange, authority, communal association and discourse.

Later in his paper, Münch has an important passage that describes social change:

> we can take cultural patterns to be a genetic code which during the process of socio-cultural evolution obeys, *internally*, a logic of rational argument and…approaches a cultural pattern with increasingly universal validity. *Externally*, this cultural pattern has to be converted into particular institutional patterns by interpretative procedures.[7]

We may say that the Welfare State developed out of the 'logic' generated by mass unemployment in the 1930s as embodied in and interpreted by the Beveridge report of 1942. This interpretation enabled the Welfare State to be legislated institutionally after the war. The present dilemma may well be that change is occurring because of the 'logic' of Britain's declining power as an industrial and manufacturing nation. This is supported *externally* by a new interpretative process associated with 'New Right' thinking with its emphasis upon the need to free individuals so that they can create wealth.

Implications for the Use of the Old Testament

The following questions seem to be pertinent:
1. As a system in ancient Israel, was welfare provision poorly or strongly developed, and were the mediating systems poorly or strongly developed?
2. Given that welfare provision in many developed societies has not been wholly successful, was provision in ancient Israel successful or not, and if so, why or why not?
3. The past sixty years have seen changes in attitudes to welfare provision in Britain. The Old Testament spans *hundreds* of years. Can we expect to find one continuing attitude or mode of practice? What, for example, of the social changes occasioned by the Babylonian exile and the return?

7. Münch, 'Parsonian Theory Today', p. 137.

To what ideal do we aspire in our society in terms of systems integration? Is our context marked by such different conditions, for example, of the global market economy, and political democracy, compared with ancient Israel, that to make transfers from the Old Testament to our society is impossible?

Chapter 12

THE ENEMY IN THE OLD TESTAMENT

In an essay entitled 'Segregation and Intolerance' Bernhard Lang asks:

> Is it possible to find in the sacred scripture of Judaism and Christianity an alterna-
> tive to the religious segregation and intolerance that fills our modern world?[1]

His answer is no. The Jewish community, like other ancient societies, needed to
identify itself in opposition to its neighbours, and it therefore instituted laws concerning marriage and religious practices in order to maintain and strengthen the
boundaries that separated Jews from non-Jews. In the literature of the Old Testament the Jews were accordingly presented as

> a militarily powerful people who would annihilate polytheistic nations that
> threatened its unique religion. To the regret of the modern mind, such fantasies
> became part of the Bible.

Lang allows that this is not the only strand in the Old Testament. At the end of his
article he mentions a 'trajectory that, although not opposing separation, was more
tolerant'. The examples he gives are the book of Ruth (the possibility of marriage
with Moabite women), the book of Judith (conversion to Judaism of an Ammonite)
and Esther, where a Jewish girl becomes a Persian queen. However, Lang regards
these voices as isolated, and 'not accorded the status of Deuteronomy'. 'In the Old
Testament', he concludes, 'the separatist attitude prevails.'

Lang is not writing about the enemy, but about segregation and intolerance; but
they amount to the same thing. A society that erects the kinds of barriers described
by Lang will not feel kindly towards enemies; and some of the narratives of Deuteronomy seem to bear out his point about the brutal treatments of enemies. Consider
the following passage from Deut. 20.10-14:

> When you draw near to a city to fight against it, offer terms of peace to it. And if
> its answer to you is peace and it opens to you, then all the people who are found in
> it shall do forced labour for you and shall serve you. But if it makes no peace with
> you, but makes war against you, then you shall besiege it; and when the LORD
> your God gives it into your hand you shall put all its males to the sword, but the
> women and the little ones, the cattle, and everything else in the city, all its spoil
> you shall take as booty for yourselves...

---

1.   B. Lang, 'Segregation and Intolerance', in M. Smith and R.J. Hoffman (eds.), *What the
Bible Really Says* (Buffalo: Prometheus Books, 1989), p. 115-35.

This injunction applies to cities that are far from Israel. The inhabitants of cities of foreigners in the land of Israel are to be utterly destroyed (Deut. 20.15-18). The fact that, as far as we know, these commandments were never carried out, but were part of a religious object lesson warning readers against worshipping the gods of their neighbours, does not alter their seemingly horrid content. They convey the sense of exclusiveness and intolerance about which Lang writes.[2]

But has Lang said the last word? In two respects, no. First there are several incidents that can be mentioned in the Old Testament that show more generosity towards enemies than the Deuteronomy passage indicates. Second, by far the greatest amount of material on the subject of enemies is in the Psalms.

Among narratives in which enemies are treated generously the following can be mentioned. First, although the Midianites are Israel's enemies in Judges 6–8, it is noteworthy that Moses is portrayed as fleeing to exile in Midian, of marrying a Midianite woman Zipporah (Exod. 2.21), and of being supported by his Midianite father-in-law Jethro when he reaches Mt Sinai after the Exodus (Exod. 19). Second, Elijah went to live with a pagan woman in Zarephath during the drought in the reign of Ahab and brought her son back to life (1 Kgs 17). Third, in the midst of the narratives about war between the northern kingdom Israel and Syria, the Syrian commander Naaman was healed from leprosy by the prophet Elisha (2 Kgs 5.1-19a). These two last narratives were given prominence in Jesus' sermon in Nazareth (Lk. 4.20-29) to the distress of his hearers.

However, the bringing of such examples begs the question of how we should use the Old Testament in regard to the matter of enemies. Lang's approach is essentially historical and sociological. He sketches the development of Israelite religion from the perspective of his belief that there was a prophetic 'Yahweh-alone' movement from the ninth–eighth centuries; and he develops a model in which exclusiveness necessarily plays an important part.[3] But this reconstruction (assuming it to be correct—and it is certainly controversial) places the emphasis on Israel's development as apparent to the observer. A quite different approach, by way of the Psalms, opens up what the enemy meant in the religious experience and worship of the Old Testament. From this perspective we are in the realm of theology rather than of history and sociology and more likely to find a way from the Old Testament text to our own situation.[4]

---

2. For a recent discussion of these passages from Deuteronomy, which, while tracing their literary and social history, does not gloss over their difficulty for modern readers, yet which makes pertinent observations for today's world, see G. Braulik, *Deuteronomium* (Die Neue Echter Bibel; Würzburg: Echter Verlag, 1992), II, pp. 146-51.

3. See further Lang's stimulating monograph, *Monotheism and the Prophetic Minority* (Social World of Biblical Antiquity, 1; Sheffield: Almond Press, 1983).

4. For the enemy in the Psalms see especially O. Keel, *Feinde und Gottesleugner* (SBM, 7; Stuttgart: Verlag Katholisches Bibelwerk, 1969), and section 5, 'Die feindliche Mächte', in H.-J. Kraus, *Theologie der Psalmen* (BKAT; Neukirchen–Vluyn: Neukirchener Verlag, 1979). An article by Professor G.W. Anderson, 'Enemies and Evildoers in the Book of Psalms', *BJRL* 48 (1965–66), pp. 18-29, provides a characteristically balanced survey and notes the possibility of a wide range of interpretations. It is in this spirit that I take the approach that I do in this paper. For a

A cursory glance at the Psalms will show how frequently one of the Hebrew words for 'enemy' occurs: twice in Psalm 3, once in Psalms 5 and 6, twice in Psalms 7 and 9, once in Psalm 10 and so on; and where a word for enemy does not occur at all, as in Psalm 2, enemies are nonetheless prominent. In what follows I shall deal with examples of three types of Psalm—Royal Psalms, Psalms of National Lament and Psalms of Individual lament.

Psalm 2 is about the threat to the rule of God's king in Jerusalem on the part of various enemies:

> The kings of the earth set themselves,
>   and the rulers take counsel together,
>   against the LORD and his anointed, saying
> 'Let us burst their bonds asunder,
>   and cast their cords from us'. (vv. 2-3)

We are not told who these kings and rulers are, nor what is meant by the bonds and cords which they wish to break. I shall return to these in a moment. The Psalm proceeds to point out how futile this opposition is. The Jerusalem king has been enthroned by God, and God has adopted the king as his son, and has promised that he will possess the nations even to the ends of the earth, and will break (or possibly rule, vocalizing *tir'am* for *tero'em*) them with a rod of iron, and dash them in pieces like a potter's vessel.

At first sight this seems no better than Deuteronomy 20; but it has to be read as part of the Zion theology of the Old Testament. This theology is not about Jewish national domination of the world, but about the universal rule of the God of Israel, a rule which, when established, will draw the nations to Jerusalem and give them the desire to

> beat their swords into ploughshares
>   and their spears into pruning hooks.

God's rule will put an end to enmity because

> nation shall not lift up sword against nation
>   neither shall they learn war any more. (Isa. 2.4)

But this will only happen in the latter days. For the moment the hope that the world will be thus transformed is kept alive by the people of God in Jerusalem, for whom the king is the symbol and pledge of God's rule in a hostile world. This is why, in the Psalm, the kings and the rulers are not identified. In actual historical fact, Jerusalem was too insignificant for the kings of the earth to plot against it; nor did Jerusalem control them such that they would conspire together to throw off the bonds and cords by which they had been bound.[5] The language is symbolic; but it is

different, and in my opinion not wholly successful, attempt to relate the question to modern readers, see T.R. Hobbs and P.K. Jackson, 'The Enemy in the Psalms', *BTB* 21 (1991), pp. 22-29.

5.   Qimḥi identifies the problem and seeks to solve it by identifying the kings and rulers as the Philistines and the cords and bonds as those which bound Israel together after David became king over the united kingdom. See R. D. Qimḥi, *Haperush Hashalem 'al Tehillim* (Jerusalem: Mossad

nonetheless real in seeing in the Jerusalem king a sign of hope for the ultimate triumph of goodness and justice in the world.[6]

Similar themes are found in Psalm 110, which opens with an explicit reference to enemies:

> The LORD says to my Lord,
>   'Sit at my right hand,
> till I make your enemies your footstool'. (v. 1)

As in Psalm 2, promises are made to the king:

> You are a priest for ever
>   after the order of Melchizedek. (Ps. 110.4)

There then follow statements about the God-given success of the king against his enemies:

> He [probably God: but there are ambiguities here] will shatter kings on the day of
> his wrath.
> He will execute judgment among the nations,
>   he will shatter chiefs over the wide earth. (Ps. 110.5-6)

Again, we see expectations on a world-wide scale which were never true in Israel's experience, and yet which transcend narrow, nationalistic aspirations and look for God's universal rule.

This perspective is seen most clearly in Psalm 97. It begins with the affirmation that the LORD is king, and calls upon the earth and coastlands to rejoice and be glad. His kingship is bad news for his enemies:

> Fire goes before him,
>   and burns up his adversaries round about. (v. 3)

But the outcome of this is that 'the heavens proclaim God's righteousness and all the people behold his glory'. Ultimately, all those (including non-Israelites) who hate evil and are upright in heart are vindicated and share in the rejoicing.

If the existence of the people of God and the Jerusalem king are signs of hope for God's future universal rule, then the triumph of Israel's enemies is more than simply a national disaster. Psalm 79, in which a word for enemy does not occur, nevertheless vividly describes a situation in which Israel's foes have triumphed:

> the heathen have come into your inheritance,
>   they have defiled your holy temple;
>   they have laid Jerusalem in ruins. (v. 1)

Harav Kook, 1971), p. 11. Rashi gives the same interpretation in order to oppose the *minim*. See Rashi, *Parshandatha: The Commentary of Rashi on the Prophets and Hagiographs* (ed. I. Maarsen; Jerusalem: Maqor, 1936 [repr. 1972]), pp. 1-2.

6.   The same point is true if, with E. Gerstenberger (*Psalms, Part I* [FOTL; Grand Rapids: Eerdmans, 1988], pp. 44-50), the Psalm is taken to be post-exilic in its extant form, expressing the hopes of the post-exilic community.

We notice here that the psalmist speaks to God about 'your' not 'our' inheritance, and about 'your' not 'our' temple. What is at issue in the Psalm is not the vindication of Israel as much as the reputation of God himself.

Why should the nations say, 'Where is their God?' (v. 10a)

The Psalmist himself is in no doubt about the lordship of God. It is God's anger against Israel that has led to the defeat, which is why, among other things, the psalmist prays for God to avenge those of his people who have been slain so that this may

be known among the nations before your eyes! (v. 10b)

Part of the prayer for help also appeals to God as the protector of the helpless:

Let the groans of the prisoners come before you. (v. 11)

Further, the psalmist prays for the punishment of those who have taunted God.

In interpreting this Psalm it must not be denied that there is a nationalistic element in it. The defeat of the nation is an occasion of national shame; reversal will vindicate national honour. But more prominent than the desire for national self-respect is the desire to see God's name vindicated in the world. If the people are restored, it will be so that, for generations to come, they will be able to worship God, give thanks to him and recount his praises.

From the National lament we move to the Individual lament. If defeat for the nation puts into question God's future rule over the world, so the defeat of the individual by his or her enemies questions the place of justice in the world. An excellent example of this point is Psalm 7. It opens with a cry to God for deliverance from the psalmist's enemies:

O LORD my God, I take refuge in you;
    save me from all my pursuers, and deliver me,
lest like a lion they rend me,
    dragging me away, with none to rescue. (vv. 1-2)

But the psalmist is not looking for rescue at all costs. He acknowledges that if he has been at fault then his plight is deserved:

if there is wrong in my hands,
if I have requited my friend with evil
    or plundered my enemy without cause,
let the enemy pursue me and overtake me,
    and let him trample my life to the ground... (vv. 3-5)

That the psalmist's prime concern is to see that justice is done is indicated in vv. 6-8:

Arise, O LORD, in your anger...
    awake, O my God; you have appointed a judgement.
Let the assembly of the peoples be gathered about you;
    and over it take your seat on high.
The LORD judges the peoples;
    judge me, O LORD, according to my righteousness
and according to the integrity that is in me.

A hope for the establishment of God's just rule is expressed in the words of v. 9:

> O let the evil of the wicked come to an end,
>   but establish the righteous,
> you who try the minds and heart
>   you righteous God.

One of the results of approaching the subject of the enemy in the way suggested here is that, for the individual, the enemy is not necessarily a non-Israelite. In Psalm 35, the psalmist says of those who threaten him,

> I, when they were sick—I wore sackcloth,
>   I afflicted myself with fasting.
> I prayed with head bowed on my bosom,
>   as though I grieved for my friend or my brother;
> I went about as one who laments his mother,
>   bowed down and in mourning. (vv. 13-14)

Now that the psalmist is in some kind of unspecified trouble, these erstwhile friends have become his foes.[7] But again, the psalmist's main desire is that God's justice will be vindicated; for the psalmist's enemies seem to be those who doubt or deny the fact of God's righteous judgment, and if they triumph it will be a dark day for those who seek to be faithful. This theme is, in fact, common in the Psalms, and there are numerous complaints about those (almost certainly Israelites) who doubt whether God can or will exercise justice and who become active enemies of the faithful accordingly (e.g. Pss. 14, 17, 22, 28, 36 etc.).

In his commentary on the Epistle to the Romans, Karl Barth marvellously sums up the point I have been trying to make:

> But who is the *enemy*? The Psalmists knew, at any rate. They saw in the *enemy* not merely a rival or an unpleasant person, an opponent or an oppressor but the man who to my horror is engaged before my very eyes in the performance of objective unrighteousness, the man through whom I am enabled to have actual experience of the known man of this world and to perceive him to be evil. The enemy is the man who incites me to render evil for evil... We can now also understand why it is that in the passionate language of the Psalmist the enemy attains before *God* a stature which is almost absolute, and why it is that they cry unto God that they may be avenged of him. The enemy...lets loose in me a tempestuous, yearning cry for a higher—unavailable—compensating, avenging righteousness, and for a higher—absent—judge between me and him.[8]

---

7.   See especially Chapter 3, 'Die treulosen Freunde', in Keel, *Feinde und Gottesleugner*.

8.   K. Barth, *The Epistle to the Romans* (trans. E.C. Hoskyns; Oxford: Oxford University Press, 1968), pp. 471-72. I am indebted to Kraus (*Theologie der Psalmen*, pp. 166-67) for this reference, the translation of which I have altered at two points with reference to the German. Barth is saying much more than I am attempting here—he is dealing with the whole problem of the temptation in the modern word to overcome evil with evil. Where he is pertinent to the present paper is in linking the theme of the enemy to the wider question of God's justice in the world.

There is much more in this vein, and the whole passage deserves close study and is important for understanding the enemy in the New Testament. For the present lecture, it leads us back to the Old Testament, because I believe that it helps us to take one final step in the discussion. If, with Barth, we believe that in the Psalms encounter with the enemy 'lets loose…a tempestuous, yearning cry for a higher—unavailable—compensating, avenging righteousness, and for a higher—absent—judge between me and him', how does the Old Testament, at the human level, take the matter into its own hands? It does so in two ways. First, it grants the enemy the temporary status of servant of God to execute his righteous judgment upon the Israelite nation, even if this involves punishing the righteous with the wicked. Isaiah 7.18-19 proclaims that

> In that day the LORD will whistle for the fly which is at the sources of the streams of Egypt, and for the bee which is in the land of Assyria. And they will all come and settle in the steep ravines, and in the clefts of the rocks, and on all the thorn bushes, and on all the pastures.

The meaning of the imagery is unmistakable—God will execute judgment on his people by summoning the armies of Egypt and Assyria against them.

At Jer. 25.9, the people are warned that they have not obeyed God, and therefore,

> behold, I will send for all the tribes of the north, says the LORD, and for Nebuchadnezzer the king of Babylon, my servant, and I will bring them against this land and its inhabitants, and against all these nations round about; I will utterly destroy them, and make them a horror, a hissing, and an everlasting reproach.

The status of servant does not last long, for, in v. 12 we are told that

> after seventy years are completed, I will punish the king of Babylon and that nation, the land of the Chaldeans, for their iniquity, says the LORD, making the land an everlasting waste.

But we notice that what is behind this language is the notion of the working out of justice on a universal scale. Babylon will punish Judah for its wickedness; in turn, Babylon will be punished for its wickedness. Thus one way of coping with the problem of evil and the need for justice as it arises in the Psalms is by seeing God at work in the historical process executing the judgment for which prayer is made. Obviously this does not necessarily help the individual's cry for justice nor comfort the psalmist who sees the triumph of the enemy as a setback for God's rule. The Old Testament does not offer a single, consistent answer to these problems.

The second way of coping is through literature such as Deut. 20.10-18. The connection between the prose parts of Jeremiah and the book of Deuteronomy has long been recognized, and the theme of utter destruction was present in the Jeremiah passages quoted a moment ago. If a deuteronomistic school is behind the prose passages of Jeremiah and passages such as Deut. 20.10-18, we have the interesting juxtaposition in which the Israel which is to destroy other peoples utterly, will itself be utterly destroyed by its enemies. Clearly, we are not in the world of reality, but in a world where enemies have become symbols for wickedness, and utter destruction a symbol for the rooting out of evil.

This study of the enemy in the Old Testament has not been completely exhaustive. It has not dealt, for example, with texts that speak of God as an enemy (e.g. Job 33.10), neither has it dealt with the enmity of personified forces of chaos, illness and death.[9] Its aim has been to argue for a theological approach to the matter via the Psalms. Such an approach defines the enemy not in social terms as the outsider or alien, but in moral terms as those who, even within the community, doubt or seek actively to undermine the justice of God. By transcending the boundaries of the local community or the nation and by placing the problem of enmity in the context of the desire for universal justice, the Old Testament provides us with guidelines for tackling the problem of enmity in our own world.

9.   See Kraus, *Theologie der Psalmen*, pp. 168-70.

Chapter 13

THE FAMILY AND STRUCTURES OF GRACE IN THE OLD TESTAMENT

To attempt to describe the family in the Old Testament in one essay is to attempt the impossible. We are dealing with a literature which, whenever it was put into its final form, claims to describe a society that existed for at least a thousand years—a period which saw enormous social changes and upheavals. Further, this literary evidence, as well as the evidence from archaeology, contains so many difficulties and obscurities that the scholarly literature is by no means agreed about its interpretation. What follows in this essay, then, is essentially a broad brush approach, and yet one that will try to show how theologically driven attempts were made to compensate for the failures of the family structure to cope with the crises of ordinary life.

The essay will be structured as follows. I shall begin by reviewing the impression of the family in the Old Testament that is gained by a surface reading of the literature. This will be followed by a sociological and archaeological analysis which, thirdly, will lead to a social-historical review of the family in ancient Israel designed to illustrate what, in the title, is called 'structures of grace'.

1. The Family in Old Testament Literature

The families that we read about in the Old Testament are almost entirely ruling or leading families, the notable exception being the family of the Bethlehemites Naomi and Elimelech. This should not surprise us. The recorded story, even the religious story, of a nation such as Israel is the story of its rulers and leaders; and if we wish to learn about the ordinary people who lived in small villages we have to interpret the mute evidence discovered by the archaeologist. And we also have to recognize that if our literature is concerned mostly with ruling families, the picture that we get from a surface reading will reflect *their* interests, and not the interests of the ordinary people. What picture do we get?

The most striking thing about the leading Israelite families is that they were polygamous. Leaving aside Abraham's servant-woman Hagar, by whom he had a son although already married to Sarah, Jacob married the two sisters Leah and Rachel (and also had children by their servants Zilpah and Bilhah), while the so-called judges must have had several wives. It is explicitly said of Gideon that he had many wives (Judg. 8.30) and we can assume that the same is true of Jair the Gileadite who had thirty sons (Judg. 10.4), Ibzan of Bethlehem who had thirty sons and thirty daughters (Judg. 12.9) and Abdon the Pirathonite who had forty sons

(Judg. 12.14). Seven wives who bore children to David are listed at 1 Chron. 3.1-9, to whom we must add the childless Michal, daughter of Saul. The Chronicles passage also mentions that David had concubines. With regard to Solomon we are told that he had seven hundred princesses as wives in addition to three hundred concubines (1 Kgs 11.3).

In the narratives following the reign of Solomon less stress is placed upon the number of wives of the kings, and we might even conclude from the study of the illness of Jeroboam's son Abijah, that Jeroboam, at least, was monogamous. The narrative refers consistently to 'his wife' or 'the wife of Jeroboam' (e.g. 1 Kgs 14.2, 4). Yet the accounts of the palace revolutions in which the houses of Jeroboam and Baasha are completely wiped out suggest that this was a bigger job than simply eliminating a small family (cf. 1 Kgs 15.29; 16.11), and we are told that Ahab had seventy sons whose slaughter by Jehu needed to be carefully organised to ensure that none escaped (2 Kgs 10.1-11). This indicates that Ahab had wives in addition to the notorious Jezebel.

There is no more mention of polygamous leading families after the story of the destruction of the house of Ahab. But two late passages indicate the persistence of polygamy. Deuteronomy 21.15-17 explicitly legislates for the case of a man who has two wives, ensuring that his inheritance will pass mainly to the firstborn son, even if that son is born to the less favoured of the two wives. The other passage is in Lev. 18.8, a text prohibiting sexual relations with members of the family. The statement 'You shall not uncover the nakedness of your father's wife' following on from the prohibition of sexual relations between a man and his mother clearly envisages a situation where a man will have more than one wife. On the other hand, material dated towards the end of the Second Temple period points strongly towards monogamy. Thus, in the book of Tobit, Tobit's father and son and Tobit himself are monogamous; and the same can be concluded about Mattathias in 1 Maccabees.

The fact that ruling families were polygamous should not surprise us. The kings needed to ensure that they had male heirs, and polygamy assisted that, as well as enabling treaties with neighbouring small states to be cemented by marriage. The 'judges', with their many sons, no doubt exerted political control through having these sons as rulers of small towns in an area presided over by the 'judge' as a sort of chief. But the 'judges' also had responsibilities to the people as a whole, and especially the obligation to defend the people from attacks from their enemies. This, indeed, is a principal function of the 'judges' in the book of that name; and in return for these and other civic responsibilities they could claim the right to several wives.[1] How far ordinary families were monogamous is difficult to say. The story of Ruth implies monogamy, while the story of Samuel, reminiscent of the law in Deuteronomy about a man with two wives, recounts how Samuel was born to Hannah, the favourite of the two wives of the Ephraimite Elkanah (1 Sam. 1.1-2).

---

1.   Cf. the article by C. Lévi-Strauss, 'The Social and Psychological Aspects of Chieftainship in a Primitive Tribe: The Nambikuara of Northwestern Mato Grosso', *Transactions of the New York Academy of Sciences* 7 (1944), pp. 16-32 (reprinted in R. Cohen and J. Middleton [eds.], *Comparative Political Systems* [New York: The Natural History Press, 1967], pp. 45-62).

If the literature of the Old Testament presents families whose structure is mostly polygamous, its glimpse of how families worked in practice is not always reassuring. The story of Cain and Abel is one of fratricide, with Cain acting totally against the claims of kin support that his brother might reasonably expect from him (Gen. 4.1-15). Jacob and Esau are similarly brothers in conflict, albeit with less drastic consequences, while the relationship between Jacob and his maternal uncle Laban has strong undercurrents of suspicion and trickery (Gen. 27, 29). Nor is conflict within the family confined to males. The two sister wives of Jacob envy each other, so do the two wives of Elkanah in the story of Samuel. The story of David's family is even more alarming, as his firstborn son Amnon rapes his half-sister Tamar. In turn, Amnon is later killed by the servants of Tamar's brother Absalom, on Absalom's instructions (2 Sam. 13). David appears to be powerless to prevent or punish these actions. Again, where the head of a family suffered misfortune either by illness or by destruction of property at the hands of an invader, the rest of the family could turn against him. In ch. 19 Job complains that:

> He [God] has put my family far from me,
>> and my acquaintances are wholly estranged from me.
> My relatives and my close friends have failed me;
>> the guests in my house have forgotten me;
> my serving girls count me as a stranger;
>> I have become an alien in their eyes.
> I call to my servant but he gives no answer;
>> I must myself plead with him.
> My breath is repulsive to my wife;...
>> all my intimate friends abhor me,
> and those whom I loved have turned against me. (vv. 13-19)

These words of Jacob precede, of course, the famous passage in which Job declares that in spite of his alienation from his family he has an advocate or *goel*, namely God, who will vindicate him. This reminds us of the other side of the family in the Old Testament, to set against the negative stories that I have mentioned so far. It was the family that was meant to protect the individual within it. Through the institution of blood revenge, a kinsman of anyone who was murdered had the right to pursue the murderer and exact vengeance by killing him (Num. 35.9-34). This kinsman was called the *goel*. Families also had the duty to ensure that a childless widow bore a child by having sexual relations with a brother-in-law (Deut. 25.5-10). Also, smaller units within the larger family that fell on hard times were to be supported materially by the larger family. These aspects will be discussed later; but they need to be mentioned here in order to prevent us from getting a one-sidedly negative view of the family from this surface reading.

When we look at the picture as a whole it appears as follows. The family is a natural unit which, ideally, supports and protects the individuals and smaller groups within it. But its members are human; which means that the ideal is subverted by rivalry, ambition and inadequacy. To what extent all families were like the ones whose failings are recounted in the Old Testament we cannot say. How do families in our society compare with the families whose failings are described daily in our newspapers and on radio and television? Was David's family as typical of Israelite families as 'Brookside' families are typical of British families? The answer probably is that neither was or is entirely typical, but that stories of family breakdowns have an appeal and entertainment value that unites cultures separated by time and space. One thing at least should be clear from the survey so far. If anyone wishes to appeal to the Old Testament family in support of a view about how society should be organised in the West today, the appeal cannot operate at the level of a surface reading of the literature. That reading simply gives us a picture of ruling, polygamous, families that were more often than not the setting for rivalry and inadequacy, for all that there are also positive aspects in the ideals of support and protection.

2. *The Sociology of the Israelite Family*

This leads to the main section of the essay, that dealing with the sociology of the family in ancient Israel. At the outset, a question has to be addressed that has so far been deliberately ignored, namely, what are we talking about when we use the word 'family' in connection with the Old Testament? That question can be partly answered by poising another question: What are *we* talking about when we use the word family in connection with modern British society? Do we mean the nuclear family contained in a single household, or do we mean an extended family with the very strong ties that certainly existed in Durham and surrounding villages in the not-too-distant past when I worked there, and which most likely still exists? Do we mean leading families such as may exist in shire counties with social activities and networks that are very powerful? If reflection upon possible answers to these questions helps us to see that, even without sociological rigour, the matter is far from straightforward, we shall be well on the way to understanding something about the family in the Old Testament.

There is no clear equivalent in Biblical Hebrew for the English 'family'; there are three main designations in Hebrew for social units, of which one, *shevet*, usually translated as 'tribe', can be disregarded if we are considering the Hebrew family. The other two terms, *bet 'av*, father's house, and *mishpachah*, often (misleadingly in my view) translated as 'clan', can be translated by 'family', depending on the context.

Bet 'av, or simply *bayit* (house), has several senses. First, it can refer to a nuclear family living in one household. This appears to be its sense in Gen. 50.7-8. These verses record the burial of Jacob whose interment is witnessed, among the Israelites, by Joseph's *bayit* (house), by his brothers and by his late father's house (*bet 'aviv*). According to the story, Joseph had a wife and two children (Gen. 41.50-52), so that his *bayit* would consist of four people including himself. His brothers, who are mentioned separately, each presumably had his own *bayit*, while Jacob's *bait* or household presumably consisted of his one surviving wife Leah, his two servant wives Bilhah and Zilphah, and any daughters that they might have had. Genesis 50.22 implies that these women henceforth lived under Joseph's protection in the words: 'So Joseph remained in Egypt, he and his father's household' (*bet 'aviv*).

Against the use of *bet 'av* to designate a nuclear family living in a single house-hold, there is the instance of Gen. 7.1 where Noah is instructed by God to enter the ark together with his *bayit* (house). However, in this story Noah has three married sons who are included in the term *bait*, which therefore designates in this context an extended family. So far *bet 'av* has had a primarily territorial meaning, covering people living together or in close proximity. In Gen. 24.38, however, *bet 'av* has the meaning of a descent group. Abraham instructs his servant to travel to Meso-potamia to his father's house (*bet 'avi*) to seek out a bride for Isaac. He cannot be thinking of the house in a territorial sense, but as a descent group or lineage from which he has separated, setting up in the process his own *bet 'av*.

In this same passage, the Hebrew *bet 'avi* is followed immediately by *ve'el mishpachti*, translated by NEB as 'my family' and NRSV as 'my kindred'. Both ren-derings get the general sense. The reference is to relatives generally, as we might talk about our own families, meaning to include aunts, uncles and cousins, some of whom we may not have seen for years, or even ever. Certainly, in the story, Abra-ham will never have met his nephew Bethuel, whose daughter Rebekkah becomes Isaac's wife.

A *mishpachah*, then, is best thought of as a family in the sense of a descent group whose members are linked by descent from a common ancestor who may no longer be living, such as a great-grandparent. Sometimes the ancestor can be too remote to be designated genealogically, but can nevertheless be a real factor in helping people to establish their identity. At Amos 3.1 the prophet addresses 'the whole family (*kol hamishpachah*) that I brought up out of the land of Egypt'. Here, the whole people is described as a *mishpachah* that is conceived as descended from the ancestor Jacob.

A much discussed question is whether a *mishpachah* owned land, given that a *mishpachah* could be a territorial unit as well as a widely scattered descent group. The answer probably is that while a *mishpachah* did not itself own land, it had a responsibility to ensure that land remained the property of the smaller units, the father's houses, that were part of the *mishpachah*. This is illustrated by the case of the daughters of Zelophehad in Num. 27.1-11 and 36.1-9. Zelophehad had died in the wilderness leaving five unmarried daughters and no sons. They were thus mem-bers of a *bet 'av* without a male head. Although in the story the Israelites had not yet possessed any land, some of them were soon to gain land on the eastern side of the river Jordan, among them the group to which Zelophehad's immediate family belonged. The daughters thus appeal to Moses that when land is apportioned they should receive some on behalf of their deceased father. The ruling that is given by God to Moses is informative:

> If a man dies, and has no son, then you shall pass his inheritance to his daughter. If he has no daughter, then you shall give his inheritance to his brothers. If he has no brothers, then you shall give his inheritance to his father's brothers. And if his father has no brothers, then you shall give his inheritance to the nearest kinsman [*haqarov elav*] of his clan [*mimishpachto*] and he shall possess it. (Num. 27.8-11)

Thus land, according to this passage, belongs to a *bet 'av* and must be inherited by a *bet 'av* within the *mishpachah*. However, this ruling raises a further problem, dealt with in Num. 36.1-12. If a female inherits land and then marries a man from another tribe, the husband becomes entitled to the land, and it is added to his tribe and lost to the tribe to which the woman belongs. It is thus ruled that a female who inherits must marry within her *mishpachah* so that land is not lost from one tribe to another.

This leads conveniently to a consideration of the incest law of Lev. 18.7-18 and its implications for the sociology of the family in the Old Testament. The person addressed (Ego) is forbidden to have sexual relations with the following people (italics):

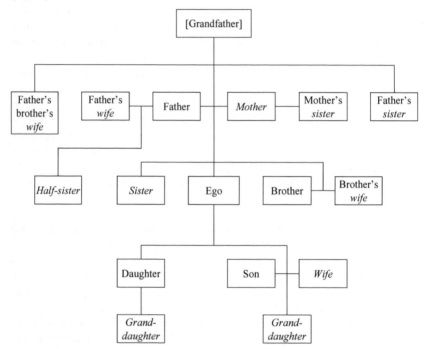

In terms of what has been discussed so far, we have an extended family (the *bet 'av* of the [deceased] grandfather) which is itself made up of at least five smaller *bate 'av*, those of Ego's father, uncle, brother and son, as well as Ego himself, while, of course, Ego's father's *bet 'av* considered as a descent unit will include Ego, Ego's brother and Ego's children, while Ego's *bet 'av* considered as a descent unit will include his own son. Territorially, as we shall see shortly, such a group would probably occupy two or three houses, assuming that Ego's sister, half-sister and daughter lived with their husbands. This extended family is a small exogamous unit, but it does allow marriage with cousins on both the father's and mother's side. To what extent people married only within their *mishpachah* or tribe we cannot say. The story of the daughters of Zelophehad envisages marriage with members of another tribe; but in practice people probably married within their own territorial areas whenever possible. We notice that the family system as described advantaged males and disadvantaged females. Only males could inherit; even females who inherited lost their inheritance to their husbands on marriage. Women, upon marriage, were expected to leave their *bet 'av* and become a member of their husband's *bet 'av*. It was also possible that they would not be the only wife of their husband.

How do the results so far fit in with the recent findings of archaeology? Bearing in mind that archaeological findings are mainly from the period Iron Age I while the literary evidence that we have been considering may be much later, the following points can be made. In the pre-exilic period two thirds of the settlements in the northern hill country of ancient Israel were hamlets or villages.[2] The hamlets had only between 20 and 50 residents and would therefore comprise two or at the most three extended families. Villages had up to 100 residents comprising four or five extended families. These settlements were mainly agricultural and self-sufficient, growing cereals, vegetables and herbs, and pasturing sheep and goats. The cities were more densely populated with a thousand or more residents, the more prosperous of them living in superior dwellings.[3] Whereas the hamlets and villages were primarily agricultural, the cities were the home of the trades and professions, including potters, soldiers, merchants and administrators. Undoubtedly some or most of these trades were family concerns, and such families would come to form a wealthy and powerful group within society in comparison with the families in the hamlets and villages that were entirely dependent upon agriculture.

3. *The Israelite Family in Social-Historical Perspective*

I now come to the social-historical account of the family. In the pre-monarchic period in Israel, we must envisage a primarily agricultural society ruled locally by prominent families whose leaders had a number of wives and who controlled the larger settlements, as in the case of the 'judges' Jair, Ibzan and Abdon mentioned earlier. Theirs was probably a genial style of leadership which did not tax or oppress the families that constituted most of society, but which enjoyed privileges in return for responsibility. They were probably also judges in the strict sense, adjudicating disputes where these could not be settled within the family. This situation was changed by the expansion of the Philistines eastwards towards the end of the eleventh century BCE. The Philistines began to tax the people in the form of exacting agricultural produce and setting up garrisons which had to be fed by the ordinary Israelites. A new form of leadership developed to cope with this threat, with the implication that the leader could make demands upon families to supply fighting men and food to support them. Whether or not it is appropriate to call Saul a king,

---

2.   See I. Finkelstein, *The Archaeology of the Israelite Settlement* (Jerusalem: Israel Exploration Society, 1988), pp. 185-204. There is a useful summary of the evidence in H.L. Bosman *et al.*, *Plutocrats and Paupers: Wealth and Poverty in the Old Testament* (Pretoria: J.L. van Schaik, 1991), pp. 144-53.

3.   See generally, V. Fritz, *Die Stadt im Alten Israel* (Munich: Beck, 1990).

his leadership ushered in a long transition period which led to Israel becoming two states, with significant implications for the family.

Historical and archaeological orthodoxy tell us that it was in the tenth century, in the reigns of David and Solomon, that what we might call loosely the Israelite state came into being, with all the demands of such a state upon its citizens, such as conscription for civil and military purposes, and taxation to support an increasing number of state officials. Further, an increase in the number of merchants and traders inevitably put pressure on the food-producing agricultural families. This orthodox picture is beginning to be challenged by excavations and by reassessment of evidence, particularly from Judah and Trans-Jordan, and it seems increasingly likely that it was not until the ninth century or, in the case of Judah, the eighth century at the earliest, that small states began to emerge in ancient Israel, Ammon, Moab and Edom, with the appropriate centralised administration.[4] There are complex issues here for experts to resolve. For our purposes, whenever these small states may have emerged, they certainly began to make demands upon agricultural communities, and we must remember that these communities were often living on a knife-edge of existence, given the agricultural conditions in the land and its unreliable rainfall. An attentive reader of the Old Testament will notice how often the word 'famine' occurs in its stories. At random, the stories of Abr(ah)am and Sara(i) (Gen. 12.10-20), Joseph (Gen. 41), Ruth, and Elijah (1 Kgs 17) come to mind, while the stories of Gideon (Judg. 6) and the Philistines (1 Sam. 13) are a reminder of how an invader could disrupt and appropriate the production of food. Whether or not these stories are historical, they imply a credible and familiar world on the part of the presumed author and readers.

Famine would be a double blow for agricultural communities and the families of which they consisted. Not only would there be insufficient food to feed the families; it would be impossible to pay the taxes in kind levied by the king. In order to pay them, it would be necessary to borrow from rich landowners or merchants. If the famine continued and the debt increased, members of the family might have to be sold into slavery. Ultimately, the family could lose its land and the former landowner could be reduced to being a hired worker working his own land, or he could become a landless unemployed worker seeking casual work wherever he could find it or he could himself become a slave.

There is plenty of evidence for the existence of this state of affairs in the eighth century from the prophetic critiques that we find in Isaiah 5 or Amos 2 and 4. Isaiah criticises those who join house to house and field to field, the reference being to landowners who acquire ever larger estates by taking land from poorer families that have fallen into debt (Isa. 5.8). Amos criticises those in Israel who

> sell the righteous for silver,
> and the needy for a pair of sandals

---

4. See D.W. Jamieson-Drake, *Scribes and Schools in Monarchic Judah: A Socio-Archaeological Approach* (JSOTSup, 109; Sheffield: Almond Press, 1991). For Edom and Moab see the essays in P. Bienkowski (ed.), *Early Edom and Moab: The Beginning of the Iron Age in Southern Jordan* (SAM, 7; Sheffield: J.R. Collis Publications, 1992).

...who trample the head of the poor into the dust of the earth...
[who] lay themselves down beside every altar on garments taken in pledge (2.8)

where the reference to the garment taken in pledge is to the practice of a man pawning his cloak, probably as a deposit against his wages for a few days' work as a casual labourer.[5]

This state of affairs is also mirrored in those parts of the so-called Book of the Covenant (Exod. 21.1–23.19) that come from the pre-exilic period. Exodus 21.2-11 accepts that a Hebrew might buy Hebrew men and women as slaves, and the law seeks to mitigate that situation by specifying that men must be released after six years, and that women slaves who are married by their owner or his son cease to be slaves and receive the privileges of being wives.[6] In Exod. 22.25-27 [Heb. 24-26] it is decreed that any loan made to a poor person must be interest free, and that a cloak taken in pawn must be restored to its owner before nightfall, 'for it may be your neighbour's only clothing to use as a cover; in what else shall that person sleep?' (Exod. 22.27 [Heb. 26]). Such a person who has to pawn what does double duty as a garment and bedding is indeed in dire straits.

The framework of Exod. 22.25-27 is important for the purposes of this chapter for it brings to us what I call a 'structure of grace', that is, a social arrangement designed to mitigate hardship and misfortune, and grounded in God's mercy. Exodus 22.25 [Heb. 24] begins 'If you lend money to *my people*, to the poor among you ...', where the phrase '*my people*' indicates God's concern for and involvement with those whom this law envisages. The passage ends with the words, 'and if your neighbour cries out to me, I will listen, for I am compassionate' (Exod. 22.27). In a series of articles and, most recently, in his *Theologische Ethik des Alten Testaments*, Eckard Otto has investigated the process of composition of the Book of the Covenant, and argued for a bringing-together of secular laws and theological principles such that, in its pre-exilic form, the Book of the Covenant is an expression of the practical implications of the compassion of God. As Otto says in an important passage:

> In the Book of the Covenant the individual is addressed directly and confronted by YHWH as the merciful one... Humans must thus practise solidarity not because the king commands it, but because God is in solidarity with humankind.[7]

The ordinances of the pre-exilic Book of the Covenant arose, according to Otto, in the family before becoming (if they did become) the responsibility of the state. They were ultimately theologically based and justified, and were designed to

---

5.   On this point see the Hebrew text from Mesad Hashavyahu, normally dated to the last third of the seventh century BCE, where a worker complains that his garment has been taken from him by a supervisor, and has not been returned. For the most recent edition, together with bibliography see J. Renz and W. Röllig, *Handbuch der Althebräischen Epigraphik* (Darmstadt: Wissenschaftliche Buchgesellschaft, 1995), I, pp. 315-29.

6.   There is a famous *kethiv* and *qere* variant in the passage which, although affecting the interpretation slightly, does not affect the overall point.

7.   E. Otto, *Theologische Ethik des Alten Testaments* (Stuttgart: W. Kohlhammer, 1994), p. 90 (author's translation).

operate when the existing social structures broke down in the face of economic pressures.

The strictures of the prophets seem to indicate that these structures of grace were often, if not largely, ignored, and in the second half of the seventh century, in the pre-exilic edition of Deuteronomy, the attempt was made to re-emphasise and indeed extend the structures of grace. Whether or not there had been a complete breakdown of the social structure in terms of the family in its narrower and broader senses in the early seventh century,[8] Deuteronomy is remarkable in the way in which it assumes that duties that were hitherto the responsibility of the family are now the responsibility of each Israelite to his [*sic*] neighbour.

The most famous illustration of this is Deuteronomy 15 where, incidentally, readers of the Old Testament who do not know Hebrew need a translation that has not been edited for gender-free language in order to understand the point. Accordingly, I quote from the RSV:

> If there is among you a poor man, one of your brethren, in any of your towns within your land which the LORD your God gives you, you shall not harden your heart or shut your hand against your poor brother, but you shall open your hand to him, and lend him sufficient for his need, whatever it may be. Take heed lest there be a base thought in your heart, and you say, 'The seventh year, the year of the release is near', and your eye be hostile to your poor brother, and you give him nothing, and he cry to the LORD against you, and it be sin to you... therefore I command you, you shall open wide your hand to your brother, to the needy and to the poor, in the land. (Deut. 15.7-9, 11b)

What is striking is the repetition of the word 'brother', which occurs four times in the verses quoted, and is common elsewhere. The phenomenon has been called the 'brother-ethic' in Deuteronomy; the point is that any needy Israelite, regardless of family or genealogy, has a claim upon his more prosperous neighbour, a claim grounded in the fact that the people as a whole are called by God to be a holy people. The term 'brother' is even extended to include one's enemy. Thus, if Exod. 23.4-5 ('If you meet your enemy's ox or his ass going astray, you shall bring it back to him') is compared with Deut. 22.1 ('You shall not see your brother's ox or his sheep go astray, and withhold your help from them; you shall take them back to your brother') it is seen that in the deuteronomic revision of the law, enemy has become brother. There are no enemies in Judah, only brothers.

Another feature of the late pre-exilic edition of Deuteronomy is its more positive attitude to women compared with the Book of the Covenant. Thus female slaves are given the same right of release as male slaves in Deut. 15.12, and there is a regulation about not taking a widow's garment as a pledge. Further, regulations that protect a newly married bride against the allegation of her husband that she was not a virgin when she was married, or that protect a betrothed or unmarried woman against rape, have led to parts of Deuteronomy being called a 'Frauenspiegel' (women's charter) although its provisions fall far short of what we today would

---

8.   So Otto, *Ethik*, p. 192.

understand by a women's charter. Otto sums up the aims of this version of Deuteronomy as follows:

> An ethics of brotherhood, theologically grounded and also anchored in the laws
> protecting individuals stemming from YHWH's sovereignty over the people and
> the land, is opposed to the breakdown of the communities, in which a natural,
> genealogically based ethics of brotherhood has its place. Every Judahite, including
> enemies and adversaries at law, and not just a relative, is a brother, to whom assis-
> tance borne of solidarity comes, when it is needed. In particular, the landless, for-
> eigners, widows and orphans are the objects of the solidarity that is given concrete
> expression in the third-year tithe, the year of release, in the freeing of slaves and in
> emergency loans that are interest and pledge free. Also in family law the weaker
> members are the objects of solidarity, especially women.[9]

In my terminology, Deuteronomy is an attempt to introduce a whole series of
structures of grace.

The composition of Deuteronomy in the second half of the seventh century was
followed within a generation by the massive upheaval of the destruction of Jerusalem in 587, preceded ten years earlier by the transportation of the so-called cream
of society to Babylon. It may well be that for those remaining in Judah, the exilic
period was one in which ordinary family life was able to recover from the pressures
of the two previous centuries. The nobility and the wealthy had gone, and perhaps
there was little or no taxation on the part of the Babylonian authorities. For those in
exile, it was necessary for new social structures to be developed, and the exilic
period thus saw the rise of the *bet 'avot*, which is not a plural of *bet 'av* but a term
meaning 'house of fathers'. In practice it was an extended family similar to a *mishpachah*, but named after a leader or founder. In Neh. 7.7-38 some of the names of
these leaders or founders are given as Parosh, Shepatiah and Arach. The *bet 'avot*
probably enabled new groupings to be formed where existing families were deliberately dispersed in exile, or had been virtually destroyed by the fighting with the
Babylonians and the executions that followed the Babylonian triumph. It is also
likely that on their return to Judah, these new extended families took over the
leadership of the community and began once more to exert pressure on the agricultural families. The Persian government also expected heavy taxes to be paid.[10]

By the second half of the fifth century, the situation had once again become
desperate for some, perhaps many, families. Nehemiah 5 records the outcry made to
Nehemiah, the governor of Judah:

> There were those who said, 'With our sons and daughters, we are many; we must
> get grain, so that we may eat and stay alive'. There were also those who said, 'We
> are having to pledge our fields, our vineyards, and our houses in order to get grain
> during the famine'. And there were those who said, 'We are having to borrow
> money on our fields and vineyards to pay the king's tax. Now our flesh is the same
> as that of our kindred…and yet we are forcing our sons and daughters to be slaves,

---

9. Otto, *Ethik*, p. 192 (author's translation).
10. See R. Albertz, *Religionsgeschichte Israels in Alttestamentlicher Zeit* (Göttingen: Vandenhoeck & Ruprecht, 1992), p. 539.

and some of our daughters have been ravished; we are powerless and our fields and vineyards now belong to others'. (Neh. 5.2-5)

We are told that Nehemiah ordered the nobles and officials responsible to stop charging interest on loans and to repay the interest paid, as well as restoring the houses, fields and vineyards that had been acquired.

It has been observed that the actions of Nehemiah seem to imply the enforcement of the year of release as described in Deut. 15.1-7. It has been argued by some (e.g. Kippenberg[11]) that the Jubilee Law in Leviticus 25 was the later response to the crisis in Nehemiah's time. Whether or not this was so, and whether or not it was ever enforced, the Jubilee is another of the structures of grace in the Old Testament. It decrees that if an Israelite needs to sell land, or cannot maintain himself, or needs to sell himself as a slave, then any fellow-Israelite has certain duties towards him: to buy the land, or to let him live with him as an alien, or to employ him as a hired servant. It is forbidden to enslave a fellow-Israelite, although non-Israelites may be enslaved. When the Jubilee year comes, all debts are cancelled, all land is returned to the original owners, and all Israelites who are dependent on their fellows can return to the lands that were once theirs and be once more free. The Jubilee has been described as a reworking of Deuteronomy 15.[12] We notice the same use of the term 'brother' in order to transcend family and genealogical limitations (again, gender-free translations such as the NRSV obscure this), while the whole set of ordinances is grounded in the fact that God freed the Israelites from Egypt and gave them the land of Canaan (Lev. 25.38) and that the Israelites are the servants or slaves (*ᵃvadim*) of God whom he brought up out of Egypt. Because Israelites are slaves to their heavenly Lord they cannot be slaves of human masters. God did not deliver them from one form of human oppression so that they could become the victims of other forms of human oppression.

4. *Conclusion*

With the material before us it is possible to conclude that anyone who wishes to reflect theologically on the family in the Old Testament, or who wishes to use what is said about the family in the Old Testament in order to draw lessons for today's society cannot do this at the level of the letter. The family in ancient Israel was a natural social mechanism that developed initially to meet particular circumstances. It was often polygamous, especially in its leading families and in the pre-exilic period, and it could be the context for rivalry, jealousy and even fratricide. It was far more advantageous to men than to women. Although it tried to generate mechanisms such as blood revenge, and the responsibility of the *mishpachah* to support the smaller family units if their members fell on hard times, it was often powerless in practice to prevent the incursion of the state and of powerful landowners or merchants into its sphere of interest, with the result that families became debt-ridden

---

11. H.G. Kippenberg, *Klassenbildung in antiken Judäa* (Göttingen: Vandenhoeck & Ruprecht, 2nd edn, 1982), pp. 62ff.

12. Otto, *Ethik*, p. 255.

and lost their land and freedom. Anyone who would want to suggest that the Old Testament family as just described should in some sense be a model for the family today could only do so by means of a highly selective and superficial use of the text.

What is really important is that theologically driven efforts were made to counteract the forces that undermined the family. These included most notably the 'Bruder-ethos' of Deuteronomy and of Leviticus 25. Also, substantial attempts were made to improve the position of women. These attempts were grounded in the compassion of God and the need for that compassion to be actualised in inter-human relationships, in the solidarity of God with 'my people', and in the redemptive action of God in freeing the Israelites from slavery in Egypt. These structures of grace transcended family ties, but were not intended to abolish the family; rather to support and sustain it. If the Old Testament says anything to us today, it is that we need to devise theologically driven structures of grace appropriate to our situation that will sustain those aspects of family life which, from a Christian perspective, we deem to be most valuable, and which may be most under threat from the state and powerful interests. This is not something that biblical scholars or theologians can do, without the expertise of lawyers or sociologists. The sort of questions that have to be asked are the following: What is the effect upon children of the break-up of marriages? What sort of strains are put upon families by the need for both partners to earn substantial salaries in order to pay for a mortgage? What style of family life is appropriate if the aspirations of women are to be met to combine a career with raising a family? How should housework, whether done by a male or female, be regarded in relation to paid employment? These are all new questions which are not envisaged in the Bible and yet which demand a solution in terms of structures of grace. If the Old Testament is instructive, it will be by way of example rather than precept.

Part IV

OLD TESTAMENT ETHICS AND CHRISTIAN FAITH

Chapter 14

Exegesis and World Order[*]

That the University of Cambridge has sponsored a series of lectures about the application of the New Testament to certain modern social problems will undoubtedly cause surprise or even annoyance in some circles. Every time that a church report is published which appears to be critical of any aspect of the ordering of present-day life, the cry goes up that the church is meddling in politics. No doubt a group of academic biblical scholars will not be noticed by the media; but they may nonetheless be accused of trespassing into areas which they have no right to enter.

I do not intend to offer a defence against the charge that the lecturers in this series will be meddling in politics. Rather, it is my purpose to consider some weighty objections that can be brought from within theology and biblical studies to the possibility of relating biblical exegesis to world order. These objections can be summarized under two headings. The first is that the teaching of the New Testament is directed to individuals as private citizens, and is not directed to governments or to individuals who may be occupying specific offices in the state. The second is that biblical criticism has, for various reasons that I shall spell out in a moment, made it impossible to study the New Testament other than as an attempt to guess at the original form of the teaching of Jesus and its adaptation to their needs by the earliest Christian communities.

The view that New Testament teaching, especially that of Jesus, is directed solely to private individuals is attractive, because it seems to make sense of moral dilemmas familiar in our modern world, and it enables us to escape from some of the radical and impractical implications of the teaching ascribed to Jesus. All of us would agree that it would be a crime if, as private individuals, we were to order someone to kill another person, and that order was carried out. I remember from many years ago that a young man named Bentley was hanged because he allegedly urged his accomplice Craig to shoot a police officer. However, if we are not a private individual but a captain or a corporal in the army and we give the order to fire at an enemy, we are not held to be committing a crime if we are carrying out the duties of our office within the generally accepted rules of war. The injunctions of Jesus not to resist evil or to turn the other cheek seem absurd when viewed from

---

[*]   This study was delivered as a public lecture delivered in Cambridge on 15 October 1986 as the first in a series entitled 'Peace, Poverty and Freedom: A New Testament Perspective'. The presentational style of the original has been retained.

the duties of certain offices, and the problem of this absurdity is certainly resolved if it is assumed that the teaching of Jesus does not apply to states or to office holders.

I hope that, at the end of the lecture, I shall be able to put this dilemma into a perspective that will help us to view it differently. For the moment I shall observe that if Jesus came merely to impart teaching to private individuals for the sake of their future salvation, then he is not in that great succession of Old Testament prophets who were certainly addressing themselves to office holders and states, proclaiming to them words of judgment and hope, and explaining what was expected of them in the moral sphere. F.D. Maurice, in a sermon preached in May 1851, indignantly rejected the idea that whereas the Old Testament is concerned with the ordering of *this* world, the New Testament merely projects the minds of individuals into a region beyond death:

> Is it possible [he exclaimed], that this is what the writers of the New Testament meant when they proclaimed that the Son of God had taken flesh and become man, and that thenceforth the Lord God would dwell with men and walk with them, and that they should be His children and He would be their Father? Do such words import, that the world in which God has placed us has lost some of the sacredness that it had before; that the visible has become hopelessly separated from the invisible; that earth and heaven are not as much united as they were when Jacob was travelling to the land of the people of the east: that now earth is merely a forlorn place, in which men are forced to stay a certain number of years, engaged in a number of occupations with which Heaven has nothing to do, while yet it is held that the preparation for Heaven is the great business of those who dwell here? Surely there must be terrible contradiction in such language...[1]

The difficulties in relating exegesis to world order raised by biblical criticism come from the fact that historical critical study of the New Testament has focused attention on to the historical particularity of the teachings of Jesus, and have made it difficult to see how we can get from these particularities to general or universal principles. The saying 'render unto Caesar the things that are Caesar's and to God the things that are God's',[2] has been used to define relations between church and state and between citizens and their country; but however it may have been used in the course of church history, it was a saying directed to the following explicit problem: Should a people under military occupation pay a poll tax to the overlords in a coinage bearing symbols that are offensive to their religion? It is arguable that the effect of this saying of Jesus depended on the fact that his opponents produced the offensive coinage when asked to do so, thereby compromising themselves and giving Jesus the chance to make his reply. Whether or not this is correct, the question is raised as to what principles exist, if any, whereby such a saying with its very specific reference can be applied to the mutual responsibility of a state and its citizens, or a state and the church.

---

1.   F.D. Maurice, *The Patriarchs and Lawgivers of the Old Testament* (London: Macmillan, 2nd edn, 1855), pp. 251-52.

2.   Mt. 22.15-22 and parallels.

A slightly different problem raised by biblical criticism occurs when a passage thought to have a clear application to world order is interpreted in a way damaging to such application. Twenty years ago it was common to hear sermons in support of Oxfam or Christian Aid based on Mt. 25.40: 'as you did it to the least of these my brethren, you did it to me'. Today there is a growing body of opinion that, in the so-called parable of the Sheep and the Goats, it is not individuals but nations that are judged, and that the brothers of Jesus, that is, the hungry, the sick, the naked and the imprisoned are not the poor in general but the disciples of Jesus. On this view, the parable is not about the need for the wealthy to support the underprivileged; rather, the nations of the world are judged by what notice they took of Christian disciples suffering for the sake of their master.[3] If this is correct, is it not then a mis-interpretation to use the parable to support causes such as Third World aid however good these causes may be?

A third problem raised by biblical criticism is that it has emphasised the eschato-logical dimension of the teaching of Jesus, that is, his expectation that a new age was breaking into the world, or was about to break into it. In the work of Albert Schweitzer, to name the most famous example, Jesus was presented as so con-vinced of the imminent end of the world that his teaching was at best interim ethics, that is, good advice for what little time remained before the world ended.[4] The attempt of C.H. Dodd to stand this view on its head by presenting a Jesus who preached that the Kingdom of God had actually arrived was not, however, any more successful in showing how the ethical teaching of Jesus and the New Testament might be understood and applied.[5]

It might seem as though we have reached an impasse, with no obvious way of relating exegesis to world order even if we want to do this. However, where tradi-tional biblical scholars have hesitated, interpreters starting from materialist assump-tions have boldly and energetically sought to use the Bible in a way that makes it speak to all who, for whatever reason, seek a new world from which injustice, oppression and poverty are eliminated. I want to outline these materialist approaches in some detail, not because I agree with them—in fact I do not—but because they raise important questions about method and indicate ways in which the biblical text can be applied beyond the confines of the ancient world.

In 1974, a laicised Roman Catholic Portuguese priest living in exile in France, Fernando Belo, published his *Lecture matérialiste de l'évangile de Marc* in which he argued that in the Old Testament there are two radically opposed ways of life. The first was embodied in the tribal system in which the members enjoyed equal status and were free from absolutist forms of government; the second was a priestly, kingly centralised and absolutist form of religious and political life which threatened the autonomy of the tribes. In the New Testament, Jesus challenged the embodiment of the centralised and absolutist form of life, namely, the temple. He

3. The matter is discussed fully by W.J.C. Weren, *De broeders van de Mensenzoon* (Amster-dam: Ton Bolland, 1979).

4. A. Schweitzer, *The Quest of the Historical Jesus* (London: A. & C. Black, 3rd edn, 1954), p. 352.

5. Cf. C.H. Dodd, *Gospel and Law* (Cambridge: Cambridge University Press, 1951).

died in the attempt, and his trial and execution meant a victory for the temple and what it embodied; but his attempt pointed the way to what needed to be opposed if exploitation and inequality were to be eliminated.[6] Belo's book was followed by Michel Clévenot's *Approches matérialistes de la Bible* (1976) which similarly presented a Jesus who sought to abolish the temple, who challenged the priestly laws of purity, opposed absolutism, and stood in the tradition of those parts of the Old Testament, such as Deuteronomy, which envisaged greater equality in society based upon an economic system of mutual exchange.[7]

Writings such as those of Belo and Clévenot led to the formation of study groups consisting mainly of left-wing church organisations, trades unionists and socialists, students and the like, in Europe and North and South America. In November 1978 a conference on materialist biblical interpretation was attended by over 100 representatives from sixteen countries, and some of the material prepared for study by the conference appeared in two volumes in German entitled *Der Gott der kleinen Leute*.[8] The delegates were addressed by an open letter from a German pastor which urged them to avoid 'idealistic' concepts such as 'sinner', 'justified' and 'the New Adam', and to recognise instead that the people who were addressed by Jesus were living in situations in which they faced economic and social uncertainty and oppression, and in which he encouraged them with hopes and expectations for a better life. If this was done, the pastor claimed, this would re-establish the Bible as a book addressed to mankind today and would do away with the need for people to learn a special 'idealistic' theological vocabulary before they could begin to read the Bible. It would bring back into view the central theme of the Bible—the Kingdom of God.[9]

The materialist approach, especially as we find it in Michel Clévenot, is a sophisticated position that owes something to French literary structuralism and to the Marxist theory of a text and its interpretation as manufactured products, an expression of the work of the group responsible. The approach is less interested in discourse than in narrative, that is, it is not concerned with what Jesus said, but with what he did. Clévenot declares that it was not what Jesus said but what he did that brought the crowds to him (cf. Mk 3.8—'a great multitude, hearing all that he did, came to him'). The word, in the parable of the soils, is the narrative of Jesus' deeds, and indeed the Gospel as such is the narrative of the actions of Jesus. Jesus is not seen as a person to whose life and teaching the text bears witness; what is important is the events of which his deeds were part, the interpretation of which can affect the process of changing the world order.

---

6. F. Belo, *Lecture matérialiste de l'évangile de Marc* (Paris: Cerf, 1974); English translation, *A Materialist Reading of the Gospel of Mark* (trans. M.J. O'Connell; Maryknoll, NY: Orbis Books, 1981).

7. M. Clévenot, *Approches matérialistes de la Bible* (Paris: Cerf, 1976); English translation, *Materialist Approaches to the Bible* (trans. W.J. Nottingham; Maryknoll, NY: Orbis Books, 1985).

8. W. Schottroff and W. Stegemann (eds.), *Der Gott der kleinen Leute: Sozialgeschichtliche Auslegungen* (2 vols.; Munich/Gelnhausen: Burckhardthaus, 1979); English translation, *The God of the Lowly* (trans. M.J. O'Connell; Maryknoll, NY: Orbis Books, 1984).

9. Schottroff and Stegemann (eds.), *Der Gott der kleinen Leute*, I, pp. 13-19.

It is here that the view of a text as a material production becomes important. Just as in the purely material sphere specific useful objects are produced from raw materials, so a text is produced by the transformation of the raw materials of conversations or accounts of actions into finished literary works. But the *interpretation* of texts is also a mode of production, in that, through interpretation, a text can be seen in a completely new way affected by the conditions and insights of the interpreting community. Jut as a text, at the time of its initial production, is an expression of the social ideology from which it emanates, so an interpretation is a new product which expresses the ideology of the interpreters. On this view, it is in order for a community which seeks for radical social change to read the New Testament in such a way that this reading or interpretation becomes an expression of hopes for the establishment of a new order, and an encouragement to social and political action. There is more that can be said about the theory underlying materialist use of the Bible, for example, the use of the theory of the 'asiatic mode of production', but I leave that idea aside in order to give an example of an interpretation of a parable in *Der Gott der kleinen Leute*.

It is Luise Schottroff's interpretation of Mt. 20.1-15, the parable of the Labourers in the Vineyard in which the workers who worked for one hour received the same wage as those who worked a full day.[10] Parable interpretation usually looks for the 'main point' of a parable, and in this case the main point is said to be that God rewards people according to needs not deserts, or that there is no such thing as a twelfth part of God's love. Schottroff starts out from a detailed analysis of the economic situation implied in the parable. Why were some workers not able to get work until the last hour? Why did the employer not employ his entire workforce from the outset, as opposed to his successive visits to the market place to engage labour? Why was no rate of pay agreed for those hired from the third hour onwards? What emerges is an economic situation in which there were many unemployed men even at a season when casual labour was needed, thus giving an employer the power to dictate what terms he wanted. The employer agreed the usual day's wage with as few men as possible, those who started at the beginning of the day, and then added to the work force from time to time knowing that there was no agreed wage for people who started form the third hour onwards, and who were thus entirely at the mercy of the whim of the employer. Schottroff argues powerfully, and in my view irresistibly, when she says that if the economic conditions had been other than as she has reconstructed them, the parable would have meant little to the original audience.

What does the parable mean? Taken in isolation it indicates that a worker's highest duty is solidarity with his fellows. The totally unexpected generosity of the employer in offering all the workers the same wage leads to division among them, and reveals the awful fact that, instead of being united by a common humanity and a desire for social justice, they are motivated by the selfish greed which leads those who worked for twelve hours to complain against those who worked for only one hour, but who nevertheless had the same need for money to feed and support their

10. Schottroff and Stegemann (eds.), *Der Gott der kleinen Leute*, II, pp. 71-93.

families. But Schottroff does not only take the parable in isolation. The passage is preceded by Peter's question about what the reward will be for those who have followed Jesus, and it is followed by the request of the mother of James and John that her sons should receive preferential treatment in the Kingdom of God. By juxtaposing these passages, Matthew is warning against the desire for superiority over others in the Kingdom of God. Just as the workers who worked twelve hours were wrong not to practise solidarity with their fellows, so it is wrong not to practise solidarity in the Kingdom of God, by wanting to be superior to others.

Subsequent to *Der Gott der kleinen Leute* there has appeared a volume in the first of a series entitled *Traditionen der Befreiung*, in which there is an important methodological essay by Helmut Gollwitzer on materialist exegesis.[11] Gollwitzer considers in detail the materialist approach to history writing in which history is interpreted from the standpoint of the economic circumstances of societies, the distribution of wealth and power, the factors that bring about economic change. From this point of view religion, if it is considered at all, is simply *a* factor in the complex economic process; and Gollwitzer is certain that what must be given up is the 'idealist' view of history in which events are caused by great personalities or influenced by 'ideas' that are completely unrelated to the social and economic matrixes in which they have their roots. Biblical interpretation must therefore be materialistic in the sense that it sets the great personalities and 'ideas' of the Bible into the social and economic matrixes of their times, and does not extract them out of the real world into some timeless, idealistic world. If this is done, Gollwitzer argues, the gain will be great, because it will become apparent how biblical preaching and activity affected and challenged the economic and social conditions of the biblical period.

I want to save the climax of Gollwitzer's article for the end of this lecture, and now give another example of a materialist interpretation of a well-known text in order to illustrate the difference between treating texts as though they teach an 'ideal' truth and interpreting texts in the light of their social and economic background.

In the book to which Gollwitzer's chapter is the methodological introduction, Wolfgang Stegemann writes about the saying of Jesus 'Let the children come to me' and the incident in which it occurs.[12] Stegemann believes that it is possible to discover what he calls 'the oldest tradition', then the tradition as it came to Mark, then its use in Mark, and finally its use in Matthew and Luke. In seeking for the 'oldest tradition' Stegemann investigates in detail the position of children in the Graeco-Roman world. He notes that various texts exist from the Graeco-Roman world that speak of tender relationships between parents and sons, but he argues that the reality was that children were on the whole greatly abused. They could be sold as slaves by their parents, and there were special markets for the sale of children. They could be abandoned at birth to die, or even condemned to death in Sparta by a special commission. Female babies were especially at risk. Various

---

11. W. Schottroff and W. Stegemann (eds.), *Traditionen der Befreiung*. I. *Methodische Zugänge* (Munich: Chr. Kaiser Verlag; Gelnhausen: Burkhardthaus, 1980). Gollwitzer's article, 'Historischer Materialismus und Theologie', is on pp. 13-59.

12. Schottroff and Stegemann (eds.), *Traditionen der Befreiung*, I, pp. 114-44.

reasons for the killing or exposing of children existed, and the matter was widely discussed. Stegemann notes that child killing could be justified as a form of euthanasia, or as a means of controlling the growth of the population. Another justification for getting rid of children, especially in wealthy families, was that children were a burden to parents, and that if only the firstborn were allowed to survive, this would enable *him* (the word is used deliberately) to inherit wealth without having to share it with other siblings. Stegemann makes the interesting point that although there is evidence that the *idea* of children or childhood could be valued in the Graeco-Roman world, the fate of many individual children was determined by economic necessities, and this meant slavery or abandonment.

According to Stegemann the story of children being brought to Jesus consisted, in its earliest form, of a saying of Jesus promising the Kingdom of God to children, just as it is promised to the poor in the original (Lukan) version of the Beatitudes.[13] In the form in which it came to Mark it was transmitted by a Christian group which practised the care of abandoned children. From this point it began to be spiritualised and idealised in the Gospel tradition. Its primary meaning, however, when viewed against the economic plight of children in the Graeco-Roman world, is that the Kingdom of God is promised to this endangered and defenceless group; and so far as its modern application is concerned we do not have to look far in the world to see children endangered by famine, war and poverty, and to apply to their plight the implications of Jesus' promise to the children of his own day.

I have dwelt at some length on materialist interpretation of the New Testament, not because I accept it—I do not. I find far too much unverifiable guesswork in Stegemann's positing of the 'original' and the 'pre-Markan' forms of the tradition, for all that I find it most illuminating to read the Gospel narratives in the light of the elucidations of the social and economic background. I have dealt with materialist interpretation because I think it may help us to see why we have experienced the hang-ups about applying the Bible to modern situations that I outlined at the beginning of the lecture.

We might complain that the materialist approach succeeds in applying the Bible to modern problems precisely because it starts out from a position from which it is *determined* to see the Bible in economic and social terms, and is determined that it shall be brought to bear on economic and social problems. But that raises the question whether traditional methods of biblical interpretation *fail* to address economic and social matters because they set out from a position that is determined *not* to address these matters. When I say 'determined' I do not mean that traditional methods of biblical interpretation *deliberately* set out to avoid facing up to social issues. What I am suggesting, however, is that many of the hidden assumptions of traditional biblical scholarship militate against linking exegesis to world order. What do we mean when we say that biblical scholarship is a neutral and value-free exercise in which we are simply trying to discover the intentions of the biblical writers? When we claim this as biblical scholars—and I include myself among those whom I am implicitly criticizing—are we not in fact declaring that we engage

13. Lk. 6.20-21.

in our scholarship from secure and privileged positions, untouched by poverty and hunger, and not exposed to many of the dangers and uncertainties that were all too familiar to ancient Israel and the earliest Christian community? What right have we, as academic biblical scholars, to claim a veto over how the Bible is to be used by others, and to deny to those engaged in the struggle for a better world order, as they see it, the possibility of seeing the Bible as a document of liberation?

And yet there *is* something to be said for traditional biblical scholarship, because it is not good enough to say that anyone can make the Bible say what they want it to say. It is all to the good that we are becoming increasingly aware of the hidden assumptions of biblical scholarship; of the fact that even if we can guess reasonably certainly about what the biblical writers meant this does not mean that we have exhausted the full significance of the texts; that our modern scholarship is not so much the assured results of the biblical criticism but a brief moment in an ongoing process of interpretation, a brief moment that owes much to secular and external factors. Yet when all this is said, it does not absolve us from doing our utmost to interpret the biblical texts in such a way as to discover an authentic, not an arbitrary meaning.

In my view, the great value of materialist interpretation is that it has shown traditional biblical scholarship that it is no longer possible to ignore the social and economic backgrounds of the texts, and indeed the 'social world' approach has begun to be a burgeoning area of research in both Old and New Testament studies. Also, we have become aware of the special privileges we enjoy as scholars, in the powerful and rich West, living in communities far removed from those poor and underprivileged groups that first spread the Gospel and formed the New Testament. But can we go further? I believe that we can.

In certain areas of New Testament scholarship a consensus seems to be emerging that we must take seriously the apocalyptic element in the teaching of Jesus; that is, his belief in the in-breaking of a new age into the present world, and the implications of this for ethics and the world order. Whether or not Jesus and his followers expected the world to end shortly is now seen to be less important than the fact that the promises of a new age were now taking effect in the present world in the words and work of Jesus. An important attempt to present an 'Ethics of the New Testament' has been worked out along these lines by Wolfgang Schrage,[14] but the best formulation of this that I have seen comes from a paragraph from Gollwitzer:

> In the…biblical sources the kingdom and will of God are so described, that these aim for an immediate alteration in individual human action in the world, as well as an immediate alteration in community action; action that entails a new relationship between people in society, and which expresses itself in a new community that is not confined to members of the group, but which works its way out to affect relationships with every fellow human being, and has the universal perspective of a renewed common life which embraces the whole of mankind.[15]

---

14. W. Schrage, *Ethik des Neuen Testaments* (NTD Ergänzungsreihe, 4; Göttingen: Vandenhoeck & Ruprecht, 1982).

15. Gollwitzer, 'Historischer Materialismus und Theologie', p. 47 (author's translation).

If this is a fair summary of the intended effect of the in-breaking of the Kingdom of God into our world it must have social implications, and set up a position from which we interpret biblical texts. Gollwitzer would want us to see how the praxis of the New Testament communities was a challenge to Graeco-Roman society and an attempted embodiment of the new power of the Kingdom of God. Schrage re-opens questions that might be thought to be closed. For example, even if Jesus did not engage in political action, are we justified in supposing that his teaching has no political implications? If he did not pronounce on the economic reordering of life are we justified in supposing that his teaching has no economic implications, especially when the workaday world of his day and its economic conditions figured in some of the parables?

But if the teaching of the New Testament has political and economic implications it does not provide us with economic and political blueprints for the ancient *or* the modern world. If the Kingdom of God is among us (Lk. 17.21) it is far from being fully realised. Christians are thus called to live in two ages at once. We must take seriously the world in which we live, but we must see it as a world in which the Kingdom of God is present, bringing with it values that may often contrast sharply with those of the world. This paradox is my answer to the problem of the absurdities of the teaching of Jesus when applied to the office of a soldier or a statesman. In my view, we cannot say that the soldier and the statesman are exempted by their office from the claims of the Kingdom of God. Rather, the soldier and statesman, if they are Christians, may have to carry out the tasks of their office fully conscious that what they are doing is contrary to the demands of the Kingdom of God, and committed to do all in their power to change that which makes the performance of their office come into conflict with the values of the Kingdom of God.

Christians who believe that exegesis is related to world order do not have superior knowledge about how the world should be reordered, or what political and economic systems are to be preferred. They are, rather, salt to the earth, light to the world, leaven to the dough. They are groups who stand on the side of the oppressed against the oppressors, who protest against dehumanisation, who strive for peace and wholeness, and for the breaking down of discriminatory barriers between male and female, black and white, rich and poor. To undertake biblical exegesis from this point of view is, in my opinion, not an abandonment of standards of academic objectivity; it is rather an attempt to rediscover the impact that the Christian message had upon the world of its day. This can become an inspiration for the impact that it could have on the world of our day.

Chapter 15

JOHN ROGERSON: PERSONAL REFLECTIONS
ON THE CHRISTIAN FOUNDATIONS OF OLD TESTAMENT ETHICS

[Editor's note: The purpose of this final chapter is to allow Professor Rogerson to recount in his own words the development of his Old Testament ethics. His pilgrimage has been a rich one, one in dialogue with biblical, theological, and philosophical studies that have influenced his appreciation of how Christians are to use the Bible and live in the world within that tension that lies between the demands of the Gospel and modern realities. This personal narrative can serve as a stimulating illustration of how dynamic the process of ethical thinking can be and how rich the field of Old Testament ethics is becoming. More personal details can be found in the Preface.]

My first exposure to ethics came in my second year at Manchester University (1958–59) when I studied Moral Philosophy with Professor Dorothy Emmet and indeed, this course of study laid the foundations for my subsequent thinking in this area. Of the various approaches to ethics that we studied I was most attracted to the intuitionist or deontological view, the view that holds certain things such as justice to be self-evidently right. I could also see the importance of aspects of utilitarian ethics, especially where moral actions could be framed or justified in terms of the achievement of a *summum bonum*. But if there was a clash between the two principles, for example, in the case of the so-called Caiaphas principle, that it was expedient for one person to die for the nation so that the whole nation did not perish, I had to side with the view that the justice owed to the one person must override the expediency of preserving the nation.

Of the texts studied, Kant's metaphysic of the groundwork of ethics seemed to me to provide philosophical justification for my intuitionist preferences, and that formulation of the categorical imperative, that people should be treated as ends and not means, has remained important to me. Another text that made a profound impression on me was A.D. Lindsay's *The Two Moralities: Our Duty to God and to Society*[1] for this enabled me to see how Christian faith related to ethics. Lindsay contrasts what he calls 'the morality of my station and its duties' with 'the morality of grace' and argues that while a society must take certain actions to preserve itself,

---

1. A.D. Lindsay, *The Two Moralities: Our Duty to God and Society* (London: Eyre & Spottiswoode, 1940).

such as imprisoning those who disobey its laws, the morality of grace will always challenge such actions, by insisting, for example, that we must love our enemies. Lindsay also insists that the morality of grace has a prophetic role, and that its insights have often played a crucial role in changing the morality of my station.

The following year (1959–60) I studied Christian Ethics with Ronald Preston, and found the course most disappointing. I came expecting to study how Christian beliefs provided principles on the basis of which moral decisions could be made. Instead, the course dealt largely with the history of Christian Ethics, with little or no attempt being made to deduce or examine any underlying principles. However, the course provided an important overview of one aspect of the history of theology and of biblical interpretation. Two books of importance that I read subsequently to my undergraduate studies were N.H.G. Robinson's *The Groundwork of Christian Ethics*[2] and Helmuth Thielicke, *Theological Ethics*.[3] In Robinson I found the concept of 'natural morality' which I took to be the equivalent of Lindsay's 'the morality of my station and its duties'. Robinson argues that Christian ethics must always acknowledge its debt to 'natural morality' and must be in some kind of partnership with it, albeit a critical partnership. Thielicke's exposition of the Lutheran dialectic of Gospel and Law seemed to me to be an elaboration of Lindsay's contrast between the morality of my station and the morality of grace. From these sources, as well as from technical studies of Old Testament texts and related issues, the following general position that I hold has emerged:

1. The search for moral principles, and ethical reflection upon this process is an activity common to humankind. It can be called 'natural morality' or 'the morality of my station and its duties'. It will differ in societies according to time and place.

2. The Bible contains the 'natural morality' of certain circles in ancient Israel as well as that of the early Church. In many cases, for example, the prescription of the death penalty for adultery or for working on the Sabbath in the Old Testament and the prohibitions against women speaking in church or teaching men in the New Testament, the 'natural morality' of the Bible has been superseded by the 'natural morality' of modern Western society.

3. The distinctive role of the Bible and Christian faith is to confront 'natural morality' with the 'morality of grace'. This process can be seen in the Old Testament in prophetic denunciation of 'crimes against humanity' (Amos 1.3–2.3) and social injustice, and in the Pentateuch in attempts to legislate what I call 'structures of grace', that is, social and administrative arrangements which seek to treat people graciously and to enable graciousness to govern social interaction. In the New Testament 'natural morality' is confronted by the values of the Kingdom of God, for example, in regard to the definition of greatness as servanthood, and the priority of individual need over what is prescribed (cf. Mt. 20.1-16). The life of Jesus as presented in the Gospels is the challenge of grace to natural morality.

4. Christians must live dialectically and eschatologically. They are embedded in 'the morality of my station' and must be loyal to it as far as Christian conscience

2. N.H.G. Robinson, *The Groundwork of Christian Ethics* (London: Collins, 1971).
3. H. Thielicke, *Theological Ethics* (3 vols.; Grand Rapids: Eerdmans, 1966, 1969, 1979).

allows. They will also have to accept that there are many situations that they will not be able to affect because of their powerlessness. As and how they can, they must confront 'natural morality' with the challenge of grace. The Bible will help them by example rather than precept; that is, they will not be able to apply directly to their situation laws that presuppose that they own slaves or are peasant farmers. They will be challenged to ask what 'situations of grace' are appropriate to their own situations in the same way that the Parable of the Good Samaritan challenges us to identify 'the neighbour' in our own situations and to act accordingly.

5.   Christian moral action will often amount to trying to apply absolutes to contingent situations. The result will inevitably be compromise. In the case of war, for example, it must always be wrong to wage war; but there may be circumstances in which not to wage war will lead to a greater evil than war itself. In this case, war cannot become 'just' in any sense. It must remain evil and be treated as such. It must be regarded as a necessary evil, and as a sign that the world, and with it the human race, is in need of redemption. This brings us back to a central theme of the Bible: the fallenness of humanity and the need for re-creation, which only God's grace can bring about.

6.   In recent years my thinking has been greatly stimulated by my study of members of the so-called Frankfurt Critical School—Max Horkheimer, Theodor Adorno, Walter Benjamin and Jürgen Habermas. Horkheimer's and Adorno's *Dialectic of Enlightenment*[4] is for me a profound account of the modern dilemma of humanism and amplifies my point in numbered paragraph '5' above about human 'fallenness'. Habermas's work on discourse ethics and on communicative action has led me, first, to point out examples of discourse ethics in the Old Testament (e.g. Gen. 18.22-32) and second, to see similarities between Habermas's 'ideal speech situations' and what I call 'structures of grace'. I am attracted to Habermas's rejection of relativizing approaches to ethics, as well as to Adorno's negative dialectics, in which he emphasizes the uniqueness of each individual and has as an ideal that has been called the 'coercionless synthesis of the manifold'.[5] In different ways, members of the Frankfurt School seem to me to be articulating secular versions of what I understand by the Kingdom of God.

The most fundamental ethical and theological issue, in my view, is 'What does it mean to be human?'. The answer to this question has implications for medical ethics, and social and world issues, as well as for the issues of sexuality and gender that are currently dividing some of the churches. The answer that is implied in political decision-making, and which drives research especially in the medical sphere, is that humankind is *homo economicus*. Many activities, including education and the creative arts find their justification and rationale in their ability to

---

4.   T.W. Adorno and M. Horkheimer, *Dialectic of Enlightenment* (London: Verso, 1997).

5.   [Editor's note: for more details concerning Rogerson's appropriation of Adorno, see his 'The Potential of the Negative: Approaching the Old Testament through the Work of Adorno', in M.D. Carroll R. (ed.), *Rethinking Contexts, Rereading Texts: Contributions from the Social Sciences to Biblical Interpretation* (JSOTSup, 299; Sheffield: Sheffield Academic Press, 2000), pp. 24-47.]

generate national wealth. Yet this drive to achieve greater wealth is destroying the planet, degrading the value of human life and shows no sign of dealing with the fundamental issues of poverty and ignorance in the Two-Thirds World. Christians, members of other faiths, and people of 'good will' are faced with the challenge of saving the human race from its rush to self-destruction. Within this coalition, Christians will draw upon the resources afforded by the Bible and Christian tradition—belief that each individual is made in the image and likeness of God, that in his incarnation, Jesus identified himself fully with humankind, even to the point of suffering in death, that the resurrection of Jesus, as well as much Old Testament tradition, witnesses to the possibility of hope and transformation—here and now and beyond our limitations of time and space.

INDEXES

INDEX OF REFERENCES

OLD TESTAMENT

NEW TESTAMENT
AND OTHER EARLY
CHRISTIAN SOURCES

INDEX OF NAMES

DATE DUE